THAT'S HOW THE L

'Anne has created a uniquely African template of love, dignity, care and compassion for people in the end stages of life. Her pioneering model of care reaches 90% of the districts in Uganda and is making its presence felt in Tanzania, Nigeria, Cameroon, Sierra Leone, Malawi, Ethiopia, Sudan, Rwanda and Benin. The model is, by design, culturally and spiritually inclusive. It is an organic African, Ubuntu-centric approach to caring for the dying that could be used across the Mother Continent and beyond. There is no doubt that it is work that makes God smile.'
Archbishop Emeritus Desmond M. Tutu, 2018

'A captivating journey of a super generous lady who is filled with compassion and a great spirit that shines brightly – lighting up the lives of others. Dr Anne's simplicity, humility and joyful spirit has served and touched many, and through her tolerance and thoughtful actions she embodies the true essence of generosity, which has made a positive impact on the lives of many weak and less privileged across Africa.'
Queen Sylvia Nagginda, Nnaabagereka Buganda Kingdom

'Dr Anne's simple but ingenious formula for compounding morphine solutions not only revolutionised how we treat pain in Uganda, but it also transformed how we care for patients across Africa. She exemplifies the many phrases she taught us at Hospice Africa Uganda ... "attending to detail" ... "fire in the belly" ... "going the extra mile". This is just who she is.'
Dr Eddie Mwebesa

'Anne has been the single most motivating person I've ever met in my life. If you'd forgotten your "why", she'd remind you of your purpose. She turned on a light that at that time was so close to being turned off forever. I could have floated through my career doing far less good. I wanted to chase that light. She provided the model on which I wanted to base myself and my practice.'
Dr Ged Faulks, UK

'Anne was and remains an inspiration as I am called to service in palliative care. Only when I began full-time hospice work did I realise she had sowed early seeds within me. I am eternally grateful and feel blessed that our paths converged at pivotal points in my life, both personal and professional.'
*Dr Chong Poh Heng, Medical Director,
HCA Hospice Care, Singapore*

'Against all of the odds, Anne succeeded here in Uganda. Her determination, persistence and persuasion has enabled palliative care to be integrated into the Ugandan health care system. Anne's love and care for her patients goes beyond doctor/patient responsibilities. The seeds she planted in 1993 are flourishing and palliative care is here to stay.'
Rose Kiwanuka, Uganda

'Anne was not afraid to step on people's toes and push for what she saw needed to get done to get hospice care in Singapore off the ground. Without Anne there would be no palliative care in Singapore. Definitely no oral morphine in Africa without Anne either.'
Nurse Leekiang Chua, Singapore

'Anne has a strong faith and really knows who the master is of all storms. She is a fighter, never giving up, and always smiles under any circumstance.'
Martha Rabwoni, Uganda

'We faced many challenges when we began. I remember Anne saying. "We need to take the high road! We need to rise above the situation and act differently – that's what makes all the difference in palliative care. The spirit of how we work." Anne imbued the ethos into everything she did. She had the biggest heart for people suffering and wanted to do everything she could to help.'
Fazal Mbaraka

'I first met Anne in March 1954, when we were both setting out on the extraordinary adventure of Missionary life. Perhaps what never changed despite our roads diverging and reconnecting was Anne's deep compassion combined with a mischievous humour, with which she met all situations. She became undefeatable and remains so, consistent in commitment, loving in friendship and with her never changing cheeky smile, "a chink of the Grandeur of God". I'm proud to be one of her really old but ever young friends.'
Sr Dr Brigid Corrigan, MMM

Books by Anne Merriman

Audacity to Love: The Story of Hospice Africa
(1st Edition, Irish Hospice Foundation, 2010;
2nd edition, Aesop Publications, 2023)

International Geriatric Medicine, 1989, Singapore

THAT'S HOW
THE LIGHT GOT IN

Dr Anne Merriman

with Autumn Fielding-Monson

AESOP Publications
Oxford

AESOP Publications
Martin Noble Editorial / AESOP
28A Abberbury Road, Oxford OX4 4ES, UK
www.aesopbooks.com

First edition published by AESOP Publications
Copyright (c) 2023 Anne Merriman and Autumn Fielding-
Monson

www.annemerrimanfoundation.org
www.hospiceafrica.or.ug

First edition 2023

ISBN: 978-1-910301-70-8

Disclaimer:
This book is a memoir. It reflects the author's present
recollections of experiences over time and some of those
recollections may be inaccurate. Some names and characteristics
have been changed, some events have been compressed, and
some dialogue has been recreated.

CONTENTS

PART III   THAT'S HOW THE LIGHT GOT IN

Foreword

Y EARS before I would meet Dr Anne, I found myself
crumpled up in a ball on the ground. It was my senior
year at Kennewick High School in Washington State,
USA, and I had been suddenly overtaken by a blinding pain.
By pure luck, my younger sister stumbled upon me on her
way to class and managed to get me to the nurse's office.
Something was terribly wrong. Sweat poured down my
face and my stomach cramps came in convulsing waves. It
was some of the worst pain I had ever experienced. Yet,
somehow, while laying in the nurse's office waiting for my
dad to pick me up, I felt an immense gratitude for the place
of my birth and the socio-economic status of my parents. I
knew I'd go to a doctor and we'd get to the bottom of it. But
I also thought of the people around the world not so
fortunate. So, while I lay there in the kind of pain that
makes you want to pray to God, I, well, began praying to
God. I made a promise to help others, also in immense pain,
who were not as fortunate as I was.

I would soon be diagnosed with a fast-growing non-
malignant tumour on my ovary. (Years later, in Uganda, I
would see patients with non-malignant tumours that were
bedbound and helpless, due to the size and evasive
characteristics of their tumour.) My tumour, the size of a
baseball, had completely overtaken my ovary and was still
growing. The tumour, and consequentially my ovary, were

surgically removed and I was given treatment. I recovered and went on with my life.

I thought about this promise often and went into my first year of university as a pre-med student. Between playing collegiate basketball and my studies it soon became apparent that my interest leaned more towards the social aspects versus the physical and medical aspects of humanity and inevitably my future career. I graduated with a psychology major and sociology minor. My promise with God didn't fit my current trajectory. But I kept it in my heart and carried on with life. Upon graduating, I went travelling and worked for a time in a hotel in Ireland on a work visa.

And that is where I met Dr Anne. God had not forgotten the promise.

An older woman, short with light blonde hair, wearing a soft purple wool shawl, kept coming into my café. I'd bring her some coffee and hours later she'd still be working away on her laptop. One day I commented on how much I liked her shawl and with that conversation a lifelong friendship began. Dr Anne, with her thick British-Irish accent, was a spitfire and I found her wildly interesting. As we talked, I learned that she worked in Uganda at a hospice and was spending a week away on 'spiritual retreat'. After spending the whole week in the café working, and not much 'retreating', she gave me her card and invited me to come out to visit her in Africa. That chance encounter changed the entire trajectory of my life. Ten months later, after working multiple jobs to save up for this trip, I found myself at last in Uganda, volunteering at Hospice Africa Uganda for the next six months. Not having a medical background and not knowing how I'd be useful, I pledged to help in any way I could.

Little did I know, Dr Anne was kind of a big deal. She didn't just work at Hospice Africa Uganda, she had actually *founded* the first palliative care service in Uganda, which served as a model for all of Africa, and had been a trailblazer for palliative care in South-East Asia and Sub-

Saharan Africa. Previously, Dr Anne had worked in Ireland, Nigeria, United Kingdom, Malaysia, Singapore and Kenya, and now had found a great need in Uganda.

I arrived in Uganda greeted by a warm welcome. Dr Anne was kind, funny, and had flickers of wildness in her eyes. Adventurous and wildly intelligent, she wasn't like any seventy year old I had ever met. She also drove like a bat out of hell and once gave a passenger a black eye when the jeep went airborne after she slammed into a speed bump at high speeds! To add to the intrigue, I learned she had once been a nun! Even though I was five decades younger, we connected easily. She felt like another sister, albeit older and even crazier than myself!

Have you ever met someone truly incredible and thought, 'Wow. How did you do so *much* with your life? How did you create such a positive impact on so many thousands of lives ... and yet, still manage to have so much fun and fill your life with such joy and meaning?' I found myself thinking just that as I listened to her stories over dinner. When I stayed with her at Andrew Kaggwa House, Dr Anne would have the dinner table roaring in laughter over her adventures and sharp wit. I found myself thinking on multiple occasions, 'This needs to be in a book!' At seventy-three and counting, she was not getting any younger.

I began encouraging Dr Anne to write a book and eventually she agreed. I spent three months helping her write *Audacity to Love*, a book about Hospice Africa Uganda and palliative care. That was the book Dr Anne wanted to write; that was her passion and her life's work. I, however, was much more interested in the fascinating person behind the organisation. At the time, I was young and searching for my own path in life, and I knew there was a wealth of wisdom to be gained from hearing her story. I wanted to know about her struggles, how she'd handled them, about her relationship with God, the crossroads she faced, what influenced her, who inspired her and all the other adventures I had not yet heard about. I wanted to know how she did it – how she threaded the needle of life. How did it all come together? But that book would have to wait.

After my six months working with Dr Anne, I left Uganda to go back to university. My experiences in Africa led me to get my Masters in Conflict Resolution in the UK. (Thanks to the recommendation by Christine Colledge, a UK social worker student volunteering at HAU!) Over the next ten years, Dr Anne and I kept in touch and I continued to volunteer my time, building the Anne Merriman Foundation website and the HA-USA website, and also collaborating with others on writing her nomination for the Nobel Peace Prize.

Years later, in 2017, Dr Anne asked if I'd come back to work with her for a year. Timing is everything. I had spent the last five years working as an analyst for a nonprofit mediation organisation that resolved complex safety, health, environmental and related retaliatory issues at the Hanford nuclear site. But the organisation had recently been closed and I was in-between jobs. I knew this would also be the chance for us to write *this* book. I agreed and would spend the next year travelling with her to Uganda, Ireland and the UK. Needless to say, we spent a lot of time together. Although not without its challenges, I look back on that time as a very special year in my life.

Now, at eighty-two years of age, even as things were becoming more difficult for her, Dr Anne still lived her life with so much passion and dedication. She was still quick to laugh, curious and constantly challenged herself by keeping up with the latest technologies. Deeply spiritual, her relationship with God went beyond a Sunday spent at church and the basic Narrative of the Catholic Church. Although she has many disagreements with the Catholic Church, she continued to be a deeply devoted Catholic. While attending a midnight Easter Mass with her in Uganda, she asked me if I was going to get communion.

'Well, I'm not Catholic. I don't think I'm supposed to,' I whispered back.

She smiled at me and her eyes sparkled like she had a secret. 'Well, I'm pretty sure my Christ wouldn't care. You're just as Christian as everyone here.'

And so, I went up and took communion with Dr Anne. She had a deeply inclusive nature and she readily loved and accepted others outside of her 'tribe', a Christ-like characteristic that I think many religious people sometimes forget. She had a lionheart, and in the end, used it to care for those in the greatest need.

But not everything was deep and serious with Anne. She was lighthearted, great fun and on occasion enjoyed the finer things in life. She loved fashion, painted nails and bright, beautiful clothing and earrings. She loved her food and when returning back to the UK or Ireland, could spend hours walking up and down the isles picking out her favourite biscuits and chocolates – hours! She loved TV programmes and movies, and we enjoyed long stretches of watching *Sex in the City* while writing the first book in 2007.

But Dr Anne had another side too. She could also be quite bull-headed and stubborn. To get things done, she sometimes felt like she had to be a fighter and she'd come out swinging. Quick to anger, she could fly off the handle for something minor a driver did or didn't do. Like so many of the 'movers and shakers' of the world, Dr Anne did not always have an 'easy' personality. But her saving grace was always that, if earnestly confronted, she could reflect, acknowledge any wrongdoing and make amends.

We didn't want to write a book about a saint. We wanted to tell the story of someone who is human. Complex. Dynamic. And has contradictory aspects to her nature, like we all do. And as we wrote about Dr Anne's life, it was clear she'd had just as many challenges in her life as she had victories. And often, it was during the times of blinding despair or grappling around in the unknown, that the shift manifested. A small trajectory change that led her down a path she could never have imagined for herself. Leading her to grow into the person she was meant to become. The cracks created space for the light to get in.

This book did not get completed during our year together. As busy as our lives became, it has taken a giant's effort to finish it. Yet, only God can plan the timing. As Hospice Africa Uganda celebrates its 30th Anniversary in September 2023, coinciding with this book's publication, I feel I've kept true to the promise I made to God years ago. Dr Anne has truly lived a hero's journey, and her story stands as a beacon of light and inspiration, not only in the palliative care world, but for everyone else.

Ultimately, I believe, the universe will conspire to help you if you hold something quietly in your heart and stay true to yourself. Life is magical and mysterious. We all have more creative power than we realise. What will you create? Where will your heart lead you? What path will you walk? I hope Dr Anne's life shines a light for you on your own journey.

Autumn Fielding-Monson

Dedication
Anne Merriman

We all have different paths. Unique purposes.
Distinct endowments, gifts.
And imperfections.

My life surprised me.
I was shaped and hardened into a vessel that could carry
something, something more.
Beyond me.

Looking back, I see the touch of God's hand throughout my
entire story. Omnipresent.
Sometimes coming through in bold strokes.

Yet, while living it, many of the pages felt empty from Grace.
My purpose found me after a long road of twists and turns.
But it is in the twists and turns that it happens.
Unfolding. Evolving.

I dedicate this book to the bravehearts embarking on this
journey,
adventuring into the dark unknown,
to seek your purpose and soul's inner call.

May you remain open to the miraculous, to life's whispers and
serendipitous encounters, to love and to heartbreak,
the arduous challenges, failed expectations
and the winds of change.

May you find and fulfill your inner path. Your inner possibilities.

Be open to every moment and experience. Be yourself.
Courageous and with joy. Go where the fire burns.

The birds they sing, at the break of day
Start again, I heard them say.
Don't dwell on what has passed away
Or what is yet to be…

Ring the bells that still can ring
Forget your perfect offering
There is a crack, a crack in everything
That's how the light gets in…

Leonard Cohen, Anthem

Prologue

Guts

Faith is taking the first step
even when you don't see the whole staircase.
Martin Luther King, Jr

Whatever you can do, or dream you can do,
Begin it. Boldness has genius, power, and magic in it.
Johann Wolfgang von Goethe

Kampala, Uganda, 1993

A S DAWN broke, sun flooded through the window, bathing the bedroom in warmth. I had been in Uganda for a few weeks and was starting to acclimatise to the heat, having spent last year in cold, rainy England. I lay awake in bed waiting until I heard the knock on the front door. Tap tap tap came the hand on the hollow wood frame.

I threw off the thin sheet and slowly pulled my creaking body upright in the small single bed and slipped my feet into my plastic orange flip-flops. At fifty-eight, life wasn't getting easier. Starting somewhere new again, in a different culture, and far from home was *never* easy. But my inner furnace was roaring, ignited by a new vision that had drawn me here. Despite reaching an age at which most people would be considering retirement, I was to be known for my endless energy for the next quarter of a century.

I was currently living in Nsambya Hospital compound. The Sisters of Franciscan Missionaries of Mary had graciously offered me a two bedroom-house to work and live free of charge while I began the first palliative care service[1] in Uganda: a place where people could come and seek relief from the gripping pain with which they had been struggling as they faced an impending and painful death from cancer and other diseases. In places like Uganda, 95 per cent of people with cancer never reach treatment, and for the 5 per cent who do, it is often already too late. In Uganda and places with similar socio-economic infrastructures (LMICs), cancer and other illnesses are not only a death sentence but a very painful death sentence.

This kind of pain – and the lack of dignity accompanying it – is not something that most of us are familiar with. We consider pain relief as an afterthought, as an expected basic treatment. But the dark rendezvous with pain and death is set in stone – for millions – merely based on the geography of their birth. For these unfortunate people, who form a significant fraction of the world's population, simple relief from agonising pain still doesn't exist. Cancers disfigure the body. Wounds emit unpleasant and foul smells. The ceaseless crying and screaming may even get the person exiled to an outside shed, side by side with the animals. Death becomes longed for. Prayed and wished for.

---

[1] Other services, especially for those dying of HIV, had already commenced in Uganda, but were medically known as 'support services' through HIV services like Taso and Nsambya Home care. But because they did not have effective pain control. We started the first palliative care service in Uganda because we helped effect the laws to import oral morphine, and from the start, we administered oral morphine to patients to control pain at Hospice Africa Uganda.

However, this two-little bedroom house, locally known as the VMM House,[2] would be one of the first places in the entire country where that kind of pain would stop. The pain would stop. The crying would cease. A deep breath could be inhaled. A conversation with loved ones could finally take place again. And, they would be sent home with a treatment plan so they could die in dignity. Or, if they were the fortunate 1 per cent[3] they would receive treatment and recover. This place had the chance to be a seed of light and love. Uganda was to be a model for the rest of Africa.

The rap at the door came again. 'I'll be there in a few minutes!' I replied.

I threw on my clothes and went out to answer the door. The patient standing before me was starting to serve as my alarm clock. In this field, people were often dealing with more than physical pain: they also needed to find the courage to face death and learn skills to cope with depression and fatigue. This man didn't suffer from the intense physical pain so many others did, but his emotional and mental wounds were causing terrible anguish and he needed holistic care and attention.

I was currently running the two-little bedroom hospice solo. Fazal Mbaraka, a young Kenyan nurse of Pakistan descent, who had worked with me at my previous post in Kenya, fully embodied the spirit of hospice. When asked if she would leave her job, her home and help me start a new organisation with no financial security – she quickly agreed. However, death and the loss of death, escapes no one. While I was in the UK securing funds and while Fazal was in Uganda working to set things up, Fazal received sad and unexpected news that her frail, elderly father had been murdered back home in Kenya. Although she would return,

---

[2] VMM, Volunteer Missionary Movement. The house was named VMM after a volunteer of Nsambya Hospital who paid for it.
[3] 95% of cancer patients don't receive treatment. Of the 5% who reach treatment, many reach it too late or receive inconsistent therapy. Only 1% of cancer patients are cured in African countries.

Fazal needed to return to Kenya for a period to help with funeral and family matters.

Arriving in Uganda, I scrambled to get it all going. But those who have overcome obstacles know that they are merely a part of the path. As Marcus Aurelius once wrote, 'The impediment to action advances action. What stands in the way becomes the way.' I became the de facto doctor, nurse, executive director, secretary, accountant, driver and cook. This may explain so much about who I was and who I still am.

Although it felt like I was alone in Uganda, it was taking a village back in Liverpool to keep things going out here. Successful non-profits are usually fuelled by the quiet, unsung heroes working and volunteering tirelessly in the background. I knew this and felt grateful for the invisible support that laced the mission. I stared up at my metaphorical mountain, ready and excited.

Uganda would be my greatest test yet. After 58 years of preparation I was ready for battle. Unknown even to myself at that time, I had spent my life preparing myself for this mission and hardening my armour.

Every person wears armour, unique to their strengths and weaknesses, individuality, and chosen purpose. My armour was an eclectic blend, forged by my natural personality traits, the period and place in which I was born, my family, my career path and the unique experiences these factors created. It has always been important to me to have a big heart, to be compassionate, and to be a hospitable host. Although grounded deeply in my faith I tried to be open-minded. I was fearless in my pursuits, and I laughed easily and often. But with light comes the darkness. At times, I could be brash, arrogant, stubborn, quick to anger, and I often spoke my mind, just as I thought it. All of these traits would be invaluable to my purpose. The light and the dark coalesced to form a sharp sword that I would utilise to fight for others. Twenty-four years later I would be quoted in *The*

New York Times, 'sometimes you have to kick and scream to keep things moving!'

But on that hot day in Kampala, there was no kicking and screaming; instead, my mind wandered to a letter I had received informing me that a package was waiting for me at the airport. Was it the first shipment of morphine powder? It would have to wait til morning as darkness descended. Before deciding to set up in Uganda, I had talked with the Minister of Health, Dr Makumbi, asking for his support in allowing the importation of powdered morphine. I could not start a hospice without effective pain-control medicine. Dr Makumbi knew that his people were suffering. Despite opposition from other members in the government he agreed to help get me the powdered morphine. 'Our people here are suffering so much from cancer and from AIDS. Please bring palliative care and your affordable morphine to our people.'

Powdered morphine, reconstituted into oral morphine, is the key that unlocks the door to severe pain management in low economy countries. It's cheap, easy to make and people who don't have regular access to hospitals or doctors can take it in their homes. A week's worth of oral morphine costs less than the local cost of a loaf of bread. It is so simple to manufacture that it can be made at the kitchen sink. Filled into recycled water bottles, the lids and a 5 ml syringe are used to measure the liquid, accommodating for resource-poor areas and homes. Before 1993, Uganda was importing morphine injections and tablets – expensive, scarce, and only used for emergencies and post-operative pain. Everyone else with cancer, AIDs and other terminal diseases suffered unrequited pain until their disease mercifully took them. In Africa, extreme suffering and pain, which human rights activists equate to torture, is epidemic.[4] But I planned on doing something about it.

---

[4] In 2017, oral morphine is still not available in 34 of the 54 African countries. Further, the affordable essential medicines needed for palliative care, which include internationally controlled medications such

The last patient left just as dusk began to set in. I sat outside on the cement steps, filing my pink-painted nails as a small lizard went flying by into the bushes. I was going to have dinner with my dear friend, Sister Brigid Corrigan, a Medical Missionary of Mary (MMM). Brigid had been in East Africa for the last twenty-four years and was visiting Nsambya Hospital to see the work in the AIDS division. She was visiting from Dar es Salaam where she was involved in the Catholic AIDS organisation, PASADA. Brigid and I became close friends thirty-five years ago, when we both joined the MMMs only two months apart.

My stomach growled. 'Where on earth do you think Brigid is?' I said out loud to Turkey Lurkey as he went gobbling past. Mr Lurkey wasn't an especially beautiful or smart turkey but was a gift and had now become the infamous m'zungu turkey. M'zungu, the Swahili word used by the locals for 'white person'. Only a white person would have a turkey for a pet. And he too was white! And to add to the mystique, I collected Turkey Lurkey every evening, scooping him under my arm and walking him back to my compound to ensure my pet turkey didn't end up in someone's boiling pot of stew.

'There goes the crazy m'zungu and that m'zungu turkey of hers,' the locals would mutter, laughing under their breath.

Skipping lunch was often a necessity under the current workload and my stomach let out another grumble in protest. But I didn't notice this time as my mind began to whirl with the challenges I foresaw in a country far away from my own. With only three months' worth of funding, Fazal and I had a lot of work to get done if my vision had any chance of coming to fruition.

What I wouldn't give for a cigarette just then.

---

as morphine, are unavailable in more than 80% of the world. This continues in 2023, often more due to the strict rules in place by uninformed health professionals, who advise the governments.

PART I

THE DECISION

1

The Merrimans

In every conceivable manner, the family
is a link to our past, bridge to our future.
Alex Haley

THE SNOW fell hard. Hardly commonplace for Liverpool, and almost a rarity for the middle of May. The large snowflakes layered Queen's Drive and decorated rooftops in white. This would be Josie's first home delivery. The weather was too treacherous to get to a hospital and conversely the doctor and midwives couldn't get to her. This would be her third. Miss Heeny (Neeny to the family), a close friend of my mother's, sat holding Josie's hand as the first strong contraction hit. Josie let out a scream and Neeny's eyes went wide with fright as the responsibility of a healthy mother and baby landed directly on her unprepared shoulders. After a long night of sweat, wailing and heaving, Neeny caught a little baby girl.

I was born on 13 May 1935 in a small upstairs room in one of the new corporation houses on Queen's Drive, Liverpool, UK. I was born to Thomas Joseph Merriman (Toddy) and Josephine Dunne (Josie) in a strong Catholic family. Mum and Dad were both born and raised in Liverpool by Irish Catholics immigrants. My parents would grow up as true Liverpudlians – also known as 'scousers', named after the pot of Irish stew (scouse) cooked by the Irish immigrants who came over during the Irish potato famine in the late 1840s. Liverpool saw a great influx of Irish immigrants and the scouser accent reflected the descent – harsh, nasal tones, with both vowels and consonants affected – making it 'one of the most recognisable accents in the country, if not the world'.[5] And luckily, the welcoming culture of the Irish had infiltrated the stiff upper lip of the British shores, giving the scousers a kind, welcoming reputation, albeit paired with the likes of low-class criminals, and to that extent correspondingly stigmatised.

Dad was tall and thin. He had great feelings for Mum but was rather reserved and strict with us children. His clever nature and intelligence earned him a BSc degree, uncommon for those born in the early 1900s. Despite having the potential to garner a high income, his passion for teaching led him into primary education. He initially began teaching at St Brigid's RC primary school in Liverpool, known for its abject poverty. Children would show up to class in the dead of winter with no shoes on their feet and no lunch in their haversacks. With Dad's low-income, penury was never far away from our door and I remember the tension between Mum and Dad on the vexed issue of scraping by. 'If only he had gone into scientific research,' Mum would mutter.

But despite my parents' financial difficulties, our family life was stable and secure and whatever we may have lacked materially we made up for in other ways. Mum and Dad enjoyed making music together and most nights would include a few Irish folk songs and plainchant. Dad was a gifted musician and could play the piano and organ by ear, often playing at church services. The three younger children would eventually follow in our parents' piano-playing fingers, but for Joseph the eldest, he took up the screeching violin. Thankfully it did not last long.

As a result of the formal relationship I had with my dad, I don't remember any deep personal affection between us. I did not seek my dad's lap to cuddle in or run to him with my fears. Quite the opposite. Although lively and energetic amongst my friends and even my mum and siblings, when my dad came around I'd get uncharacteristically shy and quiet. (This stage didn't last forever as my dad would later comment on my unruly adolescent behaviour.) But despite our lack of closeness, my dad's actions and values would leave an indelible mark on me. Even if I wasn't aware of it as a child, my father's strong character was to be a decisive influence on my later life.

---

[5] https://www.ukessays.com/essays/languages/liverpool-accent.php

My mum, Josie, was the youngest of seven children. As is often the case in big families, she was raised mostly by her siblings and due to the early death of her father, her mother was constantly working to try to feed her children. As a young girl, Mum heard rumours about her father's death. Apparently, he came home one night after a long, physically exhausting shift, and sat relaxing with nightcap in hand next to the open fire. Although it was difficult for Mum to know for sure what happened next, she believed her father, having dozed off, then fell into the fire and burned to death. The family would eek out a living – but his death meant that everyone had to learn how to work and contribute. Her two brothers became priests and one of her sisters became a nun, while Mum decided to become a typist. Her career choice, however, didn't reflect her true nature as she was a deeply spiritual person. (Although her career was shortlived and ended with the arrival of her marriage which was common for that time.)

'When you four grow up,' Mum would later tell us, 'I'm going to send your dad off to a be a monk and go join the nuns!'

To be a nun in the early to mid 1900s – in a family of Irish descent – had a rather different connotation to that of today's world. The best and brightest often went off to serve in the Catholic Church. In the Irish tradition, it was a blessing if at least one child from each family became a priest or a nun. Mum was my spiritual rock. She regularly went to Mass in the mornings before breakfast and often took me with her. I remember getting bundled from head to toe and walking as quickly as my skinny legs could carry me down the dark street with nothing but Mum's hand guiding me. At a time when children were taught to fear God, I learned from Josie to love and feel a personal relationship with God. So much so that as a little girl I was constantly having conversations with God – even over the smallest things.

My little brother, Bernard, entered the world fifteen months after me, completing the family of four children: Joseph, Oonagh, me and Bernie. Despite wanting to have a large family – which at that time could even have numbered over fifteen children – this would be the last child Mum would have. After Bernie, Mum had three late-term miscarriages. Even when I was three I remember Mum's misery as she asked me to pray with her for a new baby. A short time later a new baby arrived in Uncle John's house and I was so upset with a God who had sent our baby to the wrong Merrimans!

After her last miscarriage, Mum was told she should never get pregnant again. She was devastated. She even apologised to us, weeping, that she wouldn't be able to give us more brothers and sisters. This must have been hard on her marriage in an age when birth control was condemned by the Catholic Church, except for the 'safe period', unknown and untrusted by most.

But darker forces were at work at this time: the deadliest war in human history was about to be unleashed on all of us.

2
Run to the Bunker, Baby: World War II 1939–45

You have power over your mind, not outside events.
Realise this and you will find strength.
Marcus Aurelius

ERMANY invaded Poland on 1 September 1939. Two days later, Great Britain and France[6] declared war on Germany. Before the war was finished over twelve countries would be involved. The greatest and most horrific war in human history – spanning the next six years – had just begun. My early childhood would be engulfed and consequentially shaped by World War II.

The UK immediately passed the National Service Act, enforcing the conscription of all men between the ages of 18 and 41. Boys, not yet men, and men with wives and children, said their goodbyes. They swarmed onto trains and buses, leaving behind crying women and children. Over 3.5 million men would serve in the British army over the course of the war.[7] Many of these men

---

[6] France, Australia and New Zealand.
[7] Men joined the British Army from the mainland and the colonies.

29

would never be seen by their families again. Nearly half a million British lives[8] would perish.

A limited number of exceptions kept a man out of a soldier's uniform. However, a severe case of asthma might and did in Dad's case. He had suffered asthma attacks as a teenager and into his adulthood and was exempted from conscription. He remained in Liverpool with us while teaching in St Brigid's and other schools in downtown Liverpool. When I was nine (1943) he was to become Headmaster of 'St Matthew's Junior Mixed' our local Catholic school, where his three youngest children were still attending. He also volunteered for the local ARP, a community position commissioned by the national war effort, to protect the local people in disasters. Every night I'd watch him leave our house in Uniform to survey the streets and help bomb dropped areas.

Although there would be intermittent times apart, our family would be a rare wartime family unit. Living through the war in Liverpool, our family of six would need all the solidarity and stability we could get.

Liverpool had the largest transatlantic convoy port on the west coast of Britain. The enormous commerce, naval activity and supplies passing through the Merseyside port allowed the British to sustain the war efforts and keep putting food on the table. As such, it became a central target for the German attacks. The Germans would carry out air-raids on this little island, unable to attack by land. Over the course of the war, over 30,000 civilians would die and another 87,000 were injured from the German Blitz attacks on the UK. Liverpool received the full wrath of the German air force, second only to London.

Targeted cities began evacuating woman and children to safer areas in the countryside. The plan to protect the prosperity of the nation was known as Operation Pied Piper. Over two million children would be packed up, wrapped with identification tags, and shipped away to bomb-free zones. Liverpool was no exception. As a teacher in St Brigid's, Dad would have to leave his family and accompany his school to the city of Chester, a town approximately 28 miles away. Joseph and Oonagh were to evacuate with his school and go with him. That left my mum with

---

[8] Includes military and civilian deaths.

two small children, too young to go to school, to face the bombs alone.

'Mum? Why are they leaving?' I asked as I watched Joseph and Oonagh pack their haversacks with their nursery rhyme painted tin dishes.

'They need to go with Daddy for now. But don't worry they'll come back soon,' she soothed me, stroking my hair.

I watched Joe put on his gas mask.

'Do you think we'll have to use this?' he said, looking at it.

I remember the feeling of excitement as my brother proudly displayed his mask. I also had a wonderful little bright red and blue Mickey Mouse gas mask.

'Take that off and put it back. The bus will be here any minute!' Mum snapped. Although she tried her best to hide it, the tension was increasing and becoming palpable.

The brakes juddered as the bus pulled up, crammed full of young children – and Dad. We all came out of the house to greet him. It was a cold, grey morning and Bernie and I, holding hands to comfort ourselves, watched the whirl of activity in front of us. Dad walked up to the door, where everyone was hovering, gave Mum a kiss and crouched down to speak to Bernie and me.

'Now you make sure you take care of each other,' he said softly. He gave us a hug and stood up and locked eyes with Mum one more time.

'Alright, time to go,' he said, a grimace form on the side of his mouth as he turned away.

Oonagh and Joseph fell in line behind him.

I watched the children on the bus watching us.

As Mum stood viewing the departure of half of her family, she let out a small sob. I looked up at her to see the tears streaming down her face. Her chin was trembling and before I knew it, Mum was racing down the road.

She ran to Dad, blocking the path of her two older children.

'They can't leave,' she sobbed, clutching Joseph and Oonagh to her sides.

I'm not sure what happened next. There was a lot of crying by Mum and hushed conversation between her and Dad. And then Mum, Joseph and Oonagh all walked back to the house together. Together, we all waved goodbye to Dad as the bus slowly crawled away.

Sometimes, it's better to be united – come what may – bombs and all. But the bombs didn't come. Not initially – and it wasn't long before Dad came back and the entire Merriman family was together again.

*

During the first few months of war, life was surprisingly normal. Several of the younger children that grew up in Liverpool during this time would later recount that they weren't afraid and easily adjusted to wartime life because 'we knew no different ... and accepted everything as normal life'. What I remember is the cold. It pierced through my clothes and into my bones. The only coal fire was in the living room. We kept a pile of coal outside our house and used it sparingly in the evenings to keep the living room warm and pneumonia at bay. But it was freezing in the hall and the landing in winter. My sister and I shared a bed, cuddlingly close for body heat.

Overall, I also adjusted quite quickly to the changes. I remember flipping through Mum's magazines in the living room, continuing to walk to Mass in the mornings and playing in the back garden and on the drive, with my little brother, Bernie, and the neighbouring children. However, the one indelible mark in my memory involved food – and the lack of it – especially the limited rations of sweets.

Food and clothes rations began a few months after the start of the war. Every person had a ration book with coupons in it based on their age. I still remember the different colours of the small books in green, blue and sandy brown, marking the age classifications. As a four-year-old, I began with the little green book. Sweets were few and far between, except on the occasional 'extra sweets day' when Mum's friend would send her extra coupons. Families were encouraged to grow their own vegetables and fruit was a rare sight. 'I don't think I saw a banana the entire war,' one of my childhood friends later said. No sugar for tea. Eggs came in a yellow powder sent over from America in wax-coated boxes. If you were lucky, you might have a friendly neighbour who might have a hen. And I was lucky.

As small and as skinny as I was, I still made it a habit to feed leftover bread crusts to the neighbour's hen. The neighbour must have watched me befriend and feed her hens because she would occasionally reward me with a beautiful brown egg. Cupping the egg reverently in my tiny hands, I'd carry my prized possession directly back to Mum beaming from ear to ear. Smells and sounds have an incredible ability to recreate past emotions. The cooking of an egg sends my serotonin levels flying – the crack of the egg as the shell breaks, the sizzling hiss as the egg hits the hot pan; the eggy smell mixed with salt and butter; and the warm yoke breaking across the plate that I would delightfully mop up with my bread. Eighty years later, eggs and chips are still one of my favourite meals.

On an island that sometimes doesn't see the sun, anything fortified in vitamin D was important. It was especially essential in places like Liverpool where the smog emitted by the factories blocked the sun, covering the sky in an uninterrupted grey haze. It was common for children to get rickets, colloquially referred to as 'bendy legs' – the bones went soft and the legs would develop an outward curvature. At one point, Joseph began to have early signs of rickets and had to seek extra nutrition before it became permanent. As a precaution, we all drank the free Government supply of fortified orange juice, only obtainable with a green ration book!

But overall, things were normal. Or at least, us wartime children perceived things as normal. And one day, during the first months of the war, I said a rather strange thing to Mum.

She received a monthly magazine she had subscribed to called *Echo from Africa* – a religious magazine that illustrated the work of the missionaries in Africa and I found myself drawn to the pictures of the children. They depicted a world entirely alien to me, and yet I knew that the children were worse off than me. On this day, Mum noticed that I had become transfixed by one particular child. It was as if me and that child had locked eyes on each other and were communicating in a different time-dimension, the way only a child's imagination could conjure. I slowly lifted my head and stared at Mum in the same way as I had been staring at the picture.

'Mum.'

'Yes, love?'

'When I grow up, I'm going to go here. I'm going to help these children.'

Mum looked down at me, her little four-year-old, but I had already returned my gaze to the picture. As she later told me, a strange feeling swept over her. A moment of strange wonder when your child says something precocious, with unwarranted compassion for others at the very same time as the rest of the world was trying to blow each other to bits and pieces.

'Mum?' I said again.

'What is it?' she said, wondering what on earth I would say now.

'When is breakfast?' I said staring up, eyes wide and hungry.

Mum smiled. I was back to being a four-year-old.

Bombs and Bunkers

The Battle of Britain of 1940 began as the fight for air superiority exploded over the English Channel. If the Germans gained an advantage in the air they'd be able to send thousands of troops and invade British soil. In only a few weeks, the British Royal Air Force (RAF) Command in the South was completely exhausted of resources, ammunition and at the end of their means. But the remaining RAF fighters decided not to waiver, and fought on in peril. In the final hours, it was the Germans who retreated. With greater losses than expected and no progress, the German leadership decided to implement a different strategy. Instead of infiltrating by foot – they would target key industrial cities from the sky. With one country left in their sights, the German's rained down hellfire on the small island.

Defence preparations for British civilians had begun immediately. Cheap bunkers, made of corrugated metal, were distributed to the entire population of Great Britain. Commonly referred to as Anderson shelters, the bunkers were buried four feet underground with an arched roof and disguised with grass or soil over the top. A family of six could snuggly fit in the shelter, even with a few sleeping bunks. By the time Germany began dropping bombs, over two million shelters were erected.

Nearly a year after declaring war, the first major air raid hit Liverpool on 28 August 1940. I was lying in bed sound asleep when the siren pierced through my consciousness, snapping me upright in bed. Oonagh wiggled next to me. (The two of us would share a bed until I left home at the age of eighteen.) The sirens were positioned throughout Liverpool so everyone in the city could hear them. An alarm would be sounded, signalling the incoming of planes, but no one cared about the planes really – it was the bombs. If a bomb dropped close to you, the sound would rip through your heart the same way they'd rip through the earth, buildings and sometimes people.

Just as my eyes began to adjust to the darkness Mum ran into the bedroom.

'Wrap a blanket round you! We are going to the shelter!' She already had Bernie scooped on her hip and shone a small light on us girls.

'Hurry, girls, stay warm.' Her breath was short. Mum had managed to throw on a big woolly hat and a trench coat over her pyjamas.

Oonagh and I shot out of bed and grabbed a blanket as we fumbled for our slippers.

Having arrived outside, Joseph handed us another blanket as we entered the shelter with Mum and Bernie. The five Merrimans huddled together in the dark. Dad was typically out on air-raid precaution (ARP) duty. Although I sensed the fear coming from Mum, I couldn't help but feel an edge of excitement. Getting pulled out of my bed in the middle of the night. Sleeping underneath the ground. It was great fun. Mum encouraged us to sleep if we could and sleep always came easily to me after the excitement had worn off.

When darkness fell, the entire city became black. There were no shop lights, streets lights or house lights. ARP wardens would patrol the streets, searching for any detectable light that might give advantage to the enemy planes. Curtains would be drawn, torches were always half-covered and pointed at the ground, and doors had light traps installed. If any light was detected, wardens would bang on the door. 'Put the light out!' they'd holler. The black curtains over wooden blinds always had light gaps. Many families would seek shelter in their bunkers, and some would huddle under the staircase. For once, the smog, clouds and grey overcast became Liverpool's ally. Of course, on moonlit nights, all was revealed.

We would trade stories about the night's events. First came the rising wail of the airaid siren, then the planes would sound over the city like drones, and although a lot of it was exciting, hearing the planes was frightening, because you didn't know if it was going to come right down on you. Finally, would come the relief siren to let us know we could return to our homes.

On one night, a German bomb fell on a train full of ammunition. Those of us who had been children from all over the area still recall the explosion. It was like fireworks exploding into the night sky – fountains of bright lights and sparks – and many bangs as well. A friend of mine who lived about a mile away from the explosion had a neighbour who discovered a length of railway line in her backyard the next morning.

Another morning, they awoke to an unexploded bomb hanging on the roof of a nearby school. My friend Pat had to evacuate her home with her family and stay in a large house crammed full of people in similar situations. Families would bedhop between homes and churches for dry places to sleep at night.

A friend, Frank McGurk, recalls a night when, huddled under the staircase, he heard a sound wave hit his family's house. The soot dropped down the chimney, and black ash exploded into the living room covering everything. The slates and tiles from the roof had ripped clean off and the windows had shattered. They awoke to find that a large landmine had exploded 500 yards from their house. A large salvation army home, five houses down, took the major impact of the explosion.

'We went out the next morning... the building that had been there, vanished, just smoke and big craters remained.' The four houses next to the Salvation Army Hall hadn't been touched. 'If the Hall hadn't been there and taken the impact of the explosion, the first four or five houses would have been flattened,' he says. Having missed the likely target of the nearby railway bridge, Frank remembers the tramlines coming out of the ground 'like a rollercoaster'. I remember my Mum's sadness as our family friend, Mr Peacock, had been killed that night while out on ARP duty.

Liverpool received heavy bombing in the final months of 1940. As Christmas approached, so did tragedy. Between 20 and 22 December, the Germans targeted several large shelters and killed over 300 people.

Father Christmas didn't come that year to the Merriman household. I accepted this bitter pill until I heard that Father Christmas was still going to the wealthier kids' homes! I was five years old when Mum broke the news that Father Christmas was Dad! I couldn't believe it! For a child, that indeed was difficult news.

It wasn't until May 1941 that the Germans again hit hard. The Luftwaffe pounded Liverpool and nearby Bootle for eight days – laying devastation to homes, hospitals, churches, the Merseyside port, and other important buildings. Over 1700 people were killed and over 1500 people were injured.

After the first onslaught, the family decided to sleep in their underground shelter without prior prompting from the sirens. We'd get dressed in warm clothes, boil flasks of hot tea and make our way out as the sun was setting. There was hardly any standing room in the dark, musty hole and we younger kids were directed to go straight into our bunk where we'd stay for the remainder of the night. My sixth birthday was about ten days away. I lay in the cold, staring up at the dark board above me. Would we still be sleeping in the bunk on my birthday? I wondered, 'would everyone still be alive on my birthday?'

In daylight, the horrors and danger of war could be turned into fun and games. Every morning all of us children would go hunting for shrapnel. The small, jagged shards of metal would get traded and prized for its uniqueness in size, shape, and colour. We would even take pride swapping stories about the events of the night. But as the light from the day began to fade, the fearless masks of the day vanished and fear coursed through the veins of children and adults alike, not knowing what each night had in store.

It would be the first time I truly met fear. That night the entire family stayed in the shelter. I liked having my dad around, he must have had the night off from ARP duty. Just as I was starting to doze, a high, whining whistle grew louder and louder ... a deafening sound erupted in the shelter, sending out sound wave compression shocks. The colossal noise was followed by the sound of shattering masonry. Something had been hit. Even for me, a five-year-old, the naïve excitement of ignorance was now long gone. Dread. Confusion. Shock. What had just happened?

I opened my eyes and peered around in the dark, trying to find the glint of other eyeballs.

'Is everyone OK?' Dad's voice punctured the silence. Everyone began chiming in. 'Still here.'

Bernie began to whimper, and Mum wrapped up her youngest in a bear hug.

'What just happened?' Joseph piped up. 'Did our house get hit?'

'I don't know, son. We'll just have to wait till morning,' Dad replied, his voice calm and matter of fact. The tone held just enough confidence to reassure the shaken family. No one slept the rest of that night.

The thing about fear is once you allow it in its pervasive quality besets its host. Dread crept into my consciousness – the not knowing – the suspense. My senses came alive. I strained to hear every little noise. I worked to control my breath and slow it down so I could hear. Anything. I wanted to know what might be coming, even though there was nothing I could do about it.

It was just after daybreak when the 'all-clear' sirens sounded the long one-tone signal. The morning siren always created a sense of relief, heralding that night was over. Did we even have a home to go back to?

Our family slowly started making their way out of the shelter. Dad left first and the rest of us followed. The air was fresh and crisp, the grass wet with the morning dew. The birds were eerily quiet that morning. And there was our home – standing in one piece. The windows were completely shattered and blown out. Rough, jagged edges of glass that lined some of the windows gave a malicious warning. But our home hadn't been hit.

'Wait outside while I go check the house.' Dad ran inside to make sure it was safe for us to enter.

'All clear.' He waved at us to come in.

'Be careful of the glass,' Mum instructed us. 'Oonagh, go get the brush and shovel.'

'Josie, I'm going to go and see if the neighbours are OK. Someone must have been hit close to us.'

Dad placed on his ARP helmet and leaned in and gave Mum a kiss before heading out of the door. Despite the situation, we were all still alive. Perspective can always change misery to gratitude.

I walked around in an exhausted daze until – *crunnncchhh* – I stepped on the shattered window glass.

'Anne! Be careful. Go sit down next to your brother.' Mum checked my shoe and then took me into the front sitting room and sat me on a clean seat as Bernie slowly fell asleep.

My mind drifted back to the moment when the bomb hit so close to our shelter. Where had it hit? I quietly slid off the chair and slipped out of the front door. It was an overcast day but appeared extra bleak and grey because of the auxiliary smoke.

As I took in the surrounding human chaos it didn't take me long to discover where the bomb had hit. The house six doors down on the left on our side of the road had been devastated. Walls were missing, the remains of beds and furniture had been scattered in all directions – iron pipes stuck out like misplaced fence posts. The dirt and dust from the explosion had left a heap of chaos. Adults were running around the debris.

'Anne! What are you doing?' Dad's voice emerged through the rubble. 'Get back home!' he shouted sternly. 'Today is not the day for your shenanigans.'

I knew better than to disobey Dad. I slipped back into the house without being noticed. Bernie was still sleeping on the sofa.

*

The bombs continued to fall, and tragedy followed the dark nights into the light hours of the day. Dad regularly partnered with another ARP warden and would inspect homes that had been bombed. That morning, his partner had discovered a land mine, while checking the house, and thinking it was either a dud or had already exploded he explored further. The bomb went off, killing Dad's mate.

Dad entered the house that evening with a slow step. His eyes were dim and his lips tight. He has been mere inches away from leaving his children fatherless. After a sparse meal, the family headed to the shelter.

The bombing continued for eight straight nights. The blitz of May 1941 left the city in ruins. I had my sixth birthday in a home with blown-out windows in a city that had been demolished by the German bombs. But I was one of the lucky ones. I had my family. I had a home. I had a country not yet occupied by enemy troops. But I now understood the danger my family and my country. I understood that death could be moments away.

Evacuation to Wales

After the dangers of the May blitz, another evacuation was carried out. This time Mum, Oonagh, me and Bernie travelled to St Asaph, a small town in North Wales, about 56 miles away from Liverpool. Joseph was now at grammar school and he stayed in Liverpool with Dad while the rest of us lived in St Asaph for about a year – on the ground floor of a large old house – owned by a married couple who lived upstairs to allow us to use the downstairs rooms. The house was next to the Plough Inn where I quickly became friends with the owner's two daughters. Playing in this huge inn, tobogganing in the snow, and hikes in the fresh country air helped us children forget the frightening nights spent in the shelter in Liverpool.

While things became darker in the rest of the world, I would always remember my stay in Wales with something like happiness. The school I attended, with one class, for five to eleven year olds, was taught by nuns in a small two-room building. Oonagh and I would take the long walk each morning to get to the school, where the day was enlivened by meeting up with other children, many of them family friends. Bernie had not yet started school and was with Mum most of the day. Dad and Joseph, now attending grammar school in Liverpool, would join them at the weekends.

This was also the time when Bernie and I would become as thick as thieves. The terror of the war had not dimmed our light, and together, it was the two of us against the world. We would create secret languages, take on phantom enemies and outsmart our foes with our wit and cunning tactics. I always felt closest to Bernie, who was turning into a beautiful little boy, smart as a whip, with dark hair and a lovely personality.

Meanwhile the bombing in Liverpool had died down considerably after the May blitz and our family was united back in Liverpool by the spring of 1942. Although I had came to Wales, frightened and worn and already awoken to the realities of war – my spirit had been rejuvenated in Wales. I would return to Liverpool the bright, giggly girl I had always been. My resilient nature was strong as a young child. Life was uncertain. Life could be dangerous. But why not smile and have fun while you still could? Whether I was born with it or had learned it during my childhood, this trait would continue to be one of my strongest assets throughout my life.

Peace in Liverpool

The peace in Wales extended for the next three years. Life back in Liverpool, would continue as normal. I had rejoined St

Matthew's School where my father later was headmaster. The school was attached to a large Byzantine church. Frank and Pat, my classmates, have described me as 'lively, clever, always happy and smiling, but well-behaved'. But I was not too well-behaved: I still let Frank copy my work in an exam.

Every morning we walked to school carrying our gas masks over our shoulders on thick string in square cardboard boxes. We often practised gasmask and air-raid drills to prepare us for any unknown situation. All of us children would get bustled outside into the big, brick air-raid shelter, a cold, and horrible smelling place, and encouraged to sing as loudly as possible. Only later would we understand that this was to block out the sound of planes. Luckily, the drill was never used for a real emergency. The class would begin every morning with a prayer. 'Dear God, please look after all of the soldiers fighting for our safety; and please bring back Marie's father.' But despite the prayers, Marie's missing father would never be seen or heard from again.

Liverpool's airbase served as a hub for arriving US and Canadian soldiers. As children, we heckled the American soldiers with their big smiles, and occassionally if we were lucky they'd throw a packet of gum in our direction and six children would all dive to get the prize. I remember seeing the Canadians in their big trucks with them – you'd get really lucky, and sometimes even get a chocolate bar.

During the war years I developed a close relationship with Pat Ruane who also went to St Matthew's. Pat, the youngest of six, was a striking brunette with a quick wit and energy to spare. Her father was a policeman who also stayed back in Liverpool. The family stability that both of us were fortunate to have during the wartime may have been a strong contributing factor to our ability to cope with adversity and maintain high spirits. Our high energy complemented each other well. Only ten days apart in age, Pat has described me as always 'giddy and larking about'.

Although I was a bright-eyed rambunctious girl, often on the edge of causing trouble, I had a completely different side to me. At the age of seven, I'd rise before the break of dawn, get myself out of bed, dress myself and walk to Church by myself for morning mass. I'd sit in the dark, cold church with its high ceilings and listen to Mass that was spoke in Latin. Unable to understand, I'd thumb through my daily Catholic missal – a book containing the daily Latin and English translations for the Mass reading of the liturgical year.

The tradition of morning Mass with Mum had stuck – even when she had become too busy working at the Mother's Union to attend. Why the devotion? Thinking back, I remember how important my first Communion was to me.

On 2 July 1942, I took the third out of seven sacred Catholic sacraments: Holy Communion. In the Catholic tradition, Holy Communion typically occurs when a child has reached the age of reason, which is seven years old. As a Catholic, Holy Communion is one of the most intimate of ceremonies, based on the belief that Jesus is entering your body and soul. During a time when it was common to teach children to 'fear God', I developed an entirely different relationship with Jesus.

Through Mum's mentorship, I deeply felt that Jesus was my friend and someone I could turn to. Yet I couldn't believe that the Jesus I had heard so much about would enter my own heart. I was taller and skinnier than Oonagh and wore her first Communion dress with lace sewed to the bottom to extend the dress past my knees. The mismatched quality of the dress was fitting for the time and place – yet I wore it as proudly as if it had been new and perfectly hemmed for me.

Two days before the big day, Bernie came down with the measles. As contagious as measles were, it was undecided if I would even be allowed to be around other children.

In the end, I was allowed to receive Communion.

After I received my blessing the priest placed a small unleavened bread host on my tongue. I felt no momentous shift, my heart did not burst open with love but instead, calmness permeated my being as the bread dissolved in my mouth. As soon as it had started, it was over. I was shown out of the door and went back home. There would be no celebrating, no food, no social time with the other children. But maybe the message of the Holy Communion wasn't spoiled for me in the way it so often is when children are showered with presents and money. Jesus was a part of my soul now and had just become my new friend. So, maybe missing a party wasn't such a big a deal.

I would begin to turn to Jesus and have a personal dialogue with him, and this practice and way of thinking would continue throughout my life. I would always be a devout Catholic, even though my opinions of the Catholic Church and their practices would diverge and vary over time.

*

The European war came to an official end on 8 May 1945 when the Allies captured Berlin (it would still take another four months for it to end worldwide). With the celebrations for VE Day – Victory in Europe – street parties exploded across Europe.

Nearly every side street in Liverpool was overflowing with people laughing and crying; drinking and eating; hugging and dancing. Banners were hung from lampposts and draped across the top of streets. I remember running around in the street and seeing Mum crying tears of joy.

Five days later, I celebrated my tenth birthday, safe and sound with my entire family.

3

Easter Sunday

Your absence has gone through me
Like thread through a needle.
Everything I do is stitched with its colour.
W.S. Merwin

Grief does not change you, Hazel. It reveals you.
John Green, The Fault in Our Stars

THREE YEARS had passed since the war had ended. It was the beginning of 1948 and life was humming again. I had taken my Eleven Plus (often referred to as the scholarship exam) and had passed. This qualified me to enter a government-funded grammar school.

The Eleven Plus was a tripartite system used in the UK between 1944 and 1976 to place children on different paths after primary school.[9] Similar to an IQ test and designed to measure problem-solving abilities, the child would enter one of three schools: grammar school, secondary modern school, or technical college. Typically, only those children placed in grammar or secondary modern schools had the opportunity to proceed to university. Secondary modern schools also provided paths to attend a technical college or seek employment after the age of 14. The competition and stress to do well sat heavy on us children.

---

[9] The Eleven Plus did not apply to those whose parents paid for their private education.

All three of the elder Merriman children were now attending grammar school – Joseph and me by merit, and Oonagh, who became terribly panicked during tests, would attend because our parents paid directly for her fees as she hadn't passed the test. As March rolled around, it was time for the final child to take the exams.

Bernie appeared to be the brightest of all the children and had tested highly in his recent primary exams. Quite different from his elder brother, Bernie was sociable, open and warm. The females in the house found it much easier to connect with him and not only was I closest to him but the family recognised without jealousy that he was Mum's favourite. The young boy with the perfect quiff was often found in the streets playing football with his friends.

Bernie left in the morning to take his Eleven Plus exam in great spirits, but the moment he stepped back through the door later that day, I knew something was wrong. He looked pale and distraught. Was he really that worried about the exams? I wondered. But the extent of his pain became quickly evident as Bernie curled himself up on the floor and cried that his head was hurting.

Even though headaches were rare in the Merriman family, Bernie had previously fainted at Mass a few months earlier. Bernie and the other boys were holding candles at the front of the church during the priest's sermon, when Bernie suddenly collapsed to the ground and his candle went flying, as another altar boy standing next to him recalls.

Sitting with my family, I remember hearing a sudden crash from the altar. One of the altar boys had fainted. Fainting was frequent in those days. Many people would fast from midnight the previous night before receiving the Holy Communion the next morning. As if guided by a sixth sense, Mum flew out from the pew and rushed to the sacristy where they had carried the boy. Refusing to let Bernie walk home, they wrapped him in a blanket and took him home on the bus. We were reminded of the harbinger of the previous event as Bernie's headache continued to worsen into the night.

The following day, Bernie still lay curled up in a ball in his room, with curtains drawn.

I went to check on him and sat next to him on the bed.

'You OK, Bernie?' I said, rubbing his back.

Bernie looked up at me. Little drops of perspiration freckled his forehead and grimace lines etched the sides of his mouth. He groaned in distress and rolled over.

'It's going to be OK. Doctor is coming to see you today,' I tried to soothe him.

The doctor examined Bernie that Friday afternoon and said he had the 'flu. Many children had it around that time of year. 'If he doesn't start improving in a week, give me a call,' the doctor instructed.

But the headache only worsened. During the following week, Bernie cried night and day. He stayed in the dark confines of his room – any sign of light would send him wailing and vomiting. The family waited as the week passed and as we watched our little Bernie suffer, we were desperate for signs of improvement but there was none.

After the long week of waiting, the doctor came back to the house to check on Bernie. Upon seeing poor Bernie and his worsening condition he immediately sent for an ambulance from the infectious disease hospital (Fazakerley Hospital).[10] The doctor's provisional diagnosis was TB meningitis. The family was terrified – TB in 1948 was a death sentence and streptomycin, which was the first cure, was only discovered that year.

A green ambulance came to the home. Bernie was wrapped in a red blanket and carried out of the house. We all went outside to see him off. I remember his white skin against the dark red blanket and tried to give him a reassuring smile as they carried him away. The pain on Bernie's face left an indelible mark in my mind.

Upon arriving at the hospital, Bernie and my parents were told at the gate that he would need to have three needles put into his spine. i.e. lumbar punctures to decide the diagnosis. Mum later relayed to the rest of us how scared this made Bernie. But the tests were carried out and TB meningitis came back negative. Suspicious of a possible brain tumour, more tests were needed. Bernie received a carotid angiogram which meant injecting dye into the carotid artery to see if they could identify any displaced blood vessels in the brain. To prepare for this, Bernie had to have his head shaved. I knew he was so proud of his hair – it must have been incredibly sad for him, I thought upon hearing the news. The

---

[10] Now Aintree University Hospital.

angiogram showed a tumour in the cerebellum – a more common tumour in childhood.

I didn't see much of my parents the following week. They stayed with Bernie day and night; and the rare hours they did come home they would relate updates to the rest of us, but these updates were not promising. Bernie continued to get weaker and was constantly vomiting. As the surgery was being planned, he developed pneumonia.

My parents, exhausted from the long days and nights in the hospital, came home for a rest on Good Friday. The Merrimans always attended the noon service together. I was with Mum in her bedroom, which faced onto the main road, when there was a knock on the front door.

'Look and see who it is,' she asked me.

'It's Doreen Faulks,' I replied, looking out of the window.

Mum's response scared me. She jumped out of bed and instantly began to cry. She seemed to be afraid to meet Doreen, and instead paced the room trying to collect herself. Unbeknown to me, Doreen's house had the nearest telephone and her number had been left at the hospital to call in case an emergency developed with Bernie. After talking briefly with Doreen, my parents rushed out of the door. I remember the cold air filling the house as the door remained open. Joseph, Oonagh and I all stood in the hall in fright.

'Let's go to the service,' Joseph finally said.

My heart was aching and there was a chill in the pit of my stomach as we walked to the church. Was Bernie going to be OK? I had the picture stuck in my mind of my little bald brother, wracked with sobs. *Please be all right, Bernie.*

On Easter Monday morning, I was having a hard time sleeping when I heard the door creak open. I rolled over to see Dad walk slowly into my bedroom and sit on the bed beside me. Before he could speak the look in his eyes said everything.

'Bernie has died,' he told me.

Despite knowing what it meant, I couldn't understand it. This was not how it was meant to be! He was only eleven and had the love of the whole family. How could he have died? And so suddenly? He was such a healthy boy. Questions continued to stream through my head. I sat there in shock as Oonagh was gently shaken awake to be told the news.

Oonagh and I, still sharing the same bed, drew closer together. How was Mum? I wondered. The three of us went out into the kitchen where Mum was getting the breakfast ready. Eyes glistening, I watched as her tears fell in the porridge. Mum, Oonagh and I held and hugged each other tightly for a long time.

After breakfast, I took out my wartime secondhand bicycle – a present I had received for passing the scholarship exam – and set off for Pat's house about two miles away in Tuebrook. I gripped my black handlebars as my mind continued to try to make sense of how something like this could have happened.

I arrived at Pat's and her Mum opened the door.

'How is Bernard getting on, Anne?' she asked.

What I said next complelety caught her off guard.

'Bernie has died,' I said numbly. Neither Pat nor I knew what to do. Pat was as stunned as I was. We sat in the garden in silence. The tears never came. The shock and disbelief were tremendous – almost numbing. Not knowing how to handle it, Pat showed me how to make drop scones on the hotplate of the stove that she learned during her domestic science class. After spending a few hours with my friend, I began my journey home through Cherry Lane. My feet slowly pushed the pedals as the bike crept along the empty road near the back of the park. The cold air stung my eyes as my mind drifted back to Bernie's face.

*

Tap, tap tap.

A stranger stood outside the Merrimans' house.

Mum was absolutely wrecked. We had all survived the war and it felt like we had made it. We were safe again. And just when things were beginning to feel easy and make sense again, her little boy had died just yesterday. And a month earlier her mother had passed away.

The knocking on the door broke through Mum's consciousness and jarred her out of her semi-trance. Maybe Doreen was coming by to check on things?

Mum heard Dad open the door. Instead, of Doreen's familiar voice, she heard a strange male voice.

'Excuse me, sir, but your daughter's been in an accident.'

And that's when Mum literally lost it.

*

I was lying unconscious in the middle of the street. My bike lay on the pavement a few feet away. Blood flowed from my temple and my stockings had ripped at the knee.

A man gently picked me up and brought me inside his house and laid me on the couch.

'Margaret, a girl's come off her bike!'

I slowly came to at this point, as he laid me down on the couch.

'Three one three Queen's Drive, Liverpool Four,' I murmured and began repeating my address. 'Three one three Queen's Drive...'

'Hi, love. What's your name?' The lady of the house gently leaned over me.

'Three one three Queen's Drive, Liverpool Four...'

Despite being totally out of it, and later having no recollection of repeating the address, I am told that I provided them with just what they needed to go to get help.

When I finally did come to, I was sitting on a strange couch and an equally strange lady was wiping my knee. Suddenly I felt ill.

'Here take this,' the lady said, holding out a bucket.

I began to vomit into the little green bucket. Looking into the bucket I realised I had been vomiting blood. *Crikie*, I thought, *was I going to die too?*

A little over a month ago, a girl from school had been hit by a car and began vomiting blood. She died a few days later. Everyone in school now knew that if you vomited blood you were done for. But before I could begin comprehending my own death, my father appeared.

Dad and the man of the house helped me to the nearest bus stop and we returned home to a very distraught Mum.

I was diagnosed with severe concussion and ordered to stay in bed for a week.

I would be forced to miss my little brother's funeral, but I would still get to see him in the coffin. Common in Ireland – and those of Irish descent – the coffin and body were brought into the home and displayed in the front room so friends and family could visit.

They carefully guided me down the steps to see my little brother in the coffin. He had a ribbon covering his head so it wasn't obvious that his head had been shaved. The scarlet ribbon around his head matched the inside fabric of the coffin. He still looked beautiful. I remember looking at his little hands and being struck how similar they were to my own. We both shared the same rigid nails and the same shape.

I stayed in my room and heard the countless guests visit downstairs; they would all come up and visit me before leaving. I remember particularly Bernie's best friend, Charlie. Charlie and Bernie were true buddies. As Mum opened the door the sobs of Charlie could be heard along the road. He was devastated.

After the funeral Mum came to sit with me. 'What would you like, Anne?' And then the tears came...

'I want Bernie. I want Bernie. I want Bernie,' I cried. The gift of tears can calm and cleanse the grief that so tightly wraps our hearts. Mum hugged me and wept with me.

*

The grief of losing Bernie never left me. Seventy years later, talking about it still makes my voice squeak and tears stream down my face. It was my first experience of the loss of someone I truly loved.

I've always understood that loss and pain can cultivate compassion and wisdom within ourselves. It's the cracks that make us human. 'There's a crack in everything – that's how the light gets in.' I would later hear Leonard Cohen's song 'Anthem' and connect instantly with it. Life's great trials, if we do the work to heal, give us perspective, depth and beauty. The cracks from these experiences although difficult, can serve as a tremendous blessing in our lives if we let it. Bernie was a bright light in the family and his death strongly impacted everyone in that household.

4

The Visitation

Sometimes an ember is all we need.
Bear Grylls

UPON HEARING of Bernie's sudden death, Father Bob came to England for a visit. Father Bob was my Mum's first cousin – the third son of her Mum's brother, Jack Callan, who married Kitty McCullagh. One of seven siblings, Bob and his five brothers would all become priests. Mum's favourite of the five Callan priest cousins, was Fr Bob. The five brothers continued to stay close despite living in different countries. Father Bob had grey hair, a medium build and a hearty laugh. His round, impish face carried a pleasant smile which contrasted his venerable black garb and roman collar. To me, priests appeared very serious and solemn. But the lightness in Fr Bob's step and the warmth he emanated brought great comfort to the house and quickly endeared him with the rest of our family.

Of all the men I had been around, Father Bob's warm and outgoing traits reminded me most of the brother I had lost. We quickly formed a special bond. He made me laugh which was not something the other Merriman men could do, or even tried to do. He made time to share in our grieving and joined me and Mum's weekly ritual to visit the small grave that sat in the shadows under a large tree. An accomplished tree-climber, Bernie would have been proud to climb on the branches that hung over him now.

Father Bob even took up the weekend tradition of wrapping my hair in rags. Having become quite fixated on my hair, maybe as a homage to my brother who never had a hair out of place, I spent Friday night's transitioning my hair from weekday plaits (braids) to weekend ringlets. I remember telling Fr Bob all the week's latest gossip as he wrapped my hair around a piece of cloth, then the cloth around the hair and then knotting it near my scalp. I recalled memories of my brother and our time in the country during the war. I'd complain about school work and my teachers. During one of the evenings I even mentioned my secret draw towards Africa. I loved flipping through Mum's magazines, *Echo from Africa*, and imagining what life would be like out there. But how on earth was I ever going to get to Africa? Protestant women had gone to Africa for years. Going to Africa as a Catholic held less oppurtunities and I had no intention to take my vows and go as a Sister. I chatted away and Fr Bob intently listened.

Despite his short stay, the bond between the two of us stuck and we would continue to correspond for years to come.

*

'Anne! A letter from Father Bob's arrived.' Mum called out from the living room.

I came rushing from my bedroom and snatched the letter off her. I loved getting letters from Fr Bob. I would delight at the black typed ink and the crisp smell of the paper. They looked ever so wonderful and were always so easy to read. I loved the '*teeeeaaaaaarrrrrr*' as I ripped open the envelope and pulled out the letter.

Dear Anne,

How are the piano lessons?

I recently met a new religious congregation of women who are medical, and you immediately popped in my mind. Although I know you aren't fond of many Sisters, these ones are quite revolutionary! They are a new Catholic order started by Mother Mary Martin called the Medical Missionaries of Mary (MMMs). They go to Africa and help look after the sick and suffering. They ride bicycles and even wear veils showing their hair! Their dresses are 8 inches off

the ground and you can even see their ankles. It may even be
something you're interested in.

Give Mummy and Daddy my love.

God bless you.
Fr Bob

Fr Bob had in fact been admitted to the Lourdes Hospital in
Drogheda, run by these Sisters and was most impressed with the
care he had received, but he did not reveal this in his letter.

Catholic medical nuns who went to Africa? Well, that was
something new! I tucked the letter away and stored it in my box
with all the rest of Fr Bob's letters.

Over a year would go by. More letters would come and go. The
leaves were starting to turn brilliant shades of red, orange and
yellow as autumn came. I looked up to watch the leaves slowly
falling from the trees. At Mass on Sunday, the priest announced a
film worth viewing that was coming to the Trocadero Cinema in
town. It was about a new order of Sisters who were working in
Africa. It was called *The Visitation*. I was always ready to go
watch any show at the cinema.

Now why did that sound so familiar? I thought. The beautiful
typing of Fr Bob's letters came flitting into her mind ... and then
went flitting out.

I went to see the film with my older brother Joseph. The crisp
autumn air went right through my jacket as we walked to the
cinema, but the warmth of the theatre put me at ease as I nestled
into my seat. It was really Bernie who would have wanted to
watch this. It had been just over a year since my little brother
passed away. Bernie was the one who had always wanted to be a
priest. The little saint of the family. Ironically, neither Joseph nor
I had much interest in the religious life. The theatre dimmed the
lights and the picture began.

I will always remember how enthralled I was by the next hour.
The mighty women working in Calabar, Nigeria, riding around on
bikes with their veils pulled back so their hair was showing! You
could even see their ankles! Not like the unapproachable,
vindictive and hypocritical Sisters always giving out at school
while wearing the garbs of Jesus! Christ almighty, they didn't
seem like any nuns I had ever known. The contents of Bob's

previous letter became clear in my mind. This was the new order he thought I would be interested in.

The film showed a completely different world over there. Nothing like I had ever seen or experienced in Liverpool. Powerful rivers, expansive countryside, red dirt roads, and the people were beautiful and black with big white smiles that spread across their faces.

And then a small shift happened in me, as a thirteen-year-old girl, I sat in my seat watching these intelligent, caring women. And *I knew*. I knew that was what I was going to go and do. I would still have five more years before I would be eligible to interview and join the MMMs. A lot could happen between now and then. Would I still want to go? Would I still have the courage in five years? I was still young.

It was a quiet knowing. I didn't want to shout it from rooftops, I wanted to hold it sacred and close. I held on to that moment – the small ember glowed – the feeling of alignment with my inner path awoke.

I walked out of the cinema with Joseph, quiet and yet excited by what I had seen and felt. I remember thinking that this wasn't going to be like all the other ideas I had. This was going to be something that stuck. I would tell only two people – Mum and, interestingly, a nun at school – one of the few I liked. Wisely, two good picks, as both of those ladies would never tell a soul. Mum even kept it a secret from Dad. That secret would need time before it could fan the flames of a great fire.

And so I went on with life and continued to be a mischievous little girl.

5

Thelma and Louise ... and Mary

If you haven't been called a defiant,
incorrigible, impossible woman…
have faith… there is still time.

Clarrisa Pinkola Estes,
Women Who Run with Wolves

M Y school years went by in a whirlwind. Only a few
months after Bernie passed away, an incident occurred
at school between my sister and the headmistress, a
horrible nun, in charge of the school. In fact, Oonagh got kicked
out of school for wearing the wrong-shaped hat, a Landgirls hat
with a dinge in it. Unlucky for Oonagh, it wasn't even her fault.
The school uniform hat wouldn't fit her head – floating on top of
her thick piles of curls – so Mum had bought her another Landgirls
hat to wear. And that was it – despite righteously supporting the
family a few months earlier with Bernie's sickness, giving us
relics of their founder and seeking a miracle, – it only took a
wrong hat to have Oonagh tossed out of the school with no notice.

My parents were so flabbergasted, angered and humiliated by
the expulsion of their elder daughter that they pulled me out as
well. But that's nuns for you, I thought. In fact, now my parents
got a taste of what I had to deal with every day! That incident
perfectly illustrated how I felt about the lot of them. Cruel, power-

hungry hypocrites that preached about Christ's compassion while flogging their power senselessly.

However, the transfer proved to be a small miracle at a time when I needed a close friend. Transferred to my best friend's school, Pat and I would be reunited and cause all kinds of chaos over the next five years at Broughton Hall. This time our condemnation would be rightly deserved. All parents seem to have a blindspot for the faults and crimes of their own children, and my dad would be no exception. He blamed Pat for my misdeeds and emphasised the influence she had on me, but not the other way around. Little did he know.

The next five years consisted of what a lot of young girls would find themselves involved in: flirting with boys (well, only with the Catholic boys, definitely not those Protestants), going to the cinema, and covertly smoking any chance we got.

Pat didn't like to smoke alone and needed the company so both of us would secretly light up when the opportunity revealed itself. Despite being rather well behaved in my younger years, times had changed. I no longer felt inclined to acquiesce to the propriety expected of me. A harbinger of the future, I often found myself caught in the crossfires with authority. I would go on to fail Latin (and the teacher refused to let me back into class!), thrown out of French class, fail French class and then fail French class again. Clearly, I did not hold the gift of the tongue.

But despite finding myself in trouble – and my inadequacy in the language department – I had taken after my parents and excelled in music. Both Pat and I were rather talented piano players. And much to Dad's lack of delight, I revelled in jazz piano no less. This bad girl reputation I had stepped into seemed to precede me so it shouldn't be a surprise when trouble found me!

Pat and I were sitting in our room, working oddly enough on our homework, when a teacher came barging into the room. She looked around the class and coldly pointed to the only girl with plaits.

'Stand up, Anne Merriman!'

I used to wear plaits. However, changing with the latest style, I had recently chopped off my hair into a short bob.

Wide eyed and unsure what to do, the girl slowly started to respond.

'Get up, girl!' the teacher shouted.

The girl quickly stood up.

The teacher continued to look around with a flare of her nostrils and pointed to another girl.

'Stand up, Pat Ruane,' she said confidently.

Once again, her finger pointed at the wrong girl. Despite the inaccurate accusation, the girl knew better than to challenge this teacher at that moment. The girl hesitantly moved her chair back from the desk and began to stand.

Pat and I quickly shot sideways glances at each other.

With the two imposters standing, the teacher really let them have it. From the sounds of it they had been totally disruptive in the library the previous day with a substitute teacher. Yesterday, the art class had been cancelled and moved to the library. However, Pat and I took music class, which occurred at the same time. So in reality, we had not even been at the scene of the crime! Reputation is a strong thing indeed.

After going on for some time, the teacher finally paused to draw a breath, the wrongly accused girl saw her chance. 'But I'm not Anne Merriman!'

And that was it. Pat and I exploded and fell on the floor laughing. Regardless of how the events played out, somehow the real Anne and Pat found ourselves at the principal's office that day.

At times, our mere reputation got us in trouble. But there was a reason we had our reputation.

French teachers may spit a little as they stress pronunciation, and my teacher was no exception. Assigned to the front row so the teacher could keep a better eye on me also put me in direct fire during pronunciation practice. It must have been the specks of spit on my face but on that morning I just couldn't control myself.

'*Passe moi le sucre*,' Miss J. said very precisely, moving her lips and nose with undue exaggeration. Before she could continue, my voice rose from the front row.

'*Passe moi le sucre*,' I repeated in the same tone, with the same vigour and expression. It was quite an accurate duplication really.

Miss J.'s blonde hair snapped to the side of her head as she glowered down at me,

'*Ferme la bouche!*' she shouted, sending more spit flying in my direction.

I looked up with almost no expression. While still making steady eye contact with her I put my finger in the inside of my cheek and flicked it outside my mouth. *POOOOOPPPP.*

The class detonated with laughter. Before I could even join in with the laughter my ear was almost ripped off my head as Miss J. (a rather large lady) dragged me out of class.

Worth it, I thought, rubbing my sore ear in the Principal's office.

And that's how things went. Pat and I got into a lot of trouble and had a lot of fun along the way. However, our lack of studious nature would soon become apparent.

Novena

Just after turning sixteen years old, I was getting ready to sit the General Certificate of Education (GCE) Ordinary Level, also referred to as the O-level exams. If I passed, I'd take the A-level (advanced) exams after further years of study. Students who typically gained entrance into university would pass four A-level exams.

After Pat and I took the O-level exams, we both knew we needed a miracle.

In Rome, there was a famous icon of Mary holding the baby Jesus, called *Our Lady of Perpetual Succour*. The girls had heard rumours of Novena miracles occurring to those who made pilgrimage to this icon. Novena, derived from the Latin origin '*novem*' meaning nine, is a Christian tradition of devotional praying for nine consecutive days or weeks. Luckily for us, Bishop Eton Church, a few miles down the road had received the first copy ever made of that icon. The gold, towering icon sat below an even larger triangle of colourfully stained glass, making Liverpool's *Our Lady of Perpetual Help* equal in mystic qualities.

In hope and desperation to improve the outcomes of our future exams we decided to set out on our own Novena. Pat and I would walk to Bishop Eton Church every morning for nine days, say the Novena prayer, attend mass, and then walk home, fasting none-the-less on our 14 km journey. Leaving our homes in the dark hours of morning, we'd meet at the cross section of Muirhead Avenue and Queen's Drive at 5 am to make the 7 am Mass.

The first morning was enchanting. Bundled from head to toe, we found a spring in our step as the cold, refreshing air hit our faces. We arrived at Bishop Eton Church with ample time to pray to Mother Mary before Mass started. Kneeling before the icon, as the morning light spilled into the church like a rainbow, I recited the Novena prayer handout.

Liverpool's Novena Prayer

O Mother of Perpetual Help, with great confidence we come before your holy icon to be inspired by the example of your life. We think of you at that moment, when, full of faith and trust, you accepted God's call to be the mother of his Son. Help us, your children, to accept with joy our calling in life.

When you learned that your cousin, Elizabeth, was in need, you immediately went to serve her and offer your help. Make us, like you, to be concerned for others.

We think of you, Mother, at the foot of the cross. You heart must have bled to see your Son in agony. But your joy was great when he rose from the dead, victorious over the power of evil.

Mother of Sorrows, help us though our trials and disappointments. Help us not to lose heart. May we share with you and your Son the joy of having courageously faced up to all the challenges of life.

Amen.

After Mass ended, we started our journey home to make it to breakfast on time.

The morning ritual continued for the next eight days. As the days went on, the anticipation and delight slowly extinguished. Tired and cold, I barely noticed as a bobby came riding towards me on his bike.

'Well, hello, miss,' said the policeman, snapping me out of my foggy trance. 'Where are you headed to?'

'Morning, sir,' I smiled. 'I'm meeting my friend at Muirhead Avenue, and we are walking to Bishop Eton. It's part of a Novena we set out to do.'

Possibly it was my impish smile or the very nature of my answer, but something made him doubt my honesty.

'Well, it's awfully dark, why don't I take you up the road to meet your friend. You can sit on my crossbar.'

I hesitated unsure if it was worse to refuse the policeman's offer or possibly break my Novena by missing my steps.

Pat had arrived a little earlier than normal at Queen's Drive and stood there waiting for me. The fog in the dark morning made it difficult to see very far away. Pat fiddled with her coat button and looked up to see me floating towards a few feet off the ground moving at good speed!

'What the...'

Pat strained her eyes as the front wheel of the bicycle and black helmet of the bobby quickly came into view. I had somehow managed to balance myself on the front of the handlebars with my legs hanging down on each side of the front tyre.

As we pulled to a stop, I awkwardly hobbled off the bike.

'Well, thank you, sir. This is my friend that I told you about. We'll walk the rest of the way together.'

Having been proven wrong in his assumption, the bobby courteously tipped his hat and smiled.

'You be safe and good luck with the rest of your Novena.'

We both giggled the rest of the way to Bishop Eton. Had I broken the conditions of the Novena by taking a lift from the bobby?

If we questioned the validity of our Novena, it was put in serious question a few mornings later after I fainted during Mass and we decided to take the bus home. (I was a regular fainter and it was most likely caused from the lack of food and all the standing and sitting.)

Having possibly broken the Novena twice, neither of us were surprised by our exam results.

6
Confirmation

'As you start to walk on the way, the way appears'
Rumi

EVERY SUMMER the Merriman family packed our bags and headed to the Lake District for two weeks in the town of Far Sawrey. The three-bedroom house sat at the base of a hill surrounded by pastures and a church at the top of the road. The green rolling hills, grey cobbled streets, stone walls, blue lakes and fresh air were a perfect environment for the frolicking teenagers and provided peace for the adults. As Oonagh and I became teenagers, we were allowed to bring our friends along. Oonagh brought her best friend Marie, and I brought my three friends, Pat, Marceline and Anastasia. As growing young women, finding a boyfriend was high on our agenda. The six of us would swoon over the brawny country lads working in the fields down the lane. Despite our eagerness to catch a boy, we never wanted to catch a boy alone! The days were fraught with gossip, giggles and gallivanting. My friends would only stay for a few days and then head back to Liverpool, leaving me wandering around on trails with Joseph, described by the famous Wainright.

I felt restless in bed and awoke in damp sweat. I cracked open the window and slowly pulled on my clothes while my sister slept soundly in the bed next to mine. Vacation time in Lake District was the only time I didn't share a bed with Oonagh. I wasn't sure what to do with all the space! The sun was rising and I could hear

Mum downstairs in the kitchen. After quickly checking in with her, I decided to go for a quick walk and see if I could see the sun rise over Lake Windermere before returning for breakfast.

Confident enough to venture out on my own, I walked down the lane to a path Joseph had shown me behind the Cuckoo Brow Inn. I arrived at the lookout point, breathless, just as the sun spread golden rays over the landscape. Looking down at the lake, I was struck by the beauty of God's creation. Quietly standing on top of this hill, the knowing I had felt five years earlier while watching the film revealed itself to me again. Difficult to put into words... I knew. Once again. I felt an unreserved call to dedicate my life to His work with a draw to Africa.

I would allow the depth of this moment to guide me for the rest of my life.

*

I returned to Broughton Hall the following autumn. After receiving average to poor results on my O-level exams, I joined the Upper Fifth form in Broughton Hall and managed to pass two more O-levels in the spring of 1952. In total, I received six O-levels. This was nothing to brag about and would not get me admitted into university. Most university students had four A-level marks or eight O-levels.

But the results of the exams didn't really matter if my goal was to become an MMM. After discussing it over again with my mum, she advised me to talk to a priest about my 'calling'. The priest I felt closest to was at Bishop Eton. I knocked on the door of the big house and explained to the receptionist that I needed to get advice from Fr Rodgers. He was a kind man and listened to me list my aspirations and my failures as a student. Before I made my decision, maybe it would be best if I further tested the waters and moved from the convent girls' school and joined a mixed college. The life of a nun is not for everyone. Better, suggested Fr Rodgers, that I really contemplate this decision by having a more informed opinion.

Dad had remained ignorant to my plan after all these years. Maybe my mum thought it would pass and there was no need to rattle his chain. In the meantime, I had publicly professed a career path as a nurse. Not satisfied with my decision and convinced I could do better, my Dad urged me to continue my education to seek A-level qualifications.

Although Dad's advice and intent differed from those of the priest, it still led to the same outcome. I applied to Byrom Street Technical College in Liverpool (now John Moore's University) and was accepted. It had access courses to A levels, medical and pharmacy classes, and boys, boys, boys.

I was already an easily distracted girl. But now, surrounded by the opposite gender, schoolwork was a mere afterthought. I did not share Dad's concern about my study habits, but I did wholeheartedly follow through on the priest's advice.

The dating began with Pachana Sambarana, a tall handsome Thai lad studying Oceanography, who halfway through our relationship assumed that I would be his English bride after I had signed a postcard to him 'Love from Anne'. But after he made assumptions about what I should and shouldn't think, he was soon passed over. As were many others. Several 'flavour of the week' boyfriends followed until Brian came along. Tall, dark, handsome and Catholic, we immediately hit it off. I had met him in pharmacy class. A previous Architecture major, Brian was older, serious and ready to find a girl he could settle down with. But the allure of Brian did not dampen the light of the little ember that had been growing for years.

*

In spring 1953, Mum, Pat and I all went over to Ireland for the Easter holidays. But there was also a clandestine reason that only we knew about – both Pat and I had an interview with Mother Mary, the Founder and Head of the MMMs.

Despite having relatives in Ireland, this would be my first time across the Irish Sea and stepping foot on her shores. We stepped off the boat as the sun sunk low into the sky. The Dublin streets were dark and I was surprised at the number of homeless people wondering about. We were greeted by my mum's cousin and safetly led to a car.

Pat and I were inseparable, and it was no surprise that Pat, too, wanted to be a nurse … which one of us had decided to be a nurse first remains lost in time. When I told her I wanted to join the MMMs she thought it might be a good decision for her as well. Pat was still at school, working towards the 'Prelim' nursing exam. After sending in our applications for the MMMs we had both received a personal letter from the founder inviting us to Ireland for an interview.

The three of us spent time with Mum's side of the family in Bettystown, and then returned to Drogeheda for an interview with the Founder herself.

Born into privilege, Mother Mary Martin was the second-born and eldest girl of twelve children. She lost her father in a shooting accident at the age of fifteen. Born Irish, her posh accent developed from her time abroad where she received higher education merits in the UK and Germany. She went on to join the Red Cross during World War I, and served in Malta and France, caring for injured soldiers.

Unsure of what path to pursue – marriage or missionary work – she had a vision that the latter would lead to helping millions of children. On her twenty-fifth birthday, she ended her relationship with her boyfriend and moved to Africa to work with the recognised Bishop Shanahan.

Mother Mary Martin's vision was to bring health care to places where there was none, particularly pregnant women, mothers and children. Obstacle after obstacle presented itself, and upon lying on her deathbed in the hospital in Port Harcourt, she was finally given permission from the Catholic authorities to found the new order. She recovered and zealously set out on her mission.

Her slight figure appeared bent forward, as if always rushing to the next place. This was an honest reflection of her character because she always was in hurry. It was also reflected in her driving. She refused to be driven by others and often broke the speed limit, parked illegally and scared the bejesus out of her passengers. But she was so well-known and well-loved she got away with everything, from talking her way out of tickets to leaving a sister in an illegally parked car with the instruction to say, if in trouble with the authorities, 'Mother will be back soon!' Despite the driving, Mother Mary Martin was to become the second most inspirational person in my life after my own mother.

Mother Mary Martin was fifty-eight years old when I met her for the first time. The order had been founded only fifteen years earlier and yet had gained such prestige and respect in the Catholic community. Both Pat and I were personally interviewed by Mother Mary Martin over a cup of tea and freshly baked scones. We were astounded that the founder of such a successful congregation would personally take time to meet and talk with us. Mother Mary talked with strength and confidence, constantly referring to the will of God and the importance of personally searching for God's purpose in one's life. The interview felt more like a discussion than an interrogation.

After we were both interviewed, we were whisked away for our medical examination. I remember laying bare under a blanket with Pat in an adjacent cubicle separated by a meager partition, and both of us were so excited to tell the other about our interview. Yet, we could barely hear each other because dozens of crows were cawing so loudly outside our rooms! Such a strange but vivd memory I still hold.

The three of us stayed free of charge in the convent, adjacent to the MMMs hospital in Drogheda. The spirit of hospitality flowed out of the convent. Every person was genuine and welcoming, and food was placed in front of us whenever there was a break in the agenda. During a tour of the facilities, Mum admired a small statue of Mary in the corridor, and immediately, Mother Mary Martin insisted on giving it to her, in spite of her refusals!

I was very interested in seeing the uniforms I remembered the Sisters wearing from the film. True to memory, the Sister wore a short grey dress (eight inches from the ground) with a sleeveless jacket over it and a simple veil with hair showing. According to the Constitution, the habit would be the nurses' uniform of the day.

Upon leaving, we said our goodbyes to Mother Mary Martin and were told we would hear within a month if we had been accepted or not. Pat and I left Ireland inspired and astounded that this famous founder, whom I had seen on the movie screen, gave us so much time!

But alas, it was time to return home. I returned to technical college and Brian, and Pat back to school to finish her Prelim. Both of us would talk about our experience for months afterwards.

7

The Journey Across the Pond

Man does not simply exist but always decides what his existence
will be, what he will become the next moment.
Viktor Frankl

O
N SCHEDULE, the letters arrived to both our homes within
the same week. I opened the letter with trepidation. I
quickly scanned the letter and upon reaching the word
'accepted' I was overcome with relief and excitement
and sat there overjoyed as I read the letter again and again. The
little secret I had held onto for years was becoming a reality. Was
I ready? Why did the life of a nun excite me? I wasn't exactly the
type of girl most people would label as 'holy', but I was devout.

Mum was delighted. She immediately set to work on getting
Dad's approval. He was far from pleased upon hearing the news.
It was common, or at least hoped for in every Catholic Irish
family, that one child would opt for the religious life. However,
my parents had already my brother, Joseph, to the Salesian order
a few years ago. It took time – but my Mum was persuasive and
eventually Dad softened to the idea of also losing his daughter.

When the letter came to Pat's house, she was not the one who
opened it, or even saw it for that matter. Pat's father saw the letter
posted from the MMMs in Ireland and took it upon himself to

open it. Upon reading its contents he went beserk! How dare she go and apply to a religious order without telling him! He would have none of it. She was to get that nonsense out of her head … and that was the last word.

*

I continued to enjoy my last term at school and my time with Brian. I told Brian about my news – but with no effect. We were both content to enjoy our last days together. We were young and lived in the moment. One day, we even snuck out of class and escaped from the school in an open MG belonging to the class playboy with two other lads and their girls. Finding ourselves tangled on the beach in the sandhills I asked him to 'remember September' and to slow things down, as that was the month I would join the MMMs.

As school came to an end, I approached the final exams knowing I hadn't studied enough. It was no surprise to me when I only passed two of my subjects at O-level, which I already had! My studies had all been for nothing. But what did it matter. I wouldn't need them as far as I was concerned.

Although I was invited to join on 8 September, it became apparent that joining so soon would not be possible. A following letter from the MMMs enclosed a list of clothing that I needed to bring, where to buy it from, and the estimated costs. The whole trousseau came to over £100, a small fortune in those days, which the family couldn't afford.

It would take time to accumulate the money. Mum wrote to her brother Pat, a Monsignor in the Catholic Church who had saved some money and was more financially secure. After discussing my future, he thought it would strengthen my vocation if I earned the money myself. A few weeks later, I found myself in a lab at Jacob's Biscuit Factory earning £2.5 a week. During the weekends, Pat and I would also provide housekeeping to Uncle Pat for an additional £1.50 a weekend. Uncle Pat was happy to oblige due to his constant turnover in housekeepers. His short temper and demanding ways may have softened for his beloved niece and friend!

At £4 a week it would take me nearly six months to earn the £100 needed. Mum delighted in the discounted chocolate marshmallows I'd bring home in a silver tin on Fridays.

'I can't let you go be a Sister now! I'm going to miss these chocolate marshmallows too much!' Mum would say with such a warm smile and soft eyes, that I knew she was actually talking about me.

Dad had accepted my decision to join the order but still had concerns and shared them with my brother in a letter!

7 September 1952

I appreciate what you wrote to Anne on the matter of her vocation, it spoke highly of the Salesians in a short time. I just wonder to what extent it will register with Anne? Who seems to me to be capable of mixing foot slogging from 313 to Bishop Eton between 5-6am, truly the spirit of the pilgrim with the facility of the inmates. All while she presents the boogy woogy tempo on the loud pedals of 313 piano. At a time when mum and I must be at our wits end. In many ways Anne is very young and Pat dominates her. She slavishly copies Pat's habits good and bad. She will suffer any inconveniences to meet Pat's wishes. And no emergency at 313 will deter Anne if her mind is set on a Ruane project.

I impress Anne the least. In a household when Anne's least doctrine of the church is practice; my fault. Not without the role of counselor. This is perhaps trespassing, yet you are both my children and it's merely technical that I want to plot Anne's happiness, contentment and peace more than even yours concern me. If you felt like kicking gold and rebelling against everything- you concealed your rebellion, but Anne does not conceal it. Anne like most girls, she gives me the impression, excluding Micky (the household dog), that much is left for consideration. Duty, loyalty, sense of obligation, service for a common a cause, fellow feeling, in short, in the Christian charity, for its own sake, has hardly awakened in her.

Carry on Joseph, for what you seek to accomplish for Anne.

News of Anne joining. It was totally unexpected. But I found immense consolation, through reading your letter to Anne,

*dated the 18th of Aug, that one of my children could show
such wisdom in what they could do for the baby of family.*

[...]

*Little Bernard found his heaven, wracked and tortured for
three weeks before he was called. Physically and mentally –
he was such a good boy. Apart from those pangs, parents
witnessing it, have much to thank an indulgent providence.
Anxiety for spiritual welfare must be the lot of all catholic
parents. Bernard blazed a trail and come what may, his
intercession has helped us, for he knew us all so well in life.*

*If Anne took Berny's place in Mummy's heart it was very
natural. The physical break will be very hard. But we can do
much with a year to work in.*

*Your Father,
Toddy*

It's always startling to read what your dad really thought of you
decades later! It gives me a smile as I think about those times.

I continued to work and whenever possible, spend time with
Pat and Brian, even though you think Brian would have given up
on our situation. But he didn't! The two of us shared a love of
ballet and its music. I cherished a record of the songs from the *Les
Sylphides* ballet and could hum it by heart. By the time I left, the
two of us had grown incredibly close.

*

As 1953 came to an end, my time to join the MMMs grew ever
nearer. The plan was set to catch the boat over to Ireland on 28
December and join the order on 6 January 1954.

Time was ticking away and there was about three weeks until
I sailed across the Irish Sea. As I prepared breakfast my stomach
began slightly cramping – almost barely noticeable. By the
afternoon I was curled up in bed as the pain began to localise on
the right side of my lower abdomen. By the evening, I was in a lot
of distress. Mum had never handled illness well again, after the
passing of Bernie.

'Darling, try sipping on this,' she said, handing me a bowl of warm soup. I had no appetite but wanted to do what I could to comfort Mum, so I took a few spoonfuls of the orange carrot soup. Within minutes it got sprayed all over my bedsheets. Children throw up all the time, but for Mum that was it. I was rushed to hospital.

Mum's anxiety turned out to be a good thing under the circumstances. I was in surgery the next morning to remove my appendix – dangerous if not caught in time, but Mum's overly concerned nature had saved the day. It was a common procedure, but surgery, nonetheless. I stayed in hospital for a week, and it was touch and go if I would still make my start date with the MMMs in a few weeks' time. But as the date drew nearer, so did my strength.

The rain fell that Christmas in Liverpool. It would be the last Christmas we would spend together as a family. Although I had to stop working in early December, the rest of the money I needed to join appeared. I went over to my second family and said my goodbyes to Pat and her parents. I also had to say goodbye to Brian. He held me in a long hug and took out a wrapped gift from his coat pocket. I unwrapped a beautiful leather bound Book of Psalms. I'd treasure it for years. He asked if he could write to me but his request was denied by the MMM superiors. We would never see each other again.

*

The morning of 28 December had arrived. It almost felt like a surprise, despite the years and months I had waited for it. Father Bob's brother, who was a curate in St Winifred's Catholic church in Bootle, came to pick me and my parents up, along with Pat who had spent the night with me. The crying started almost immediately upon entering the car. By the time we reached the boat dock, we were both sobbing as we said our final goodbyes. I was inconsolable. I watched the shore fade into the distance through my tear blurred vision. Bursts of sobs still escaped my chest. My dad came up to me and with a soft and knowing smile slipped a packet of cigatettes into my coat pocket and then walked away. And all this time he had pretended not to know!

My parents returned to the cabin to stay dry and give me some time to regain my composure. I stood on the deck of the boat and lit up a cig. The sweet smell of smoke and nicotine calmed my nerves as I stared at the bluish green sea. Wind whipped the dark wisps of hair around my face as the smell of rain grew near. The first sensations of the rain falling on my face and the cold sea air filling my nostrils brought me into the present moment and the enormity of the step I was about to take. Ireland would be the starting point of a new journey. A new and different life. I watched the tiny embers at the end of cigarette glow as the sky darkened.

We stayed with Father Bob and his parents at their bungalow on the east coast, in Bettystown, facing the Irish Sea. Our hosts continually fussed over me. Still frail from my recent surgery, I gladly accepted the doting and was served Irish food in the living room next to a lovely fireplace that kept me warm.

*

The official day had arrived. On 6 January 1954, I enter the Medical Missionaries of Mary at the age of eighteen. Excitement fluttered in my heart, yet I could feel the anxiety as butterflies in my stomach.

Father Bob has promised to go with me and my parents to Drogheda for the final send-off. On the drive to the MMMs' Mother House, Father Bob stopped at a shop on the side of the street and bought me a watch, the final item on the list required for entrance. I would always cherish the watch from my favourite cousin. It was fitting that Father Bob was there. Bernie's death had forged the solidarity of his and my relationship, and the subtle influences it would have over my life and decisions.

I entered the parlour of the MMMs' Mother House in Drogheda with Father Bob and my parents. I was one of two people entering that day. Sitting with my family, the other woman appeared much older than me, possibly in her thirties, and came from Northern Ireland. Dad could see my anxiety building. Again, he smiled warmly and handed me another cigarette from his pocket and offered to light it. Of course, at that time smoking was allowed everywhere. I smoked my final ciggie in front of everyone minutes before the other gal and I were taken away to change for the ceremony.

After I changed into the designated navy blue dress we were ushered into the small ceremony where our parents and loved ones were waiting. During the ceremony, the two of us knelt while black veils were placed on our heads. The official symbol of the MMM newcomer was complete. I rose to my feet and my head felt faint. I took deep breaths to regain my equilibrium. I was leaving my parents and the only life I had known. Well, even if I gave it twenty years – already a lifetime at my current age – that would be something, I thought.

Mum and Dad tried to hide their tears but I couldn't hide mine. Tears were to be my companion for several weeks, mainly in secret, while lying in bed.

We said our final goodbyes and took the first step into my new life. It would be a journey in self-discipline, perseverance, responsibility, wisdom, compassion, courage – and a new relationship between myself and God. Growing from child to woman, I would learn what it meant to overcome – and to turn trials into opportunities.

8

The Metamorphosis

Our actions may be impeded, but there can be no impeding
our intentions or dispositions. Because we can accommodate
and adapt. The mind adapts and converts to its own purposes
the obstacle to our acting. The impediment to action
advances action. What stands in the way becomes the way.
Marcus Aurelius

What happens to a person is less significant
than what happens within him.
Louis L. Mann

MOST RELIGIOUS orders follow a holy rule. The holy rule
is a set of recommendations, often written by the
founding saint, to help inspire the 'spirit' of the order
and those who follow it.

While Mother Mary waited for Rome to grant status to the
MMMs to do medicine and midwifery, she and a few others lived
with the Benedictine Community in Glenstall Abby in Tipperary,
Ireland. Greatly influenced by this time, the Benedictine rule was
requested and granted for the MMM order.

The spirit of the rule was one of hospitality, love and respect
for each other, for guests and all who might appear at the door of
the Monastery. To greet strangers as if they were Christ himself.
Sections of the St Benedict rule were read every morning at
breakfast.

As a headstrong scouser the first few months were an absolute culture shock for me. The Mother House in Drogheda housed approximately 200 women who were at various stages in their religious life. The MMMs, although a new order, was becoming increasingly popular with a constant instream of newcomers.

I was the only English 'postulant'. A 'postulant' is a newcomer seeking admission into a religious order. That's right, this first stage was merely a test to get in! Most of the women were from Ireland felt quite antagonistic towards the oppressing nation, and its citizens. One of the Sisters in my postulant group had lost her Dad in the Troubles, fighting against the British. She made no bones about how she felt about Britain and its people. However, I was an exception. My Irish descent and thick scouse accent differed from the posh British accent. I wasn't one of them but I also wasn't the enemy. Slowly, my fellow Irish postulants included me into the fold and treated me as one of their own.

Despite my new friendships, I missed my family and friends back home. But the tears only flowed on my pillow case at night. Life as a postulant was too busy to brood – the daily chores and checklists could barely be fitted into the daylight hours.

I would rise every morning at 5.00 am, put on my navy-blue dress, and not stop for a breath until it was time for bed. Every postulant was given different duties consisting of housework, sewing, hemming and mending, going to all the prayers, and saying the hours of the day (Divine Office). Each new postulant was given a 'Guardian Angel', a senior Sister who would answer questions and to ensure that we knew how to behave and act in our new position. There were also daily meeting with the postulant mistress with introductions to the divine office and the daily Mass readings.

The life of a postulant was intentionally designed to be tedious and difficult. But my recent surgery eased me into the bustle a little slower than most. I would be served warm milk before bed and assigned to the less physically demanding tasks. I began my duties in the sewing room and was later transferred to Sr Joseph's post natal ward in Our Lady of Lourdes Hospital. It was here, while folding nappies, I met Katherine Brigid Corrigan. We would quickly become known as the 'two little English ones'.

Brigid joined the MMMs two months after me, in March of 1954. Born in the Lake District, Brigid went to boarding school run by Irish Sisters of Mercy in the small town of Clifford just outside Leeds. She started boarding school at five years and wouldn't leave until eighteen years of age. Noticing that she excelled at science subjects, a Sister showed her a magazine article of the MMMs: 'This is something that will suit you, I think.' Brigid was only fifteen years old and soon forgot all about it. Upon finishing school, but not wanting to commit to university, she worked in a food research laboratory for two years. During this time, she began to admire the missionary movement and work in Africa but was aware of the lack of opportunities for lay people. While sitting outside a cathedral, Brigid was approached by a Catholic priest.

'Do you have a problem?' he enquired.

'No not really, no.'

'Oh, I thought you were not a Catholic but thinking about it?'

'Well, I am a Catholic and I am thinking of something.'

Brigid went on to explain that she was thinking of joining a religious congregation but wasn't sure which one or where to go. The priest brought her inside and placed the 'yellow pages' of the Catholic congregations before her. Staring down at the pages, it felt like one big jungle to Brigid. Seeing the overwhelmed look on her face, he snapped the book closed.

'To tell you the truth, to me, there is only one group.' He brought her a magazine of the MMMs. 'Any bit of money that I have, it goes to these people.'

When Brigid went home that evening, she told her mother that she was going to go to Ireland. At that time, Ireland only meant one thing, the Medical Missionaries of Mary. After personal correspondence with Mother Mary Martin, Brigid booked her trip to Ireland.

Brigid was a beauty with black hair crowning her ivory skin. I remember thinking how sad it was that her veil, although modern for any order, covered it. Warm and gentle in nature, Brigid was more conscientious and mature than me.

Brigid remembers me as laughing at things, all the time. 'I didn't think it was very funny, actually,' she recalls. 'Who knew, maybe she thought life was fun or something like that.' Brigid, however, was just trying to get used to the drastic shift in lifestyle. Little did she know that her cheery friend often cried herself to sleep at night.

The two short weeks we spent together that March were enough to solidify our lifelong friendship.

It was the middle of March, just two weeks into Lent, when Mother Oliver – the Novice Mistress – called me into her office after morning Mass. Ranking higher than the postulant mistress, I sat there wondering what she wanted with me. Mother Oliver went on about the Gospel of the day.

Her voice was steady and stern, 'The apostles had said to Our Lord at the transfiguration on the Mount, "Lord, it is good for us to be here."' She hesitated slightly and then continued, 'You will be transferred our MMM House of Visitation in Clonmel, Tipperary. Matron Phelan will be visiting a family nearby and can give you a lift. You will leave in an hour.'

With no time to say goodbye to my new friends, I quickly packed my bag. Two other women joined us – another postulant from Cork and one professed Sister who was a nurse.

'Our Lady's House of Visitation' was a nursing home where MMM postulants served as the majority of the support staff.

Possibly, this nursing home, was conceived to weed out the soft ones quickly. Or take away the troublemakers. Conceivably, the MMM authorities thought all three of us women didn't have what it took. Out of the three of us walking into the nursing home, only one of us would still remain with the MMMs in six months' time.

The life of a postulant was very uncomfortable. The rules were to be kept or else! Because I had always had issues with authority figures and following their rules, learning to be 'obedient' was a challenge. But it wasn't just the rules and regulations; I felt that some of the senior Sisters were on the verge of being psychologically abusive. As I would learn later, Christian virtues and beliefs – moulded by individual personalities and life experiences – completely differed from one person to the next. But at the time, try as I might, I had no understanding or love for Mother Patricia.

Older and cranky, Mother Patricia came from another order and needed caring for in her older age. She lived above the kitchenette. My responsibilities included caring for her while also working in the kitchenette. Mother Patricia demanded timely and exquisite service. Two oranges were to be delivered at exactly 3.00 pm sharp; and if any residue of tannic acid appeared in her tea – by God that would be the end it.

'You wretched girl! I can see the acid in my teapot! Take it back, you murderer!' she bellowed at me while lying there. Exceedingly obese and weak, yet vicious and with high levels of seniority, she could easily make someone's life a living hell! And for a period of time, that someone was me.

I had only been at Clonmel for a few weeks and was still getting used to my duties. Rushing off to attend Palm Sunday Mass and distracted by the Holy week's upcoming ceremonies, I completely forgot about the orange timetable.

Instead of receiving the tongue lashing, as I had expected, Mother Patricia went silent. But the silence was only for me. It didn't take long to find out that Mother Patricia had complained to the Sister in charge of the nursing home. Before getting a chance to explain what had happened, I was banned from attending the Easter ceremonies on Maundy Thursday. These ceremonies had always been special to me. In Liverpool, my family would attend services and pray in seven different churches in the centre of town. Now here I was, a Sister-in-training, and because of some oranges, I was being deprived of a lifelong tradition relating to Christ's resurrection! I felt emotionally transported back to my years in early grade school. These were the type of Sisters I always despised.

Ready to pack my bag, I sent several letters to my Dad saying how unhappy I was and that I was ready to come home. Even though he hadn't even wanted me to go initially, he responded with encouraging words – of resolve, fortitude, and self-discipline. The letters I received from him were just enough to keep me hanging on.

Clonmel was in the beautiful countryside at the foot of a beautiful mountain, Slievenamon. But that was about the only thing beautiful about it. My chores immediately jumped from easy to incredibly difficult. I worked in the kitchenette and scrubbed the stairs with Gumption (the scouring crème for the rubber edging on the stairs at the time} and with such personal gumption that I didn't even notice the doctors as they would trip over me trying to get past. I would take pride in quickly becoming known as one of the 'best scrubbers'. My work in the launderette was especially complicated without the convenience of modern washing and drying machines. At the beginning of every week I would trek out into the woods and gather firewood to start a fire to boil the water to clean the sheets, often soiled, from the twenty plus bed facility plus staff.

On one of the mornings me and a few other postulants were in the laundry room ironing sheets.

'Wooly-wooly-wooly-wooly.' A strange high-pitched voice was coming from one of the upstairs bedrooms. I put down my iron and strained my ear to hear the noise.

'Wooly, wooly…'

What on earth? I thought.

We followed the strange chant up the stairs into one of the bedrooms. As I opened the door the postulant from Cork, who had arrived with me, was standing over the only African Sister in the convent, rubbing the top of her hair.

'Wooly-wooly-wooly,' she said in the same high-pitched tone with a wry smile on her face.

The African Sister must have had a long night – because she was still lights out!

This must not have been the only incident with the Sister from Cork, for a few days later she was escorted off the premises by two men in white coats. We did not see her again.

At one point, I was put on hen duty. We had just received over a hundred young chicks. The cold nights caused the chicks to huddle together, often crushing each other. It was my job to find and pick out the dead little chicks the next morning. I remember hearing the horrible cries of the chicks that hadn't died yet – but had been crushed during the night. Listening to the sad little screams, I would burst into tears. One of the older Sisters, recently returned from Africa, took pity on me and the poor dying chicks and showed me how to break the necks of the ones that were suffering. And that's how it went for weeks on end. Crying and snapping, boiling and washing, oranges, and crying and snapping. Not really what I had envisioned when I imagined joining the MMMs.

The stringent new conditions of routine and order provided little opportunities for a breather – a moment to rebalance – a trice to myself. However, I found that moment at tea break. Every day at 10.00 am the postulants would get a ten-minute tea break. We were offered tea, milk and homemade bread with fresh valley country butter.

County Tipperary was renowned for its butter. Every farm had a churn and many farms and households whipped the cream by hand. Making the most of my small moment of pleasure, I could effectively eat ten slices of bread, lavished with butter, in ten minutes. One minute a slice. You know what they say: 'You can't be sad when you're holding a cupcake.' Or in this case, Ireland's delicious brown soda bread topped with golden butter.

As a consequence, I became as fat as a fool. In a little under six months, I increased in circumference by three dress sizes. Almost on cue, I received a new navy blue dress at eight week intervals.

*

Surpassing most guesses, even my own, I made it to the postulant graduation celebration, referred to as the 'Reception'. I travelled to Drogheda in late August to attend the eight-day retreat in preparation for the big day.

On 8 September 1954, my fellow postulants and I became 'novices'. We would change out of the navy-blue dress into the traditional grey habit of the MMMs (the nurses' dress of the day was a grey dress with a detachable collar covered by a sleeveless coat). As a symbolic and literal gesture of leaving our old life behind and entering the religious life, we would take on new Christian names. Choosing from the Christian saints, each woman would get to decide on her new name.

Brigid and I, now reunited, discussed our choices together. Coincidentally, we had both picked Dominic Savio as our new name! A student of St John Bosco, Dominic died from pleurisy at fourteen years of age. Bosco favoured his young pupil and eventually wrote his biography. Partially, due to Bosco's praise and descriptions of his everyday 'heroic virtue', Dominic would become the youngest non-martyr to be canonised by the Catholic Church. He had been granted his sainthood by Pope Pius XII, only three months prior, making him a new and popular saint. I had received piles of literature of Dominic from my brother, Joeseph. However, not wanting the same name as Brigid, I reflected on the qualities of the other saints.

During my silent meditations on retreat, St Christopher flashed into my mind. The legend of St Christopher, known from the West and possibly stemming from Ancient Greek mythology, says he carried an unknown child across a dangerous river. That child would later reveal himself as Christ. St Christopher, synonymous with 'Christ-bearer', would become the patron of travellers. Connecting with the image of 'Christ-bearer', I thought it would help guide my thoughts and actions. However, at the time, I didn't realise that my future would be full of worldly travels and would also need the protection of the saint.

Family members were invited to Reception before entering our 'spiritual year', a year of silence from the outside world. Mum, Dad, Oonagh and Pat all sailed across the Irish Sea to celebrate with me. As the procession of girls walked into the church, Mum began to panic. Where was her girl? It wasn't until hearing the scouse accent emerge from a rather voluptuous bodied, round-faced version of the girl that they had left only eight months ago, that she recognised her own daughter! I had gained the Postulant-Nun-Ya: 'none of your damn business ... but I made it.'

Praise the Lord.

9

The Rite of Endurance

You may encounter many defeats, but you must not be defeated. In
fact, it may be necessary to encounter the defeats, so you can know
who you are, what you can rise from,
how you can still come out of it.
Maya Angelou

The choices made at each crossroad are cumulative – and irreversible.
Stephen Cope

MANY CULTURES, traditions and groups have rites of passages that test the endurance of new initiates to ensure they have the inner strength, resilience and self-reliance to endure the unforeseen challenges of the future. Challenges and obstacles will never cease to be. The art of growing and evolving requires embracing and accepting the present moment – pain, grief, loss, frustrations, unmet expectations – and transforming it and applying it to the mastery of self. The six months as a postulant merely ensured we had the commitment and grit to enter into the 'Spiritual Year', also known as the Novitiate.

After Reception, the little group directly entered our Spiritual Year. The Spiritual Year isolated us from the outside world. Literally. We would stay within the four walls of the Mother House in Drogheda and dedicate ourselves to the study of the

Bible, prayer and meditation, the rule of St Benedict, the MMM constitution, the religious life and vows, and deepening our relationship with God to support us on our journey as missionaries. We also had general tasks and assignments each day – cleaning, cooking and waiting on tables. We were not allowed to talk to professed Sisters and were carefully watched in all aspects of our spiritual growth and assigned tasks. We were told at the start that if we left for any reason during that year, we would have to start the novitiate again. However, we were allowed correspondence with our families, unless the content of the letters were deemed 'unsuitable' by the Novice Mistress who would read and confiscate any inappropriate letters.

We all had roles in the kitchen and corresponding numbers. Once assigned, that number would stick with that person for the rest of the year. Attention to detail and diligence were required for the most mundane and monotonous tasks. Number 1 baked the bread, number 2 prepared the meals, number 3 was responsible for peeling and cutting the vegetables, number 4… and so on. We novices weren't just preparing the meals for ourselves, we were cooking and providing service for the 200 women living at the Mother House. I was number 3 and peeled sliced and diced all the veggies for over 200 women, every day, for every meal, for a year. However, technology advanced and the order received a potato-peeling machine which churned out the dirtiest of potatoes clean and peeled. This simplified my task enormously and I was able to spend more time on other tasks. I recall many funny scrapes and the joy of deepening my friendships with the other women who held the same ideals and who had chosen the same path.

We also learned a lot about the bible and its references to medical care. But when we had a chance to hear Mother Mary speak of her own relationship with God it was truly inspirational. I fell in love with Jesus during a retreat given by an inspirational Carmelite priest. I felt during that retreat that Jesus was as close to me as anyone I had loved in my (short) life. I had been given a small picture of Christ, just the face and I covered it with see through plastic and kept it beside me for guidance whenever there was a problem with others or with my studies. Little did I know how much I would soon need his comfort.

*

From the time Dad was a boy, he had always struggled with his asthma. This chronic condition kept him alive and at home during the war, but it became more difficult to manage as he got older. The smog from the industrial city of Liverpool worsened his condition. At one point, he was advised by a doctor to move out of Liverpool to the countryside, full of fresh, clean air. He refused his doctor's advice, wanting to keep his family rooted in their familiar community. But this would take its toll.

Mum wrote to me to let me know that he was terribly sick and on bedrest. My dad knew his days were limited. With the foresight of his upcoming death, he wrote to me and told me that regardless of upcoming events, I was not to leave my spiritual year. We both knew he was referring to his own funeral. Through our correspondence, my dad knew that if I left the MMMs, I would not be able to start over and thus never return.

On 13 February 1955, Brigid and I were sitting amongst a group of other novices studying the MMM constitution. It was a small, quiet room where we would gather together to study during certain hours of the day. The door creaked open and Sister Margaret entered the room with a distressed look on her face. I looked up from my book and saw that Sister Margaret was making a beeline right for me.

'Sister Christopher, can you come out in the hallway,' she said in a soft voice.

Brigid saw my demeanour change instantly. The blood drained from my face as I put down my book and slowly walked towards the door.

When I re-entered the room, Brigid remembers I was shaking. Everyone formed a circle of hugs around me. I just sat there shaking and trembling with quiet sobs, unable to do anything or go anywhere. The person whose letters and words of encouragement had provided me with the strength and fortitude during my most trying days was no longer there – would never again be there. With the loss of my dad, I felt I had also lost the external source of strength I had always relied on.

This would be the second time that after the death of a family member, outside events would keep me from attending the funeral. First Bernie and now Dad.

That evening while waiting tables, news floated around the table that one of the professed Sisters from Scotland had also lost her father that same day. I painfully overheard as arrangements were made for her to go home for the funeral. The next morning, I watched the commotion outside the window as the Sister said her goodbyes and returned to Scotland. Sister Christopher remained, red and puffy-faced, peeling potatoes and carrots.

I accepted the MMM rules and the death of my father, but my deepest sadness was not being able to be with my family and loved ones, especially Mum. After Bernie's death, Mum and I had turned to each other. Always feeling safe and loved, I shared everything with my mother. I shared with her everything from my secret calling to getting into trouble at school. Knowing that Mum was in terrible pain, it broke my heart that I couldn't be there for her. I would later discover that at age fifty-one, Mum had been left with only nine pounds in the bank when my father passed. The Teacher Association found a way to give her a weekly stipened, but with Oonagh moving away to join the WRENS, the next years would be incredibly difficult for her.

But like Dad, Mum also knew that staying and finishing the year would be crucial to my future. She sent me a letter encouraging me to stay and finish my year.

Although the MMMs' strict rules forbade me from leaving the novitiate, they allowed a Sister who needed to go to Liverpool, talk with me before leaving so she could pass on any messages I had to my family. Sister Jude would be the first MMM to go to 313 Queen's Drive and see my mother. I eagerly awaited her return and news of her visit. Upon Sister Jude's return, I was relieved to hear the messages of encouragement and support from Mum and family. And that they too were holding on and doing as well as they could given the circumstances.

Sister Jude and I remain good friends till this day.

*

Six weeks after getting the news about Dad, I received a surprised, sanctioned visit from Father Bob who worked in the Church Ardee, not far from Drogheda. I entered the parlour to see my dear cousin anxiously waiting for me.

'Oh, my dear, I am so sorry.' His kind, sad eyes comforted me.

'I came as soon as I heard.' He said softly, standing up to give me a hug. He shared his anger that he had not been told sooner! Despite our short meeting, it was a great consolation for me to spend time with him. He always seemed to appear when I needed him most.

But the pain and grief brought unexpected presents. It strengthened my friendships. I found great solace and joy from those who supported me. By losing my father, I discovered a part of myself I had not been forced to find as a young girl. Although, closest to Mum, I had drawn great strength from Dad. In his death I was forced to find a new anchor in myself and my relationship with Christ. My tears would carry me to a place of self-discovery, a place of greater resolve. When Bernie died, I had taken my pain and acted out – but now I learned how to transform my pain, endure, accept the worst life had to offer and – as the saying goes – bugger on.

Many left that year. But deciding to endure without cessation, I stayed the course.

10
A Turn of Fate

The Fates guide the person who accepts them
and hinder the person who resists them.
Cleanthes

A T THE END of the spiritual year, the novices were allowed to engage in active work. Brigid was off to medical school, others were sent to complete degrees in pharmacy, nursing, teaching, and other professions. I didn't really have a specific preference but after working at Jacob's Biscuit Factory, I knew my extraverted personality would do better around people.

Each novice was called into the Novice Mistress's office to hear our assigned profession and eventually my turn came. I sat down in suspense, yet hopeful of the life I would be given.

'Sister Christopher, please go to the sewing room for a white coat and report to the hospital,' my Novice Mistress directed.

What does that mean? I wondered nervously. I gathered my white coat and headed to the hospital. Please let it be the x-ray department, I prayed, please let it be anything but the lab. But to my disappointment, my prayers would go unanswered.

I was to assist the lovely Sister Teresita, a few years my elder, in the laboratory. Our tasks involved everything from blood counts to urine and faeces samples to cross-matching of blood. The lab was about the size of a small closet and the two of us barely fit in it together side by side. Sister Teresita's taught me the ropes of my new role and I was pleased at how well the two of us got on together.

My fate appeared set. I was on course to receiving a degree in science for my future work as a lab technician. Although it was a life I didn't want, I agreed, accepting the decisions made for me. I began my second year as a novice prepping for the pre-requisite exams needed for admission into University College Dublin (UCD). I needed to add two more subjects to the four O-levels I had received during my studies in Liverpool. Tutored by Sister Anastasia, I sailed through my Latin and Physics exams.

After completing our two years as novices, we entered the six-year stage of Temporary Profession. Every September we would renew our vows for one more year, and upon the sixth year, take our final vows. In September 1956, I completed my two years as a novice and took my first Profession.

Planning on entering UCD, Matron Sister Monica asked me to delay my studies and work in the lab by myself while Sister Teresita returned to complete hers. Sister Teresita had been forced to stop after her second year at university to fill the lab vacancy. After Sister Teresita returned, I would be able to continue to UCD as planned. Having nowhere else to go, I agreed to delay my studies. I would be left in the closet by myself for the next year facing many responsibilities.

I opened the lab at 9.00 am and set to my list of tasks. I wasn't great by any standard, but I began to perfect my craft with my mentor away and often, learning on the fly. Within a few months, I forgot how the two of us had fit together in the small space. I could barely manage the space by myself, continually knocking things over and on a few occasions setting things on fire. One time, I almost set myself on fire.

'Jesus!' I screamed, throwing my burning veil on the ground. My veil had caught fire from the Bunsen burner as I turned around to grab a chemical from the upper shelf. This closet was going to be the death of me.

A few months after working by myself, I received a request to crossmatch blood samples. The crossmatch ensured the donor's blood type was compatible with the patient. I took the donor's red blood cells and dropped it on a white tile. Next, I would add a few drops of serum from the recipient and watch to ensure the mixture of blood didn't coagulate. If it did, the blood was incompatible.

The surgeon sent down the blood sample of the donor and of a young mother who was haemorrhaging during a Caesarean section. She needed an urgent blood transfusion. I quickly performed the test and sent the results up to theatre that the donor's blood was compatible.

Halfway through another test, my peripheral vision noticed the white tile. The blood had coagulated! Panic overtook me. I immediately sent someone to the theatre with the ominous results and then collapsed on the tiny floor with my back against the wall. Tears streamed down my face as I contemplated the mother's death.

An hour later, the gynaecologist came down to the lab to find me in tears.

'Excuse me, Sister Christopher?'

I looked up to see Dr Connolly standing outside the door and broke down again. 'I can't do this any more,' I sobbed.

Dr Connolly glanced at the white tile with the coagulated blood.

'Has anyone told you that if the blood sits below the body temperature, it will coagulate, regardless?'

I looked up, slightly confused.

'So even if it is a match, it will coagulate if it sits at cold temperatures.'

Hopeful of what he might be saying, but still unsure, I clumsily rose to my feet. 'Let's put this cross-match in your incubator and see what happens,' Dr Connolly continued with a sympathetic smile on his face.

I helped him place the small tile into the incubator. Within a few moments the blood began to uncoagulate.

I could feel the blood rushing back to my head. The gynaecologist stayed with me and patiently explained how different outcomes could present under different conditions.

Except for my time as a postulant, it was the only other time I remember being ready to quit. The burden of thinking I had killed someone crushed me. Saved by one moment of kindness and a few gentle words, I kept the veil on and stayed in the lab.

So I kept working, continued to learn and started to master my craft. I developed a thicker skin and felt more comfortable with the gravity of my responsibilities. There were moments when I enjoyed what I did, but the highlight of my day always occurred outside the lab before work even started. I came in early to assist the other Sisters in the hospital. I would make beds in the private rooms, provide company to the patients, and help ensure their comfort – the only things I could do as a volunteer without a nursing degree. Between coming in early, my time in the lab, prayers and study, I was as busy and focused as I had ever been.

*

The Sisters returning from Africa always stopped to chat with the me in the laboratory. Sister Dr Margaret, a serious and dedicated doctor, had recently returned from her time in Nigeria. Always inquisitive and interested in the tales and descriptions of Africa, I asked her about her latest adventure. We talked over a period of several weeks when we had the chance. Nearing the end of one conversation, the senior Sister looked at me inquisitively.

'You know what, Sister Christopher, I don't think you should be in the lab. You should be with patients.'

I felt a light beam turn on inside of me. Interacting and caring for patients in the mornings really brought me joy. In hushed tones, guilty of being overheard I responded truthfully, 'I'd really like to work more on patient side of things. I really don't want to look at specimens the rest of my life.' Seeing that Sister Dr Margaret didn't appear disapproving, I continued, 'I go see patients an hour every morning before opening the lab. I really enjoy working with the patients.'

She could tell I spoke from my heart. Seeing that my response had aligned with her opinion, Sister Margaret continued.

'I think you should do medicine,' she asserted confidently.

Medicine, as in become a doctor, I thought astounded. I couldn't believe that such a successful doctor thought I had that potential.

Not thinking I was intelligent enough, I responded hesitantly, 'Well, I don't know if I'd be able to do it.'

'What? Well, you should try!' Sister Margaret said adamantly. 'Would you like to do it?'

I wasn't about to turn an opportunity down.

'Well, yes, I'd definitely try it if I was given the opportunity.'

'Well, I think you could do it.' Sister Margaret said again with a devilish smile.

The thought of being a doctor both delighted and frightened me. Even if I wasn't given the opportunity, just knowing that someone believed in me like that lifted my spirit.

Against all odds, Mother Mary Martin called me for a meeting.

I walked in nervously, sat down, and folded my hands neatly in my lap as I waited to see what the Mother would say.

'I hear you want to do medicine?' Mother Mary said without hesitation.

'Well, yes, if I am able…' I hadn't quite finished my sentence before Mother Mary continued.

'Would you like to?'

Nervous at the enormous opportunity placed before me, I could barely manage a reply.

'Yes, Mother.'

'Well, you can,' Mother Mary said smiling.

And that was it. It was shortest and most important interview I would have in my entire life.

In a series of conversations, Sister Margaret had talked with Sister Monica, the Matron of the Hospital. After hearing her raving compliments of the Sister in the laboratory, Sister Monica talked to Mother Mary and my life would be forever changed.

11

A Whole New World: Medical School

> You can't go back and change the beginning, but you can start right
> where you are and change the ending.
> *C.S. Lewis*

IN 1956, I entered the University College Dublin as planned –
but as a medical student. I went from my small laboratory to
joining twenty other MMM students at the MMM House of
Studies called Rosemount. This cold, large, stately house was
located in Bootestown, in the southern suburb of Dublin. With no
central heating, the Sisters would sleep with hot water bottles,
'stone jars', woolly socks and hats. Blankets were scattered in
everyone's room and the one room with a coal fireplace was
cleverly designated as the study room. The room had a large round
table in the centre where everyone would gather to study.

In alignment with Mother Mary's vision, there was incredible
solidarity between the MMM Sisters. We all were on different
journeys, focusing on different studies and in different years. But
we all supported each other and had a deep sense of community
and purpose.

It was a focused and dedicated life. But my time as a postulant
and novice had prepared me. Our daily schedule consisted of
rising at 5.30 am, attending mass, running home to eat a

substantial breakfast of porridge and eggs, grab our chutney sandwiches and flasks of hot tea for lunch, and then race off again on our bikes to the university campus where we'd study and go to class all day. We would return home in the evening after classes, eat dinner, attend evening prayer and then study again.

The thirty-minute bike ride to campus was forged in every weather condition imaginable – light rain, thick heavy rain, sideways rain, windy rain, sleet and even snow. Only on the rarest occasions, if a Sister was ill, would the bus be considered.

There was a designated 'Nuns room' at UCD where only the nuns entered. There was a spot on the right-hand side of the mantelpiece where the MMM Sisters placed their chutney sandwiches and flasks, 'There was another congregation that had a spot on the left-hand side and they had lemon curd sandwiches every day. So we use to swap!' Brigid recalls, laughing in delight, knowing the swaps were not always agreed on!

Changing from the religious habit to secular clothing (as mandated by the Archbishop of Dublin), I could have been awarded 'best dressed'. I was fortunate enough to have a sponsor from America and my love for modern clothing and style was indulged by presents from my Connecticut. Mother Mary had visited Cardinal Cushing in America and also met a few of his wealthy acquaintances. One of these happened to be a rather affluent lady from Connecticut who was inspired by what Mother Mary was trying to achieve. Aspiring that her own girls would become doctors one day, she decided to secretly sponsor a MMM Sister in medical school. Mother Mary wanted to make sure this lady had someone who was positive, cheerful and would be good at corresponding – and I was considered the perfect choice. The woman not only paid my school fees but regularly sent me books, clothing and even paid me a visit, twice!

Dressed in sheep's clothing, we seamlessly fitted in and were sometimes even flirted with by boys. Once, while gathered around the bed of a cardiac patient, the teacher began quizzing the students:

'Does anyone know what Corrigan's pulse is?'

A rather handsome young man grabbed Brigid's wrist and held it up.

'This is Corrigan's pulse!' he said, pleased as punch, as everyone bust out laughing. Good times were had but once the Sister became identified as such, it literally became hands off.

Unable to date men and engage in what one might classify as a '*normal* university life', it may not be surprising that almost everyone passed their exams with flying colours. Our outcomes reflected our one-minded purpose.

Brigid and I were reunited at Rosemount. Brigid, having been sent straight to medicine, was two years ahead of me. Brigid recalls that even as a medical student, I remained 'quite a giggly girl'.

'Anne would tell jokes and laugh, regardless of whether they were funny!' Brigid recalls, 'but Anne kept the atmosphere light and positive, which was very much needed.' But in addition to my humorous persona, Brigid remembers that I was 'incredibly determined'.

For the first time, I was excelling in school. I was coming top in my classes, proving to myself how lazy I had been before. I was second in my class in obstetrics, which is what I wanted to specialise in. Every time I witnessed a successful childbirth, with a healthy mum and baby, I wanted to burst into tears over the miraculous moment.

Due to my gregarious nature, I was nominated as the Student representative at Rosemount. Due to my responsibilities, I had the honour of updating Mother Mary Martin during her monthly visits. Over the next six years, I developed a strong relationship with Mother Mary that would continue long after medical school. I felt that she understood who I was and the challenges I faced. I would seek her personal counsel or years to come.

It took six years[11] for the medical students to complete their studies. My UCD class of 1963 graduated with approximately 100 students, of which 20 per cent were female, and 8 per cent were Sisters. I would become close with many of my classmates, especially with the other Sisters in my graduating class. Four out of the eight were MMMs. We came from all over the world: Shirley from Armagh, Ireland, Patricia from New York, Annie from Kerala, India, and I represented Liverpool, UK. Two very

---

[11] Year 1: Pre-Med. Botany, Physiology, Physics, Chemistry. Not always obligatory. Year 2: Anatomy, Physiology, Biochemistry. Year 3: Pathology, Haematology, Pharmacology. Years: 4, 5, 6: Clinical subjects and clinical attendance – Medicine, Surgery, Obstetrics and Gynaecology, Psychiatry, Public Health, including Statistics. Also Paediatrics, and Obstetric units.

posh Sisters, Maura Skelly and Noeleen Fehily, belonged to the Sisters of St Louis and were scheduled to go and serve in Africa. The final two Columban Sisters, Pauline Nagle and Irene Holocek, came from the Far East and would return upon completion of their studies. Despite the different religious affiliations, ethnic backgrounds and age, the class of 1963 was friendly and mutually supportive, as Maura also recalls.

*

The strict Archbishop of Dublin, Archbishop McQuad, appeared sceptical of the new order he had heard about. Going around visiting convents as they do, he decided to visit the Sisters at Rosemount. Escorted to the study room, he was mesmerised by the fact that we were all Sisters, as Brigid recalls. Books lay haphazardly scattered across the table and floors, grey blankets covered every piece of furniture, and the majority of the Sisters, dressed in their secular clothing, were studying around the large oval table.

'Ehhhummm,' he cleared his throat a little to gain their attention. 'Are you all Sisters? And do you have vows?' he said in a statement of disbelief rather than a question, knowing who we were.

Brigid, a senior ranking Sister, spoke up. 'Yes we are and yes we have, Archbishop.'

He raised his eyebrows as if to show his approval and began nodding his head as he looked around. Then he said in a rather patrimonial way, 'I'm going to give you the day off.'

As university students, with classes and exams, we couldn't have a 'day off'. Unsure of what to make of his grandiose proclamation, Brigid responded as politely as possible.

'That's very kind of you, Archbishop, but we can't take the day off. We still need to attend lectures and go to the hospitals.'

It must have come as a bit of a shock: he must have been expecting smiles and thankyous. His eyebrows furrowed, 'Well, what would you like then?'

A hush fell over the room and then whispers broke out as we leaned forward around the table. We had always talked about getting a scooter. 'Tell him we want a scooter!' someone whispered. 'C'mon, Brigid, say it, say it!' one of the Sisters encouraged gleefully. Once the consensus had been reached, Brigid looked up.

'Archbishop, what we really want is to ride scooters.'

'You what?' he said. His levels of disbelief kept rising the longer he stayed in the room.

'We would like to ride scooters.' Brigid said again confidently.

'Why?' He squished his eyes in confusion of the request being made.

'Well, it's a long way to different hospitals,' Brigid said. Knowing he was fond of one particular hospital, Brigid carried on, looking rather serious in her request, 'especially to Our Lady's Hospital in Crumlin. It's very important to get there on time.'

The Archbishop appeared very doubtful. 'Well, let me think about it. I'll get back to you,' he said and asked to be escorted out.

There were about fourteen Sisters around this table, and as soon as he got out of ear distance, they all broke out in laughter.

Upon reaching the front door, he looked down at the Sister with satisfaction.

'I have decided that I am going to give them the scooter,' he said rather proudly, 'and I'd like to go back and tell them right now.'

The Archbishop opened the door to hysterical laughter. The room went quiet instantly. Taking a moment of silence to amplify the moment and ignoring the previous laughing, he announced rather grandly, 'I am going to give you a scooter!'

Everyone burst into rounds of applause.

'And who will be riding?' he queried.

Brigid and Bernadette were in their final year and were making the most rounds to the hospitals.

'The two of us will be riding the scooter, sir. Thank you ever so much.'

The next day there was a letter, from the Archbishop, with his very small, definite handwriting.

'I dislike pillion riding. I'm sending two scooters.'

A man of his word, two Prima scooters arrived at Rosemount shortly after. Archbishop and Mother Mary both came to watch the scooter training. One might even say that it was through the scooters that those two high-ranking individuals developed a greater friendship.

12
Flying Nuns

You have wings because you are meant to fly.
Anon

ALTHOUGH medical school was a time of tremendous work and routine, we found moments to relax and laugh, producing extravagant Christmas skits and acting as extras in Gilbert and Sullivan operas and Puccini's *The Tryptych*. But the time flew past and before we knew it, Brigid was graduating. She and I would go our separate ways and wouldn't see each other for decades, but the times we did get to connect were as if no time had passed at all.

The next two years went by in a flurry with exams, scooters, chutney sandwiches, studying in grey woolly blankets, and monthly meetings with Mother Mary.

Immediately upon graduating, on 8 September 1963, I professed my vows one last time. Although I was supposed to have taken them two years earlier, when Brigid and the other Sisters in my group took them, it was against the rules to take final vows while still engaged in the education process. I would take my final vows by myself. But I did not celebrate by myself. I was joined by Mum, my brother Father Joseph, Pat and Mrs Jean Kennedy Stanhope who had paid my fees at university.

*

Following my graduation as Sister Dr Christopher, I began my internship at the International Mission Training Hospital (IMTH), the MMM hospital, in Drogheda. IMTH was the primary training hospital for MMMs and was attached to the Mother House. I was placed under a consultant whom I thought was a desperate man really and who was really horrible to the Sisters. Frightened by the weight and responsibility of holding others' lives in my hands, I found myself in a similar situation to my second year in the laboratory.

'Just get on with it!' the consultant would bellow bombastically to any intern's questions. Yet despite his lack of oversight, he'd make it a point to belittle a Sister in front of her peers for the smallest of errors. There were some very low points when I thought I had harmed someone because I didn't know the details of what I was doing well enough. I ended many days in tears. My saviour at that time was a new Sister from Norway, Mette Nygard. She came to my rescue many times and kept encouraging me to stay the course. The nurses were also incredibly patient and helped me find my way.

Like a bird pushed out of the nest, forced to find my wings or be crushed by the ground, I found my time as an intern more than terrifying but perhaps imbued with invisible and unexpected benefits. Learning to be uncomfortable, embracing fear and doubt, rebounding from mistakes and learning to grow on the job – would be the most invaluable skills I would take away from my internship. Sometimes, even if the fledgling feels unready and unnerved, it is time to learn how to fly.

As the end of my internship drew near, I received my calling. I would need my new set of wings more than ever. I was headed for Nigeria.

*

Sixteen years earlier, as a thirteen-year-old girl, I had been inspired by the film *The Visitation* and then received my own visitation in the Lake District, forever altering my life's path. As an eighteen-year-old, I had taken the plunge and joined the Medical Missionaries of Mary. Despite all the obstacles, travails and my father's passing, I had managed to stick it and remain true to my course. Shocking those who knew me best – the wild, ill-behaved girl that had received mediocre results in school entered

UCD's medical programme at twenty-two years of age and graduated six years later.

At the age of twenty-nine, I was about to embark on an even greater adventure, the type of adventure only my four-year-old self had the imagination to conceive.

13

Nigeria: Part I
The Maiden Voyage

A ship at harbor is safe, but that's not what ships are for.
John A. Shedd

Theology is not about understanding the world,
but about mending the world.
Miroslav Volf

BEFORE leaving for Nigeria, I was granted permission to go home and visit my family. It would be the second time I had stepped foot back on British soil in nine years. My first time had been during my fourth year in medical school when I had been given permission to attend Joseph's ordination as a Salesian priest in Kent. The ordination took place on the Ember Saturday in Lent which was also on St Patrick's Day that year!

So much had changed. Although Dad had passed away eight long years ago, it was strange to return to 313 Queen's Drive and have him gone. All three Merriman children had flown the coup. Joseph had remained with the Salesian order and continued to work with children from poverty-stricken areas. And Oonagh eventually married an English army soldier and had three children, Stephen, Paula and Jane. They constantly travelled and moved to different bases around the world.

Although the Merriman children had all scattered, Pat, my childhood best friend, continued to check in on Mum. Pat had trained up to finals as a nurse and then after experiencing a tragic incident decided to leave the profession and pivot into medical administration. Although she had several gentlemen suitors, she continued to rebuff their attempts and remained unmarried.

I would only get to spend one night in Liverpool and it would be with Mum, Joseph and Pat. Oonagh, living abroad in Germany at the time and raising young'uns would not be able to join the family reunion. When I entered 313, Mum was playing 'When I last saw Tom' from *The King and I* on the gramophone. The lead singer was passionately recalling the last time she had seen her dead husband. Although Joseph remained stoic, the women bawled for a fair bit of time before we found ourselves roaring in laughter. It was a night of tears, laughter and storytelling about the good ol' days. Joy came tumbling out of the windows and doors that evening. It was with a heavy heart that I said my goodbyes in the morning and sailed back to Drogheda to pack my bags for my maiden voyage.

*

In September 1964, I took my first steps out of the plane onto Africa soil. The Nigerian air hit my face and then wrapped around my body like a thick warm blanket, hugging me in all the wrong places. I felt as if I was breathing in a theatre full of people with bad breath! In that instant I wanted nothing more than to get right back on the plane and go running home. I now understood why hell was a firy dungeon. I had spent my entire life in a rather cold climate and my body wasn't adapting to the heat and humidity. Having never sweated, my ankles just kept getting bigger and bigger. It was like walking around in wet wellies. Despite my all the obstacles I had overcome during my spiritual and medical training, the heat had become my most formidable challenger. I was at my wits' end. On the edge of the precipice and ready to write the shameful letter asking for a change in placement, the sweat glands and pores opened. The water cleansed my spirit and provided relief and renewed strength.

I had been placed at St Luke's Hospital in Anua, a small suburb outside of Uyo. St Luke's, named after the dear and glorious physician of the Apostles, was the first hospital established by the

MMMs in Nigeria in 1937. Uyo was only a few hours drive from the Government Hospital in Port Harcourt where Mother Mary Martin, while on her deathbed, took her first vows and founded the Medical Missionaries of Mary.

St Luke's was a large, single-storey compound with detached two-story buildings to the right and left sides. In thirty years, its operating capacity grew from twelve to five hundred beds. A modern hospital, with up-to-date technology, facilities and specialties, I was astonished at finding central sterilisation with autoclaves, which had only recently been introduced to Ireland. The medical team consisted of specialists in general medicine, surgery, obstetrics and gynaecology, paediatrics, dentistry and ophthalmology. The specialists were all Sister doctors, apart from surgery, headed by Irish doctor Jack Hicky. Recognised by the British Nursing Council as a training school, St Luke's graduating nurses were not only registered nurses in Nigeria but also SRNs in the UK. It also became a teaching hospital for UCH Ibadan Medical School. The hospital served the local communities, consisting mainly of the Ibibio and Efik tribes (similar languages and cultures). As St Luke's reputation grew, many came from far and wide, including many from the Ibo tribe.

Thrown into the Fire

Surrounded by experienced specialists, trained nurses, and good equipment, I still felt vastly overwhelmed. Having mistakenly perceived my internship as intense, in reality, it only slightly prepared me for what was to come in Anua.

Under constant supervision, I began learning several different specialties: surgery, obstetrics and paediatrics, and general medicine. I was eased in and learned general surgery first. Surgery cases typically included hernias and general laparotomies but on occasion dealt with emergency strangulated hernias and perforations. The theatre (operating room) had two operating tables. If two surgical emergencies simultaneously presented themselves, Dr Hicky barked instructions over to me from the other side of the room. Although it came with challenges and a steep learning curve, this was a very special time in my life, and it taught me so much.

Dr Hicky was a kind and patient mentor. He and his wife had not yet had children of their own, so when his wife became pregnant there was great rejoicing in the compound and the baby was eagerly anticipated as the parents were so well loved by everyone. After a successful and healthy birth, Dr Hicky proudly announced, 'It was a girl!'

'Ohhhhh, sorry,' apologies echoed throughout the compound. The locals all sympathised that he did not have a precious boy, which was more highly regarded than a girl and so essential to the local cultures and traditions.

Obstetrics and Gynaecologist

My time in obstetrics and gynaecology was educational and heartbreaking. It consisted of two wards: clean and septic. The septic ward seemed to be the busiest out of the two wards and where I spent most of my time.

In the surrounding cultures, immediately after a baby girl was born, the negotiation of bride price began and a husband was declared only weeks after birth. Upon 'coming of age', the victor would marry the girl. The girls in the Ibibio and Efik tribes were having babies as twelve- and thirteen-year-olds. Pregnant at such a young age, the small, underdeveloped pelvises in these young girls resulted in many complications. Most of the cases were young, prima-gravidas (first child). Often, they had already laboured for long hours in the bush, while relatives sometimes jumped on the belly to get the baby out. Leaves and other local concoctions might be pushed into the vagina to encourage contractions. The mother and unborn child would come to the hospital in life-threatening conditions.

To further complicate matters, the tribes believed that if the baby was not born vaginally, the mother was not a proper woman. The girls, often strongly influenced by relatives, would refuse Caesarian section (CS). But the maternity unit at St Luke's attempted a solution to get around this problem by using 'symphysiotomy'. Every doctor at St Luke's was trained how to perform a symphysiotomy – a high-risk procedure that divided the fibres joining the two sides of the pelvis at the symphysis pubis. A cut from a scalpel allowed the space to expand, through which the baby could come out. Protecting the urethra (the tube through which urine is passed) from damage was critical to ensuring against devastating complications, as was post-op care. The girl's legs were tied together at the ankles and bed rest was ordered for a week. If weightbearing occurred too soon, the healing fibres could be damaged, resulting in a permanent limp and painful disability.

I watched my first symphysiotomy performed by Sister Dr Ann Ward. Even today, I remember it in stark detail, and I remember feeling that I could step in and do it – and before I knew it, I got my chance. Dr Ward walked me through the procedure, detail by detail and made sure that I did everything accurately. Given my careful mentoring and training, I would go on to perform hundreds of successful symphysiotomies. (However, this procedure was eventually banned everywhere in the developed world, due to the mistakes made by insufficiently trained doctors and the severity of complications.)

Although normal deliveries were more common amongst the Ibo women due to their natural physical structures and later childbearing ages, the symphysiotomy saved the lives of hundreds of mothers and babies from the Ibibio and Efik tribes. It also allowed the mother to have subsequent deliveries, often at home, without medical intervention. This was critical since many of the girls/women lived in rural settings and would go on to have more than ten children. St Luke's reputation spread, and many young mothers were being brought for symphysiotomies and antenatal care.

But many of the girls were not so lucky. Some arrived infected from the non-sterile treatment and delivery attempts of traditional midwives. Others arrived almost in full term with a dead foetus that still needed delivery. If a dead foetus was confirmed but the girl was too underdeveloped to give a natural birth, a symphysiotiomy was deemed too risky. The alternative was most appalling. I remember perforating the skull of the dead foetus and letting the brains come out so the baby could be squeezed out of the birthing canal without endangering the mother's life. The smell was awful. The gag reflexes were almost impossible to control. Some things are hard to imagine. This was impossible to un-imagine.

I wanted to be an obstetrician because I was always so enthralled about the miracle of life, and here I was, cracking open a dead foetus's skulls so the twelve-year-old mother had a chance at survival.

If the child had died, screams of '*Yami oh ... Yami Oh!*' sailed loudly through the wards. Tradition demanded grieving women to scream this saying, or it was assumed they had killed the child. I remember hearing '*Yami oh Yami oh Yami oh!*' ring out more times than I had ever hoped to hear.

Diabetes

Diabetic cases in Nigeria were unlike anything I had read about or had seen in Ireland. Many Nigerians were presenting with very high blood sugar levels but no ketones in their urine. They had a very dangerous condition called non-ketotic hyperosmolar diabetes (NKHD). Uncommon in Western populations, it had not yet been described in the common literature and research by the early 1960s. NKHD occurred in type II diabetes, frequently after a high carbohydrate load. In Anua, this might occur following a three-day wedding feast where many locals consumed high plant-based carbs like cassava, plantain, rice, the local potato, and – the staple and favourite among many – the yam.

Later, they also discovered something similar was affecting young children, referred to 'Maturity onset diabetes in the young' (MODY). (Again this medical condition was only described in the literature 1960s.) Traditionally, treatment in Europe for diabetes entails high doses of insulin. However, this could kill a patient with NKHD, putting them in hyperosmolar diabetic coma. The treatment for NKHD was large amounts of intra venous (IV) fluids and small, closely monitored doses of insulin – the exact opposite treatment for classical diabetic coma.

However, not all diabetes cases were NKHD. Many locals could suddenly present with type 1 diabetes (insulin dependent) and if not treated with insulin at onset, and for life, the person would die. It was customary in local areas to bury the cassava, let it mature, and eat it at its peak of flavour. However, if it sat for too long and spoiled, the cassava produced a poison that attacked the pancreas. Patients would often die while being rushed to the hospital. Since both type of diabetes presented, the diagnosis was often inaccurate, and the physician's lack of knowledge could lead to the patient's death.

I was the only doctor with enough experience to stand in for the OB/GYN specialist overnight. I often left the medical ward and diabetic clinic in the hands of the visiting Norwegian Red Cross doctors, stationed in Anua to help but also get experience. Returning the next day, I discovered my patients had died during the night. The visiting doctors, unfamiliar with NKHD cases, would misdiagnose it as ketotic coma and inject high levels of insulin. I tried to tell them about these strange cases. But I, a young Sister, new to medicine and working in Africa, did not garner the respect and attention of the seasoned physicians from Norway. The stigma of 'outsiders coming in and not listening' would haunt me and strongly influence how I perceived outsiders. Even though I myself was one and would often be the 'outsider' throughout the course of my entire life.

As a result of this complicated and misunderstood condition, I started a diabetic clinic and, together with the lead dietician at St Luke's, wrote a short book in the local language educating locals about diabetes and a diabetic diet using Nigerian foods. This would be expanded when I came back later as a consultant.

Malaria, Tuberculosis, Meningitis and Measles

In Nigeria in the 1960–70s, a high percentage of children died before reaching the age of five. I saw countless children come into the ward- many not making it out. Measles was a desperate killer due to lack of vacinations, poor sanitation and poor nutirition. The ward in the second story of the detached building on the right side was designated for open, contagious TB cases. Many would die – children and adults. I was often assigned to this ward and had no fear in contracting TB because my Heaf test still resulted in a positive response, indicating that I was resistant due to my childhood vaccination. (Although I never contracted TB, several other Sisters who had been vaccinated still got it.) Despite the high death rate, caring for the children would be one of my favourite specialties at St Luke's.

The Patient in the White Coat

On shift, many of the doctors slept upstairs in a spare bedroom. I was asleep upstairs one evening when the guards came running in.

'Za man gone crazy downstairs. Come. Come now!'

We hurriedly rushed down the stairs. One of the patients had gone totally mad and cleared out the entire ward.

'I think he's gone off his meds!' A nurse anxiously muttered to me. We both watched him through the window as he walked around talking to himself, occasionaly making violent gestures at the air.

Having awoken moments before, I was still trying to grasp the situation when Sister Doctor Pauline grabbed her white coat and put it on over her nightgown.

'I will go!' she said authoritatively, with the perfect amount of confidence. Anyone who had heard her would have believed she'd set this man straight with just the tone of her voice.

We all watched, wide-eyed, from behind the glass window as Sister Pauline marched out into the empty ward. She stopped about fifteen feet from the wild man, who was still shouting obscenities in the local language. She braced herself and with a strong, deep voice bellowed, 'Come come, my good man, calm down and let's talk...!'

The screaming ceased. With wild eyes the man slowly cocked his head and began to inch forward. Maintaining her dignity and strength of presentation, Sister Pauline stood her ground.

Approaching a few arm's lengths away, the man let out a war cry and made a dive for Sister Pauline. Unable to control her composure, she let out a frantic scream as the man made a successful grab of her white coat. Twisting and turning, Sister Pauline barely escaped out of her white coat, and ran back to the safety of the locked doors with her purple striped nightie cascading behind her.

Behind the safety of the glass and locked doors, Sister Pauline and I watched as the madman proudly held up the white coat and then put it on. His eyes gleamed with satisfaction as he stood defiantly, staring at us through the glass. In the end, he put up quite a fight and the guards had to use a tranquilliser to subdue him.

14
Maybe

There is a Taoist story of an old farmer who had worked his crops for many years. One day his horse ran away. Upon hearing the news, his neighbours came to visit.

'Such bad luck,' they said sympathetically.

'Maybe,' the farmer replied.

The next morning the horse returned, bringing with it three other wild horses.

'How wonderful,' the neighbours exclaimed.

'Maybe,' replied the old man.

The following day, his son tried to ride one of the untamed horses, was thrown, and broke his leg. The neighbours again came to offer their sympathy on his misfortune.

'Maybe,' answered the farmer.

The day after, military officials came to the village to draft young men into the army. Seeing that the son's leg was broken, they passed him by. The neighbours congratulated the farmer on how well things had turned out.

'Maybe,' said the farmer.

BY JUNE 1966, I had been in Nigeria for nearly two years and had just turned thirty-one. Although the change from Ireland to Nigeria had been abrupt and difficult, I felt my heart opening to the country and its people, as if I had always been there. I would occasionally make weekend trips to Afikpo, where Sister Dr Maeve Powell was in charge of a smaller hospital staffed by Nigerian Sisters with nursing qualifications. Sister Powell covered the maternity unit and Dr Godfrey Hinds, a dedicated long-term volunteer, covered surgery, while both shared general medicine. Overworked and exhausted from staff shortage, I offered relieve their load by volunteering on the occasional weekends to give Sister Powell a break so that the patients wouldn't have to go without emergency treatment.

I drove out to Afikpo in the little Volkswagen Beetle – a difficult journey that entailed bumpy roads and crossing a narrow bridge that hung precariously over a very fast river. The weekend had been slow with no emergency cases, so I decided to make a quick run to the market to buy a few papayas. While I exmined the fruit, Christopher, my favourite local child, skipped over to me with his endearing little smile. Christopher and I had instantly bonded when I first met him. I reached down to pick up his small but hefty little frame and as I heaved him up, a bolt of pain flashed down my back. Barely able to put him down without dropping him on his head and toppling over myself, I could feel the blood drain away from my face. On the verge of fainting and with such intense pain, my first thought was that I had ruptured an aortic aneurysm and this was *it!*

If an African sees a white person getting even whiter they get really terrified, I would say later, recalling the wide brown eyes staring back at me.

The next thing I knew, I was laying in the dirt, hanging onto a shadowy level of consciousness.

'Sorry, sorry,' the voices came cracking through. Knowing where the m'zungu had come from, a group of men managed to carry me back to the hospital.

It was the *worst* pain I have ever experienced. There was controversy on how to get me back to Anua on the bumpy countryside roads with my level of pain. But in the end, there was only one way home.

The other Nigerian Sisters working as nurses at the hospital, having tried many simpler analgesics without success, injected me with pethidine, a drug that although not great at blocking pain induces such a state of euphoria that the patient is usually too blissful to care. I was stuffed into the backseat of the Volkswagen and made as comfortable as possible. But the potholes were inescapable.

'Sorry, Sister, sorry,' the Nigerian Sisters cried out as they moved down the worst stretch of road.

'I'm fine, I'm fine,' I replied rather dreamily. In truth, I was in a beautiful haze.

*

I was on my back for weeks and continued to take pethidine to mask the pain. However, pethidine taken too long eventually stops your intestines from working, causing constipation and bowel obstruction. I worriedly watched as my stomach began to rise like a balloon and knew I had to stop taking the medication. After a few weeks of bedrest and subdued pain, I gradually went back to work. It took several months before the pain became manageable, yet after a year with no major relief, the MMM leadership decided to send me home for treatment. On 5 July 1967, I boarded a plane and flew home to Ireland. On 6 July, civil war erupted across the country.

*

The Nigerian Civil War, more commonly known as the Nigerian–Biafran War, had begun. Airports were closed; violence and chaos spilled onto the streets; and tribal relations deteriorated with distrust and animosity.

Elements of the war had been escalating for years. In 1914, the British amalgamated the northern and southern territories of Nigeria, combining over 300 different ethnic groups into what we call Nigeria. The country consisted of three main ethnicities: the Igbos of the southeast; the Hausa-Fulanis in the north; and the Yorubas in the southwest. The political, economic, and ethnic tensions that existed between the regions worsened under indirect rule and became further exacerbated during the formal decolonialisation process between 1960 and 1963.

After a series of events, Igbos were systematically persecuted in the north by government militias, escalating to a sequence of massacres in 1966 that killed approximately 50,000 Igbos. The Biafra region of the Ibos, holding key oil resources but few federal legislative seats, seceded from the northern dominated government and declared themselves an independent Republic of Biafra in July of 1967. Over the next two and a half years, the war between the Biafran state and the Nigerian Government resulted in over 100,000 military casualties and civilian suffering. Due to a military blockade around the Biafra region, an estimated half a million to two million people died from starvation.

In the end, Biafra lost and was devastated. Women were like ghostly skeletons with kwashiorkor[12] children held on their hips. The pictures of these women holding out their hands, begging for relief will always stay with me. Although I left Nigeria, the Medical Missionaries of Mary stayed in Nigeria during the war. I was so proud of my fellow Sisters, who courageously stayed to help others, despite the perilous situation they found themselves in.

---

[12] A severe form of malnutrition, most common in some developing regions of the world where babies and children have a diet that lacks protein and other essential nutrients. The main sign of kwashiorkor is too much fluid in the body's tissues, which causes swelling under the skin (oedema).

15

Finding a Voice
Where Nun Existed

Speaking your truth is the most powerful tool we all have.
Oprah Winfrey

Be true to your own mind and conscience, your heart and soul.
Theodore Parker

I FLEW straight to London and was taken to a Harley Street specialist to seek medical treatment. The specialist recommended traction for six weeks and then a brace. I then flew to Ireland and returned to the International Mission Training Hospital (IMTH) and was put in the convent infirmary for six weeks. 'Traction' meant lying in bed and slowly getting pulled apart in the hope that the disk would slip back into place. The first half of the bed angled downwards, and the traction device pulled my legs in the air and used a weight and a pulley tension system to keep the group of muscles stretched, also reducing muscle spasms. I wasn't allowed to move an inch for six weeks. My head was always lower than my centre of gravity, making eating incredibly difficult. I lay there in chronic discomfort with nothing to do but think. I spent hours thinking about my last three years in Nigeria, my patients, and the recent news about the outbreak of the war. I wondered how my religious family and the local team I had come to love were managing in such a violent and chaotic conditions. There was little time to feel sorry for oneself.

After the weights were removed, I was squeezed into a brace that clamped around my torso like a corset. For three months it squeezed my core so tightly that it gave me 'squashed stomach syndrome'. Only able to eat very small portions without feeling full and being ill, I was reduced to half my size by the time the total treatment was complete. However, once I was put in the brace, I was stable enough to slowly start going back to work.

For the next year, I stayed and worked in the IMTH coronary and metabolic units. My first assignment was as a registrar to the Coronary Care unit on the sixth floor. Instead of seeing young tribal women, I saw young Irish men, many under thirty-five years of age, who would be admitted and die shortly after from a heart attack! Most of the men were dairy farmers and lived off full cream and butter their entire lives. The same butter that put three dress sizes on me during my few months as a postulant! I remember sitting with these young men and their distressed families when there was nothing left to do.

I had developed a close relationship with Mother Mary Martin over the years. I believe our trust in each other was mutual. In secret, Mother Mary asked me to work in the newly established metabolic unit, not because of the experience I would gain or the expertise I could provide but because she was unsure if unethical practices were occurring. The metabolic unit was providing research on a new pregnancy drug that increased the occurrence of ovulation in women. This included working with patients who had stopped menstruating from various causes including anorexia nervosa. Once again, I was reporting to Mother Mary on a frequent basis. Despite the complexity of the matter at hand, her leadership always impressed me.

I continued to work hard and enjoyed working with the people around me. However, I was working with my favourite consultant surgeon (yes that one, the one who had given me a hard time during my internship). So it shouldn't be so surprising that it wasn't long before we had a disagreement. After disputing how to proceed with a case, I blatantly refused to do what he asked. He went ballistic and reported and badmouthed me to anyone who would listen.

His behaviour didn't affect me the way it once had. After what I had seen and experienced the last few years, I felt deeply responsible to my patients and felt like I needed to fight for them. Even if it meant being at odds with someone with such a favourable disposition.

I had turned a corner. I felt that what I had done was right. I had the support of others who heard the story. Gaining self-assurance and feeling support from the very top of the order, I started to regain the confidence and gutsy spirit I had had as a child and teenager.

But my time at IMTH was coming to an end. I had been encouraged to broaden my experience and after getting permission, I moved to the Mater Hospital in Dublin. I worked with senior consultant, Dr Ivo Drury, as his clinical assistant in the research of hyperthyroidism as well as taking on clinical responsibilities in the wards.

While working at the Mater Hospital, I also studied for the specialist exam: Membership of the Royal College of Physicians of Ireland (MRCPI). It had two parts. The first part I passed with flying colours but the second part I found much more difficult and failed. Advised to go further afield for more medical experience I obtained a supernumerary position with the endocrine unit at Edinburgh Royal Infirmary.

Before I left, there was a noise about Mother Mary Martin's replacement. Reaching her mid seventies and struggling with Parkinson's Disease, Mother Mary needed to be relieved of her responsibilities as the Mother General and her successor needed to be chosen. I knew that Mother Mary Martin had groomed Sr Dr Andrew as her replacement and she was incredibly competent and upheld those values that Mother Mary valued and wanted carried forward.

I attended a few meetings where they discussed a voting system to elect the next Mother General, but I felt the voting system lacked integrity. Opposition was building against Mother Mary's choice in favour of another Sister doctor who I knew had mental health issues. Not only did the choice not make sense to me, but the means to get her elected felt counterfeit. Despite my junior position, I decided to say something.

'If we don't like the result of how this process gets structured and the way the vote is carried out, how will we ever trust the person that gets put in?' I asked.

I immediately felt the disdain radiate off a few of the senior Sisters. Without heeding my comment, the meeting wrapped up rather quickly.

I went to my room still upset by the meeting's discussion and a few hours later was joined by three senior Sisters.

'Sister Christopher!' they smiled in delight. 'We hear you are accepted to further your studies at the University of Edinburgh with a senior consultant at the Royal Infirmary. You must take advantage of this opportunity and go at once! We have already called the Sisters in the Mercy convent and they will have a room prepared for you. You can remain there for the duration of your stay.'

I received the message loud and clear. It would be the first time that transportation wasn't arranged for me. With that one question, I had become a thorn to the emerging leadership. What happened shouldn't have come as a surprise. Oganisations, governments, families, and especially religious orders rarely embraced dissenters kindly. Those who speak or act upon a truth that is different from the mainstream narrative or culture are rarely welcomed. Although, I should have known this reality, still nieve, I found this to be incredibly shocking and hurtful. It was the first time I felt unwanted in my MMM family and the first 'crack' in my seamless vocation.

Tectonic shifts had been occurring in the Catholic Church. Pope John XXIII, an elderly and (considered by some) 'transitional' pope, had called for a Council of the most powerful *men* in the Catholic Church to deliberate and address the relations between the Catholic Church and the modern world. Opened by Pope John XXIII on 11 October 1962 and closed by Pope Paul VI on 8 December 1965, Vatican II sent waves of change through the Church.

There were peripheral decisions pertaining to music, artwork and the direction to face while saying prayers and mass. But there was one foundational change that would forever alter the Church's future. Mass was no longer to be read in Latin, instead, it was to be read in vernacular languages – the language of the people! People attending Mass would actually be able to understand the message! In some ways, this took the power the Church and Priests had monopolised for centuries and transferred some of it to the people. While in Anua, I read several books pertaining to the decisions made during the Second Vatican and one of the main themes that I took away was simply this: 'God has given us a brain, so use it.' Reason and logic would be new, respected pillars in the Catholic faith.

Not only did the decisions in Vatican II indirectly affect the events that unfolded at the MMM meeting that evening but it also affected my personal views and behaviour. In reality, joining the MMMs was a strange vocation for a girl who had strongly disliked Sisters and had a proclivity to fight authority. Anyone who knew me, knew I would likely struggle with the vow of obedience. But against all odds, I was obedient and was fitting in quite exceptionally! However, the Second Vatican Council gave me permission to question authority and stop blindly accepting the decisions and aspects of practice that I felt were wrong. So I did.

That meeting left an indelible mark on me. I left for Edinburgh with a heavy and confused heart.

*

I arrived in Edinburgh in the summer of 1969 and was put in an outside guest house, detached from the Mercy convent. Having been given permission to pass through Liverpool on my way up north, I was given a sacred box of chocolates from Mum and civilian clothing from Pat to wear while I worked in a non-MMM hospital. On my first day I wore long black boots that came to the bottom of a knee-length skirt with a beautiful 'midi' grey coat that wrapped around my waist with an astrakhan collar. If I didn't look half smashing, I thought to myself as I looked for a mirror. I came to discover the Convent Sisters did not believe in mirrors as it promoted vaninty. Well, they had underestimated vanity!

My appearance received unwanted negative attention from the Sisters as they caught me walking out of the compound. The Sisters of Mercy, whom I considered a pre-Vatican sort, were very strict – especially with traditions of uniform.

Edinburgh, the capital of Scotland, was nestled in the south-east part of the country. The capital had become the epicentre of education and excelled in many fields, one of which was medicine. Surrounded by the green, rugged countryside, one felt the elements of wildness and freedom. No wonder the Scots had always been so difficult to control! So it felt fitting I found myself here at this time in my life.

The independent living accommodations provided isolation for my reflections on authority to occur. The eve of discord in Ireland was the beginning of seriously questioning my vow of obedience. Who was I to be obedient to? God? The MMM leaders? Some leaders but not others? Before, it had been so clear cut – black and white – and now the lines had blurred into grey. Could I unquestioningly accept decisions by my superiors if I felt they opposed Mother Mary Martin's vision. Decisions that I felt compromised patient care?

The incident in Ireland had not only cracked my resolute loyalty to the MMMs, but the uncertainties and questions surrounding what it meant to be obedient widened the fissure, leaving room for further contemplations on other matters.

I greatly enjoyed my freedom, my smart attire and my work. Some might say, too much, others might say just as I should. Without one mirror in my place, I quickly fixed my hair while passing by shop windows on my way into work. The work was hard but full of laughs, instigated by senior consultant Dr Lesley Duncan, who had a great wit and made work as fun as it was interesting. My six months with Dr Duncan in the diabetic unit fuelled my lifelong interest in diabetes and my decision to later go on and seek the second part of my Edinburgh Membership in endocrinology.

Thoroughly enjoying my time and learning a great deal, I returned to Ireland and took the second half of the Membership of the Royal College of Physician of Ireland (MRCPI) exam in Internal Medicine. This time, I sailed through and passed, becoming one of the first Sisters in the Medical Missionaries of Mary (MMMs) to obtain an MRCPI on 5 December 1969.

But anxious as I was not to rest on my laurels, I returned to Edinburgh to prepare for the MRCPEd. However, I was soon asked to replace a Sister stationed in Nigeria in a border hospital between the fighting regions. As the war continued to rage on, hunger and starvation were becoming desperate issues with the local population. With permission to return to Liverpool before leaving to see my family, I also managed to raise over £1,000 at my local church for a malnutrition unit. Preparing to return to Nigeria for another difficult journey laden by the turmoils of war, I said my goodbyes and packed my bags, but not without a certain amount of anxiety.

And then the news broke: the war had ended! I had providentially managed to escape the Nigerian Civil War by days on each side. Although the tumultuous violence was over, I would return to a different country, riddled with unbridled fear, hate, destruction, starvation, and the other ravaging effects of war.

16
Nigeria: Part II

Do what you can, with what you have, where you are.
Theodore Roosevelt

IN LATE January 1970, I flew back to a country I barely recognised. The devastations of war had taken its toll. A middle-aged religious brother with a robust and stoic personality picked me up at the airport in a dirty green jeep. Stockpiling on city goods to take back to his rural parish, the jeep was stocked with food, essential goods and loads of cash stuffed in pillowcases and crammed under each seat. Once my luggage was squeezed into the gaps and the two passengers took their place, there wasn't room for a mouse.

Stuffed to the brim, the green jeep began its two-day journey to Obudu. It had been nearly two and a half years since I had left Nigeria. The hot, humid and bright skies of Nigeria contrasted starkly with the cold, rainy overcast regions of Ireland and Scotland. But adjusting to climate was the least of my worries this time around. Out of civilian clothes and back into the MMM uniform, my veil waived in the wind as I watched the miles roll by. The dirt roads were relatively empty with intermittent military checkpoints along the way. Halfway through the day we pulled up to a long line of cars waiting to cross the River Niger. This vast river beckoned the respect of all who tried to cross its shores. Two small platoon boats traversed back and forth with cars and people, replacing the bridge that had been blown to bits during the war.

As we pulled near, it was clear we would not get across before nightfall with all the cars ahead of us in line. Nightfall in an unfamiliar land was no place for a jeep stocked with pillowcases of cash. Turning around, Brother John remembered spotting a parish a few hours back. Belonging to a religious community, hospitality to fellow Brothers and Sisters was the rule of the land.

We backtracked to the parish and arrived at dusk as the mozzies began to take flight in the cooling night air. Warmly greeted by the parish priest, we were both welcomed inside for the night. However, unwilling to abandon the jeep to the unknown predators of the night, Brother John decided to sleep across the front seats and forgo a comfortable bed to keep watch over his supplies.

'C'mon, Sister, let's get you a room. I'll bring dinner to you once it's prepared.'

I needed no convincing and was happily escorted into the presbytery.

Exhausted from the long flight and day's journey, I wearily settled in my room. Even though I had been to Nigeria only two and a half years ago it felt like ten.

I was dozing upright in the chair when a knock at the door quickly brought me back. 'Can I come in? I have your tea and dinner.'

'Of course,' I responded gratefully.

The short elderly priest walked in carrying a tray of tea and some hot eggs, bread and local vegetables.

'I took some food out to Brother John,' the priest assured me, 'but he really shouldn't be sleeping out there. I know we have a relatively safe property, but things have become very dangerous.' He paused. 'Especially since the war.' The priest had lowered his eyes and as he looked up to make eye contact with me, I could see tears welling in the corners.

'We had a brother come out from Ireland. A real good lad. Younger. But full of energy, enthusiasm, and optimism. I awoke feeling sick one morning and so I asked him to go to the post office for me. The soldiers, unfamiliar with who he was, took him. They thought he was lying about who he was and mistook him for a mercenary. When he didn't return, we got worried and began to look for him ... we found him crucified in the field. They c-r-u-c....' his voice trailed off and the tears rolled down his dry skin.

'I'm so sorry, Father,' I said, surprised and shocked, and barely able to control my own tears. 'What a tragedy! I can't imagine how difficult that must have been even for you. I am so sorry for your loss.'

Becoming a little uneasy about my new friend sleeping in the jeep, I continued slowly, 'Do you think we should insist Brother John sleep inside?'

'I already told him that it was dangerous and men not familiar with these parts have been confused for mercenaries and killed. But he insisted,' he said, shaking his head and becoming indignant. 'He said Jesus was watching over him. You think Jesus wasn't watching over that other boy that got crucified last week?'

I was so shocked and felt my own tears grow hot in my eyes and my throat tighten.

'I'm so sorry, Father,' I whispered as my heart clenched in fear. He hadn't mentioned the detail about 'last week' in his original telling!

I felt terrible for this elderly priest. It was obvious he had cared deeply for his younger Brother and burdened some of the responsibility of his death. I couldn't imagine how shocking it must have been to find him in the field that way. I didn't even want to imagine it. It was becoming clear how dangerous things had become and that the 'religious habit or cassock' no longer acted as a protective shield like it used to. Although the war had ended a week ago the scars lay open like oozing wounds. I knew the people's hearts were still filled with bitterness and revenge.

'Brother John said he wanted to make an early start, so we'll have breakfast ready for you at 6.00 am. Sleep well, Sister. Be at peace tonight.'

'Thank you again. See you in the morning, Father. God bless.'

*

Brother John made it through the night safely. We got off early and were among the first to arrive at the river in the morning. We pulled over and had our packed lunch. Few cars passed. With no more river crossings, we should reach Obudu by nightfall. The Nigerian landscape and the people were a constant reminder of the two and a half years of brutality and violence. As we got closer to the Biafran boarder, the bodies got thinner and thinner. At one point we drove up to a big red gate. Bodies pushed up against the gate, arms shoved out through the bars and hands grasped in the air waving for what I could only imagine was food. Mothers clung to skeletal babies as their milk had dried. I realised we didn't have any food to offer them. Oh my Lord, if only we hadn't stopped so soon to eat lunch, I thought, horrified by how badly these people needed what we had just eaten. I had never seen people so thin. It was amazing and horrifying how the human body could change and still go on living. The reality of the aftermath of the war was starting to hit me in the gut. Even my knees felt weak in a sitting position.

We entered the Biafra region through what had been a bustling and shopping city of Enugu. It was eerie driving through the deserted streets. Windows were smashed, broken-down army vehicles lay in the side ditches and even the skeleton wreckage of airplanes lay in pieces on the empty roads. I was later told that the road had been used as a landing strip for the planes. (I returned to Enugu two weeks later to discover it bustling with life, people and commerce and was amazed at the human capacity for recovery and perseverance.)

Sacred Heart Hospital – Obudu, Nigeria

Brother John and I arrived in Obudu no worse for wear. I would start working at Sacred Heart Hospital, a smaller hospital than St Luke's in Anua, consisting of approximately a hundred beds. The only problem was – there were no beds, or any other important equipment for that matter. The town straddled the secession line and the hospital had been captured several times by both the Nigerian and Biafran militaries. The vacillating nature of ownership made it vulnerable to raids and looting, and as such, most of the equipment, beds and anything of value had been taken. Luckily, it wasn't long before a Canadian non-profit organisation donated a 'disaster hospital'. This consisted of a hundred camp-style beds, an x-ray machine and other necessary equipment.

I was the sole doctor and supervised seven nurses. Two of the nurses were from the MMMs and had come from Ireland, and the other five were Nigerian nurses. However, the nurses were often away on maternity leave, leaving the staff shorthanded. But it was the volunteers that kept the hospital running. There were about twelve girls, around fifteen years-of-age and with an education level equating to the UK Eleven Plus exam, but they were so willing and had an excellent work ethic. They'd work a full day and wake up in the middle of the night to assist with surgery. The next morning, they would show up on time for duty with wide smiles. There were also local volunteers from nearby parishes whose ingenious contraptions and fixes saved the day on more than one occasion.

The beds were always full. Visiting family would sometimes sleep with the patients and their frail frames could easily fit two on a twin hospital bed if need be. If not, they'd lay on the floor beside them as many had come far with no place to stay. We had an x-ray unit that only showed the positives (even though x-rays are supposed to show negatives). In the end, we just got by with what we had and did the best we could. And got by we did.

Father Jim English, a Kiltegan Father and a curate in a nearby parish, worked his magic and finally got the x-ray unit working. He also designed incubators to help save the premature babies. The five incubators had wooden bottoms and glass tops with a small hole cut into the wooden base. Next, he placed a pipe that ran along the bottom of incubators which acted like a heating system, derived from the strong lamps that generated the cold air for one of the fridges. Babies born weighing 2–3 lbs could go on to survive in these incubators. This man's genius ability to invent and utilise random materials from nothing was such a blessing and saved countless newborns.

If there was a problem, we just figured it out. That went for my driving as well. In Ireland at the time, you didn't have to pass a test, you only needed to buy a driver's licence. So I had attained my driver's license without ever passing a test (and many people who have ridden with me may have suspected this!) So, upon arriving in Obudu, I got on with learning how to drive. One of the first things I did was smash the Land Rover through the garage gate! But there was a need, mistakes were made, you learned, and got on with it.

Learning how to drive was my least concern. At times, I would learn a new surgical procedure on the go and have one of the nurses read the procedure from Bailey and Love's *Emergency Surgery*. I was the anaesthetist and the surgeon, the acting manager and one of the arms and legs of the hospital operations. But what other option was there? Just like the time I had to remove a man's leg in order to save his life. (Bone is a lot harder to cut through than you might imagine!) But if that's what it took, that's what you did.

One evening, while relaxing and having tea at Father English's home, the hospital's night watchman appeared at the door:

'Light done quench!' he cried. This meant that the electricity power had gone off. 'Woman so sick, need doctor quick, quick!

I arrived to discover the woman had an ectopic pregnancy. The fertilised egg had been implanted in the fallopian tube instead of the uterus and the growing baby had burst her tube. The woman was experiencing internal bleeding and needed surgery and a blood transfusion to keep her alive.

Unable to proceed with surgery in the dark, one of the volunteers stood over the operating table pumping an oil lamp to provide continuous light. They had no blood at the hospital to provide her with a transfusion, so an auto transfusion was the safest way to continue. The lost blood in her abdomen was scooped out and collected into a sterile basin, where it would be filtered and then transfused back to the patient.

'Buzzzzz. Blop.'

The yellow light and smell of blood in a dark building in the middle of the night attracted every insect in the area.

'Plop.' I would look over to see flies dropping into the blood pan. Eyes wide but determined to save this woman, there was nothing I could really do but continue on and have faith in the filter device. And by God did it work. This lady survived!

*

One day a family came to the hospital looking for the MMM Sisters. The man of the house – a recent patient whom everyone had liked – had died. The family begged the Sisters to come to their home and 'pay their respects' before he was buried. Obliged, we followed the family back to their home where a large gathering was underway. Many of the locals respectfully backed away to let the us through the crowd. I stopped to talk to the daughter I had got to know over the months and listen to her memories of her father.

Suddenly, a senior member of the family grasped my arm and said, 'Come and greet!' This woman would not let go and I had no other option but to follow her to the centre of the room, where in front of the fire, in his favourite armchair, sat the corpse! That would be the first and last funeral for me in Nigeria, but it struck me that it had many similarities to the Irish tradition. Upon reflection, I realised the importance of being with patients in their family settings. This is the way to learn the culture and feel the hurts and the joys of the family.

*

I remember not being able to visit a patient without being stopped every few miles by soldiers. Too often the soldiers would try to take the local nurses out of the jeep. Rape was too common.

I would make up fibs. 'No. We must go,' I would say. 'We have an important surgery. We're going to see a soldier. Must go. Can't take her.'

'Drive on,' I would shout at the driver and wave the soldier away from the window. I knew they might be persuaded to listen if it was a medical emergency for another soldier.

I was growing ice in my veins. It was an easy act for me – maybe too easy. The act slowly transitioned to real anger and disrespect. My encounters made me bold and even reckless at times as I indignantly dismissed men who could turn my life upside down. But saved by the veil, or the intrigue of an outlandish white Sister, I continued to lash out and do and say as I pleased without regards to politics, rank or gender normalities. At thirty-five years of age my natural tendencies were rising to the surface again, ranging from wise to heedless, sometimes saving the day and at other times causing trouble and disruption.

I was sitting in the outpatient clinic talking with a patient at the front of the queue. The queue was long and the problems seemed to be taking longer than normal to sort out. A soldier marched up to the front of the line.

'You must come see other soldier. Come with me.' He pointed in another direction.

I was still bent over examining my patient. I stood up and looked at the soldier.

'No. He must wait in line. Like everyone else,' I said in pidgin, mimicking his accent and pointing back to the long line of people queued up.

His eyes widened at the flat-out rejection. I bent over and continued to work on my patient. Disbelieving my contemptuous response and unsure of what to do, the soldier stormed off in a rage.

I was so tired of these bossy, arrogant men. Did I stop to think about the consequences of my actions? Maybe, but more likely not. Would that get my ward in trouble? Probably. Was I making a point and really didn't care? Absolutely.

The next day, while working in theatre (operating room), I saw two soldiers come storming in and drag out one of the Irish Sisters. Poor Sister Francis, she was in the wrong place at the wrong time and happened to be white, wearing a stethoscope and fitting the vague description of the woman who had so obdurately refused to follow military demands the previous day.

In the middle of surgery, I couldn't really intervene and let the soldiers know they had the wrong woman! I wasn't 100 per cent what was going on but knew I needed to finish my surgery before I could do anything. Besides, what would I have said? It's me you want! Moreover, Sister Francis was much more likely to make peace with them anyway and get let off the hook.

But on behalf of Sister Francis, I would need to cooperate this time. After finishing the surgery, I found out they had taken her to the local police station. Although they discovered they had taken the wrong white Sister, they wouldn't let Sister Francis go until the other one came down.

I knew it was best not to go alone. I went and told Father English what had happened, and he accompanied me to the station. As soon as the guards caught sight of me, a strange combination of glares and smiles were cast my way.

'You are the one that refused to see a soldier!' an animated soldier yelled, approaching me. Father English had prepared me on the proper etiquette of response.

Although I wanted to say, 'I didn't refuse to see a soldier! I just told him to wait his bloody turn like everyone else,' instead I said, 'So sorry. Yesterday I was very tired. I will always see soldiers first. Never again. Very sorry.'

Of course, that wasn't enough. More yelling needed to occur first and I needed to feel the fear of God. I sat there, looking remorseful, playing the part. After enough time had passed, the yelling ceased. I had made my point and they had made theirs. Possibly the soldiers would think twice about being so insistent or maybe it would make them bolder? The proof would be in the pudding. Peace was made. Sister Francis was released and all four of us drove back to the hospital.

17

The Winds of Change

Kisses are a better fate than wisdom
e.e. cummings

I T WASN'T long after I arrived in Obudu that Mum posted me a
letter. A young man from Liverpool, belonging to The Legion
of Mary group at a local church would be working near me at
a trade school. By the time I received this letter and read it, no
doubt, he was most likely already in Nigeria, she said. He was
volunteering for a new Christian organisation that had just started
in 1969, called the Volunteer Mission Movement (VMM). Mum
had become quite fond of him and wanted to make sure that, with
my previous experience abroad, I checked in on my fellow
scouser.

John Handleigh was a few months younger than me. Tall and
dashingly handsome with thick reddish dark brown hair, his
strong, athletic build had women swooning at his picture.

The broad-shouldered lad had a strong will and while
displaying machismo traits he also shared the warmhearted and
fun-loving, humour of his fellow scousers. Adhering strongly to
his Catholic beliefs, his religiosity and faith were an intricate and
important aspect of his life. As was football, like every good
Scouser and supporter of Liverpool!

The first time I met up with him was over lunch at the Ogoja
MMM convent in the Leprosy Centre. I remember that it was
comforting to find someone of a similar age, culture and history:

126

it was easy and fun to converse with him about anything and everything. John had lived in Liverpool his entire life, so it also presented me with a wonderful opportunity to catch up on what I had missed in Liverpool over the last seventeen years. That first encounter came and went like a breeze on a hot day, comforting, soothing and yet forgettable.

The hospital kept me busy. The patients, soldiers, lack of resources, malnutrition, death, exhaustion and the heat and humidity only added frustration and agitation. I took pride in my new responsibilities and continued to perform well but the stress and pressure of my current position, with its increased responsibility and leadership in a tense, wartorn environment, weighed on me. For the last sixteen years, my life had involved travelling from one place to the next, never settling, meeting new people, learning new skills, and constantly adapting and coping with new environments and new challenges. When I finally felt something comforting and familiar, I reached for it.

My friendship with John provided that little escape, like being able to take a deep breath. The gap of relating and connecting with others in a different culture is real. Words are missed. Humour is missed. Even the rhythm and flow of conversation are different. Add in the veil and the wall becomes even higher. I appreciated my time with John. It was so easy and uncomplicated. In a faraway land, it gave me a little piece of home.

When John visited, we attended Mass together. I loved to go to the church in the leprosy village, where an Irish Father gave lively and energetic sermons in the local pidgin.

'When out in the field. See Animal. Shoot. Bang. Bang!' he shouted animatedly to the crowd.

'Go up and see. What he done find? Not animal. A man deado!'

The church crowd would let out shrieks and cries as the Father carried on with his sermon. 'Murder or no murder?' he invoked the crowd.

Everyone crowded into the church to listen to the Father and his lively sermons. Afterwards, the children sang heartily, conducted by an elderly scouser (yes!) lady from Liverpool, Miss Murphy, who was volunteering in her retirement to teach in the leprosy school. The children were all speaking and singing with a Liverpool accent! I found great solace at Sunday Mass next to my Liverpudlians.

Music connects people. I loved to play and sing on my guitar. I even brought my guitar to the Hospital and the team would sing together on breaks and mealtime. I worked on new songs and even wrote an accompaniment for Mass. On one occasion, our Obudu Hospital received an invitation to take part in the Nigerian Festival of the Arts. After only a few weeks of practice our choir had come in first! So they got to go to the capital, Lagos, to compete against Nigeria's best in the finals where they received seventh place. But you would not have known as they came home joyous and still singing and telling everyone we came second! Well, it sounded the same in pidgin!

More and more, John would come to Obudu for the weekends, joining for Mass and other lively activities. As an outsider in an unfamiliar place, it was commonplace to spend the night at your friend's house if you had travelled a distance. It was even commonplace if you lived in a large city and your home was on the opposite side of town. So no one thought twice about it, when both John and I stayed at the same place, convent or presbytery. It provided a known and safe accommodation in the dangerous hours of darkness. Even to travel in the dark was not typically recommended.

The nature of these visits created a lot of time for us to spend together. We shared laughter and teasing over many breakfasts, lunches and dinners. Having just been through six months of relative isolation in Scotland, I welcomed this social atmosphere. On the weekends to escape the heat, John would even join the Sisters at Dunlops swimming baths. Sometimes a large group went and other times it was only John and me.

It began slowly and unintentionally. Thinking about it nearly fifty years later, I'm not even sure how it happened or how we got away with it for that matter. But it isn't difficult to understand how it evolved. Monthly encounters turned into weekly dinners. Someone who would only occasionally pop into your mind now began to occupy it with increasing frequency.

Over the months, the affection between us grew stronger and more palpable. We had been swimming in the river nearby the Hospital with the Fathers and were lazily basking in the sun by the shore. I heard a rumbling of vehicles in the distance and quickly climbed up a nearby tree to see who was coming.

'Oh no,' I sighed, 'there's a small line of military trucks heading into Obudu.'

John had come over to the base of the tree and looked up at me. 'Here, let me help you down. We should probably head back now.'

He reached for my hand and supported my hips as I let myself down from the tree and into his arms. As he placed me on the ground our eyes met. I knew my look conveyed more than I could ever express with words and I knew his eyes said something similar. I immediately felt ashamed. I wasn't someone who could easily conceal my emotions, and I quickly looked away.

'Yes. We should be heading back.'

At that moment, I knew it was something I still had control over. I knew I could put an end to it. But I didn't.

The relationship continued to grow. A brief, gentle grazing eventually led to lingering, longer moments. The exhilaration and fear of his new touch turned into familiar and frequent moments. A tender moment of hand holding led to a short, surprised kiss.

I knew my feelings were starting to spin out of control.

The week had been excruciatingly hot. John and I and the two other Irish Sisters decided to take a weekend trip up to a lodge in the highlands to get away from the heat. It was a beautiful place, high above the town of Obudu with gorgeous views of the surrounding valleys. The air was crisp and cool enough even to have a log fire at night. Here, a wonderful little resort run by a British couple provided the most amazing food, and their plump highland cows delivered exquisite milk and cream that reminded me of Ireland.

It had been an especially hectic week at the hospital and I was really looking forward to getting away for the weekend. The four of us packed into John's jeep and began the trek up the serpentine road to the resort. The road up the mountain was a steep, windy climb. The side of the road abruptly descended into thin air, creating breathtaking views for us passengers but requiring the full focus of the driver. As we journeyed to our destination, thick fog started to descend the mountain in cool mists of relief. But as we ascended to higher elevations the mist turned to thick patches of fog. Soon everyone was straining to see the windy road guiding the jeep up the mountain.

'I think you should stop, John,' Sister Francis said from the back seat of the car.

John slowed the jeep to a stop. The fog had fully engulfed the vehicle and surrounding road. John opened the door to step out.

'Don't get out of the jeep on the left side,' he said urgently.

At that moment, the fog swirled open, creating a gap in the thick white blanket. The jeep had crept to a stop right at the edge. The entire left side of the jeep was practically scraping the edge of nothingness and the front of the jeep was on its way off. The road had taken a sharp curve to the right but had been hidden by the fog. I would have opened my door and stepped right out into thin air. The only tyre that was fully on solid ground was the back right. We slipped out of the right-hand back door of the jeep and I looked over the edge. A few milliseconds more and we would all have been lost. The realisation absolutely terrified me and the first thing I thought was that this must be a message from God. *We could die over my infidelity!* I thought to myself.

It took John some time to back the jeep up safely. The jutting precipice on both the left and front side of the vehicle made it difficult to manoeuvre and we would let out little gasps of horror until all four tyres were firmly planted on solid ground. We all agreed to sit in the jeep and just wait until it cleared. Spooked, we all huddled together in the jeep, reflecting on how close we had been to meeting our maker. After a few hours, the fog cleared, and we carefully continued up the mountain. The food tasted amazing that evening.

I was torn. My emotions brought me great internal shame and confusion. If this isn't what God wanted for me, how could I feel this way? I desperately wanted to resist John's kindness and attention but the magnetism between us was too overwhelming. This wasn't a feeling I chose. But when you have a great love for someone, it feels like it's a blessing from God ... not a curse. Not something you would be reprimanded for.

The following week I browsed through the Catholic paper over my evening meal. A small article caught my eye about a priest who had left and married a nun! But the article went on to say he had died on their first wedding anniversary when she was pregnant with their first child. The woman felt it was God's displeasure and a fall from grace. The author of the article seemed to agree with this sentiment.

I gazed away from the paper; my mind ridden with anxiety. But John was really worried when he read it. We finished the meal in silence.

I had arrived at a major crossroad in my life. My beliefs and emotions were running counter to each other like crossing daggers.

18

Deeper into the Woods

In the depths of a forest
Secluded and wild
The night voices whisper in passionate number.
Henry Kendall

I find my soul in forests.
Kedar Dhepe

ESPITE the near death experience, my relationship with John continued. We carried on spending time with each other. On weekends we would both spend nights at the Father's house, sometimes sneaking into each other's bedrooms and stealing a cuddle and a kiss. The line continued to blur and things that once may have been considered far beyond the pale had now become the norm.

But our paths would soon divert. The Sister whom I had replaced was being sent back. I was no longer needed in Obudu. I flew back to Ireland in December 1970 and was promptly enrolled in a three-month diploma course in Tropical Medicine at Liverpool School of Tropical Medicine, starting 1 January 1971. I was joined by another Sister doctor and we lived in a convent in Everton, closer to the tropical school with less distractions than if I had stayed at home with Mum.

This would be the first time since I had joined the MMMs that I would be back in my hometown for more than a few days. However, there was little time to do anything but study. The three-month diploma course was short and intensive. The gaps between the classes, books and long hours of studying were always filled with laughs and fun, at least if I had anything to do with it. My external life was lively, full and brimming with new people, studies and visits to Mum whenever a rare opportunity arose. But in the background, John was there, never far away from my thoughts.

I was going to sit for Membership of the Royal College of Physicians of the United Kingdom. But I knew I would need more experience to pass the second part of the exam. After several considerations, I was to return to Edinburgh and work at the Eastern General Hospital.

The Scottish culture and landscape always made me feel welcome and alive. But I also found it strange, that once again, I was back in Scotland to reflect again on 'freedom', but in a different vein. My time in Edinburgh would give me a strong taste of what life might feel like outside the religious life. Back in civilian clothing and earning a wage, I lived in my own flat in the 'Gate House' of the Eastern Hospital.

I had met a devoted Catholic girl on the course who was leaving for South America for a year to work in a hospital run by a religious order of Sisters. She wanted someone to watch her car, and a car would do me greatly. Although I had more independence in Edinburgh, the car expanded the horizons of what I could do.

I took the post of an SHO at Eastern General Hospital. Originally, I had been offered the position of Registrar in Medicine but shortly before commencing, the consultant called me and asked if I wouldn't mind taking a lower post. Another doctor needed the registrar post for his CV, and the CV of a missionary Sister doctor wouldn't affect my future placements in the same way.

How could I refuse a good-looking consultant who was asking a favour of me in such a nice way? I accepted.

The question of my vows occupied my thoughts more and more. I was almost fully immersed in the fundamentals of a civilian life. While showing a picture of my time in Nigeria to one of my Edinburgh colleagues, she picked John out, 'Wow! I would like to meet this one!' she said. Although I had never thought of him that way, I couldn't help but take pride in the fact that my secret love also attracted the attention of other females.

I was to finish off the year in Edinburgh. As usual, I adapted to the change of people, pace and my new surroundings. Taking a short leave, I left for Ireland to take my annual retreat. It just so happened that John was coming to Liverpool for his annual leave. We talked briefly, and it was decided that he would pick me up at the airport in Edinburgh when I flew back.

It had been nearly six months since we had last seen each other. I arrived back in the UK in my habit and veil. Before walking out through the gate where John would be waiting, I escaped to the airport bathroom and changed into my civilian clothing. I was unsure how I would feel after not seeing him for six months. When I met John in my sheep's clothing, it felt like the six months had never occurred. The possibilities of how we could be together were opening up once more. I was surprised at the intensity of my feelings upon seeing him again but also conflicted, hoping that no one would notice that I had changed my clothes. Yet despite the time we had been apart and the difference in location, nothing had changed for either of us. I knew I had fallen for him. The reflections and renewed commitments at my retreat to the religious life were fading fast from my memory.

It was a gorgeous sunny day. We left the airport and stopped at a grassy field to enjoy a short walk. Drowsy and overwhelmed, we found ourselves entangled in the grass, holding each other. Upon hearing the laughs of nearby children, we quickly rolled apart. I could barely eat when we stopped to have dinner. Rather than go home and possibly go too far, we decided to go to a film – and the one we chose to see, the most popular movie at that time, just happened to be *Love Story*, with its haunting music. Fifty years later, the music from the film still takes me back to that day.

For nearly two weeks, John stayed in an accommodation nearby and we would see each other every day. In the evenings we made dinner at my flat and at weekends we would take trips to the Scottish countryside. At times, I almost felt like I no longer existed in a religious life. The physical boundary was constantly danced upon. At one point, wrapped up in each other, I realised how close we were to crossing a line that couldn't be erased. A willing and equal participant, yet knowing it might be the only thing that would stop us both, I burst out, 'Do you want to make a nun pregnant?'

This caused him to jolt back, wide eyes and aghast. 'I don't want to make anyone pregnant!'

'Well, then you better get off!'

Despite this little lovers' quarrel – or better yet a wake-up call regarding the reality of the situation – it didn't stop us from enjoying the rest of our time together.

I returned one evening from the hospital to find John waiting for me. An unexpected death at work had left me emotionally exhausted. Mr Duncan had whispy white hair and crinkled skin. His eyes twinkled behind his spectacles when I'd check in on him. Today, I thought he was sleeping, but as I got nearer realised he was struggling to breathe. His colour changed quickly and he didn't seem to hear me. He held out his hand and I clasped it between both of mine ... and then and there he died. It happened so quickly. I wasn't ready for it and it made me very sad. But I was also grateful I was there to hold his hand. I felt blessed that I had had the privilege to be with him when he passed to the other side.

Sitting on the couch with John, I confided in him about the events of the day. He looked at me with love and said, 'I want you to be with me when I die.'

I wanted to answer but had no words. I wanted to say, 'I will be,' but the conflict underlying our relationship left me silent. Yet despite my silence, I was deeply moved by the possibility of a life together.

When it was time for John to return, I followed him to the Lake District in my car. We stopped and went for a short walk and had a small picnic together. I returned to Edinburgh alone, and John returned to Liverpool to visit his family and friends.

Before John returned to Nigeria, he drove up to Edinburgh to say goodbye in earnest. I hadn't had this difficulty in saying goodbye in Nigeria. But the last few weeks had shown me what life might be like if I renounced my vows. I left wet tears all over his jacket and although John remained stoic, I noticed the tears in his eyes as well. I had watched wives and girlfriends cry at train stations during the war as they waved goodbye to their men. This was different, but I still felt united with these women in their greif. Saying good-bye to a loved one and not knowing how things will turn out is never easy.

As John drove away, tears came rushing out of me like a dark grey storm. I barely made the short walk back to my flat where I collapsed in sobs.

I had to put on a cheerful face with patients, colleagues and my many new friends even though my heart ached. I couldn't share this with anyone and that made the pain worse. The grief and shame – and the deep longing – made it all unbearable.

I felt a strong urge to go to confession after he left. As a child, I had strongly disliked the confessional box and the entire concept. I had tried to 'make up sins' so I could be forgiven! Why I needed forgiveness I was never sure. One of my friends went to confession one day only to have the priest yell at her. Scared to death, she changed the ending of the story, lying to subdue the tempermental priest. After she left, she was so worried about lying that she ran to another church and had to confess that she had lied to a priest!

It was stories like this that left me with distaste for the whole affair. Although my time as a Sister made me more comfortable with it all, it was never something I looked forward to. I only hoped the priest on the other side might be compassionate and understanding of my sins.

I went into the confessional box and slid the dark curtain closed behind me. I heard the Father come in the box opposite me and sit down. I opened the talking box.

'Yes, go ahead.'

'Father, I am a religious with vows.'

'Yes, please go on.'

'Father, I have committed a sin. I have feelings for a man. We have also become physical with each other.'

'Have you fornicated?'

Despite being in the medical field and delivering babies, I was still unfamiliar with the term.

'What is "fornicated", Father?'

'Have you had intercourse?'

'No, Father!' I replied, shocked but not that shocked.

'I've spent some time with him recently but he has left for another country. I won't see him again for some time.'

'Well, dear, it's good that temptation has been taken away from you, but you need to pray long and hard about this. You have given your love to a man, yet as a religious with vows this love should be given to Jesus.'

'Yes, Father.'

'You're absolved of your sins. Now go in peace.'

I walked out of the church feeling sheepish and yet relieved. I wondered if I'd need to be making the same confession again in the future.

I appeared to lose all my willpower around John. But that's not fully true because I knew my will was split. I wanted to be with John and I wanted to serve Christ and the Church. Why couldn't I do both? The feeling of love felt natural and holy. It did not have the qualities of anger, hate, and jealousy; all the feelings you were taught as 'bad'. This was one of the good ones, the ultimate feeling you were taught to embrace. It felt like a blessing, not a curse. I had several crushes and boyfriends throughout my life, but nothing that felt like this. Oh, God have mercy, I was in trouble.

Not one to stay idle, I had less than a month to prepare for my second Membership exam in Tropical Medicine. With a full-time job on top of it, I threw myself back into my work and studies. In July 1971, I walked through my exam and received my Membership of the Royal College of Physicians of Edinburgh. I had known even more than my examiners after the intense knowledge acquired through my diploma in Liverpool.

In October, I received a calling to go back to Nigeria. I wouldn't be going back to Obudu, but to Anua again. Anua and Obudu were far apart. John was in Obudu. Maybe, this was for the best.

19

The Decision

Two roads diverged in a wood, and I
I took the one less travelled by,
And that has made all the difference.
Robert Frost

The toughest choices in life are deciding between who you are
and who you want to become.
Autumn Fielding-Monson

IN DECEMBER 1971, I was sent back to Nigeria for the third
time and my second time to Anua as a consultant physician
and assistant obstetrician.

Over the last two decades, I had integrated into the MMM
community better than most people expected. I had performed
well in my work – actually, that's an understatement, I had
excelled far beyond my expected capabilities. I loved my fellow
Sisters and the Church community. Everywhere we went there
was a home, even if it wasn't with our order. Every 'calling' I
received turned into an adventure and I grew to love the new
land, culture and the people. But here I sat, having a crisis of
commitment. The crisis had been going on for several years and
I couldn't go on in limbo. It was time for a decision.

I began praying in earnest over the decision to leave or to
stay and recommit myself. I didn't feel that my lack of
commitment to stay stemmed from a lack of love and devotion
to God, nor to the communities I was serving. I still felt I was
learning and growing in faith. But my vows were constantly

being tested and the line between what was expected of me and what I found myself doing had become blurred and incongruent.

Obedience

My struggle with the vow of obedience had begun first.

The vow of obedience was always going to be the most difficult for me. It had gone against my very nature from the onset. My dominant and mischievous personality did poorly with rules and authority. I was able to slip into obedience as a newcomer but it had become less manageable as I gained experience and confidence. In the early days, I remember being indoctrinated by a story about monks who were told to plant cabbages upside down. But how could they grow? They complained to the head monk. In the end, they ended up planting them upside down because they were obedient. Be obedient and you shall understand later, came the message! But later had come, and I still had questions!

Ireland and Rome might as well have been on another planet from Nigeria. Decisions were being made from places that had little knowledge of the world I was living in. When I tried to impart knowledge about our situation, by 'speaking up', I often felt that others perceived me as defiant and disrespectful. I just wanted to ensure the right measures were being implemented on the ground.

But I wasn't the only one having problems. I would see wonderful Sisters leave the order and be very worried about why they left and what had happened! At the end of the day, I started to wonder if I could be more effective outside the religious life than I could be inside it. I believed decisions were being made without the full knowledge of the isuue, or without even seeking it, and this was stopping the congregation and our practises from moving forward in some areas. I would later recall that my 'obedience was going straight out the window'.

Poverty

My occupation was putting me in contact with money. I received a salary at Eastern General Hospital in Edinburgh. I would use what I needed for necessities and then send most of it back to MMMs in Drogheda. A bar of chocolate or a croissant for breakfast were considered excessive and extravagant, and rarely indulged in. (I have more than made up for this time in my life.)

But the Vow of Poverty was about more than money, it was about what money allowed me to do. It gave me freedom of choice and self expression. Although, I enjoyed the religious habit, I also enjoyed long black boots and bright sweaters. Once again, my time in Scotland allowed me to express my individuality. I enjoyed picking out my outfit each morning. I enjoyed choosing how to style my hair. There was also freedom of choice in having a car and deciding where to go on weekends. The accommodation I was staying in afforded me to have visitors and make weekend plans.

Even though I struggled with the first two vows, my discord with them wouldn't have been enough to leave an order that felt like my new home. I would later say that the first two gave me serious doubt but it was the final vow that was the tipping point.

Chastity

Although I was still devoted to Jesus, my heart also belonged to another man. When I wasn't with him, my mind still held him in the background. I was undeniably in love. And it didn't feel wrong as so many people would make it out to be. How dare a Sister fall in love? some may mutter. Yet despite the veil, the vows and the habit, I was still a woman. It's easily forgotten that Sisters and priests are human too.

Was it so confounding to imagine that if I were to fall in love with a man – it was not a sin or something that should elecit shame – but something that God had perfectly designed? Could one's path in life change? Who's to say that although I started on this path fully committed, it wasn't God himself that changed the course? And maybe that was part of the plan all along? Maybe so, maybe not.

I confided in a small handful of people about my dilemma to leave or stay. Stunned, the response was always to convince met to stay. But I was such a good nun! they'd say. How could I survive on the outside? How could I do anything else? One particular remark, 'You'll never exist outside of the MMMs!', still rings in my mind. I sought the counsel of Father Charlie Ryan, my confessor, to whom I felt I could not just confess but also confide in. He was the only person I told about John. He guided me without commanding me and gave me the space to think about it without judgement.

I was thriving despite all my internal struggles with my vows. It wasn't an external issue or event that others had noticed. If I wanted, I could easily have continued in the MMMs with ease and grace.

But in the end, it just didn't feel right. If I ended up with John or not, I was being pulled in another direction, outside of the MMMs. It was my path, and one I could no longer deny.

The Decision

The decision wasn't easy. I also felt I had failed my spouse, Christ. After one confession, I suddenly felt a great emotion and lifted into the arms of an understanding and loving Christ. He held me as I watched all the events, particularly my love for John, unfold and guide my way. The decision was made.

I wrote to the new Mother General – the one who I thought had been voted in under somewhat curious circumstances. In basic terms, I said that despite having appreciated my time as an MMM, immensely, and growing in my love for Christ, I now believed I could do more without the constrictions of religious life.

As one might expect, the Mother General responded by putting my request off. This was common. It made sure the decision hadn't been made in haste. 'Sisters always go through these types of emotions, but it goes away...' came back her response.

So I kept writing. Letter after letter.

While writing to the Mother General, I also wrote letters to John. I let him know that I had decided to leave and was attempting to get released. John proposed a wedding date of 13 March 1974. He knew that I would have a year of reflection before my final release and set the date knowing that my lucky numbers were 313. The date was set. Now I just needed to be released from the order.

But the Mother General's denial letters kept coming. 'Take some time to think about it,' she'd write. After months of writing to the Mother General, and with no change of response, I decided to take a different approach. In Nigeria, I had grown very close and had great respect for the Kiltegan Fathers. I had become close with Father Charlie, and he knew that I had been struggling with this dilemma for some time and had asked for permission to leave. Father Charlie had been the only person to see the trail of issues that led me to my final decision.

In the end, I didn't get released by *my* order, I got released through the application to Rome from the Kiltegan Fathers. After this long wait, it only took a few weeks. I was granted a one-year leave of absence. If I wanted to return after that one year, I could. But I knew there would be no time for reflection. I had already done that. This was it. I was out. My life as a nun was over.

*

It was a strange mixture of feelings. I had developed an amazing community and belonging amongst my Sisters and even those from other orders who had taken their vows. The Catholic community had a strong sense of solidarity. How would I be treated once I left – by the Church community and the lay community? To leave after twenty years of service was not common. Concerns and doubt and fear would waft in and out of my emotional body.

But despite all this, I was excited about new beginnings. I would have a whole menu of choices laid before me every day. I would get to decide what to wear, what to eat and where to live – the type of choices we all take for granted. Yet, one of the things I was most looking forward to was not having to hide my feeling for John any longer.

When the news broke, I wrote a letter to Mum to let her know. She was heartbroken and she wrote back asking me not to return to Liverpool. Mum had always taken so much pride in my choice of vocation. Her friends would hear about my new ventures over Sunday dinners and she knew the shame and humiliation that would cloak my return.

The consequences and social fallout hit me like a ton of bricks. Although Mum's decision and response hurt me deeply, I understood where she was coming from and that she would also face scorn within the Catholic community. Mum hadn't chosen this decision, yet she would face the negative consequences from my choice. I understood her reaction. Unsure of where to go upon leaving, I applied for a job in the West Indies.

My older brother, Father Joseph, took the news much better. He tried to understand my decision and went and talked with Mum, who respected him and his opinions. He was gracious and explained that if I felt the calling to leave, maybe it was the right decision for me. Was it not possible that this was God's plan for me? Was it not possible that she was following the guidance of the Holy Spirit, the same guidance that led her there in the first place?

Whatever Joseph said Mum gave her the courage and strength to accept my decision. She wrote a second reconciliatory letter asking me to please come home and stay with her. She confided that her health was grim and having me at home would really be a blessing. Mum had experienced a silent coronary a year prior.

I received Mum's letter before I received a response from the West Indies. I wanted to go home to Liverpool.

Leaving Anua was more difficult than I expected. During my second time on tour, I had developed a deep respect and fondness for the community and they too loved me too. I remember in particular Sister de Montfort, who had been the Mother of the community and a friend to me over many years, crying and asking, 'Why are so many good Sisters leaving?'

I officially left the MMMs on 13 February 1973. The Medical Missionaries of Mary sent me on my way with £100 in my pocket. I left the hot, humid climate of Nigeria and flew to Germany to see Oonagh and family before settling in Liverpool. Germany was freezing. The first thing I did before even visiting my sister was to stop by C&A in Frankfurt to get a winter hooded jacket. Unable to shake the cold, I even kept my jacket on inside. The jacket had cost me £9. At the age of thirty-seven I now had just £91 to my name. More money than I had ever had to my name.

No longer a nun, I joined the life as a lay person again. The world was open with opportunities, freedom and love.

Photo 1: On a bicycle made for two: Anne's mum and dad.
Photo 2: Oonagh, friend, Anne and Bernie.

Photo 3: Bernie, Oonagh and Anne

Photo 4: Oonagh, Joseph, Mickey (family dog) and Anne.
Photo 5: Pat, Mickey, Anne and Mum

Photo 6: Pat and Anne goofing around.

Photo 7: Our Lady of Perpetual Help at Bishop Eton Church.
Photo 8: Father Joseph giving Anne a blessing.

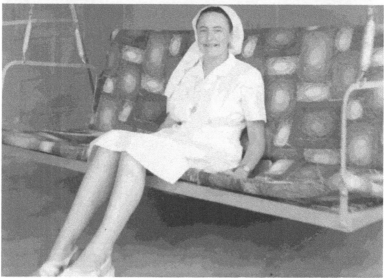

Photo 9: Front row Oonagh, Fr Joseph, Mum and Anne at
Joseph's ordination as a Salesian priest in Kent.
Photo 10: Anne in Nigeria.

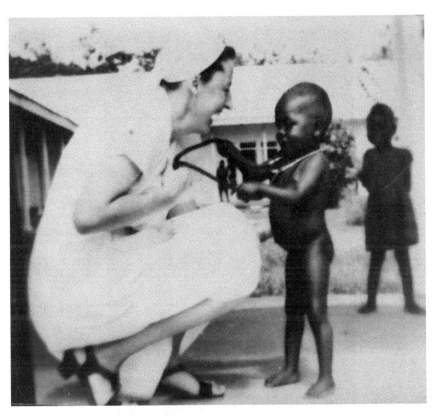

Photo 11: Anne in Obudu, SE Nigeria, 1970. She was posted for a year to the MMM hospital at the end of the Biafran war, which Biafra had lost. Starvation and poverty were rampant and Anne had been donated funds from her church in Liverpool for their malnutrition unit, where her two little friends were being treated.

Photo 12 (*next page, top*): Medical students at Rosemount Garden teaparty with guests, 1980: Anne's mum visiting, pouring the tea, Sr Rose Houlahan (3rd year); Sister Joannes, (Superior); a visiting aunt of Anne's (Mrs Buchanan); Sr Ancilla and Martha Collins (2nd year Med); three visiting Sisters from another order: Bernadette O'Brien, 4th Med, Sr Edith and Sr Elizabeth, support team.

Photo 12: Medical students at Rosemount Garden teaparty with guests, 1980. *For more details see previous page.*

Photo 13 (*left*): Obudu, Nigeria.

Photo 14 (*right*): Mother and her children, Obudu, Nigeria.

Photo 15: Patients and family in Obudu, Nigeria.

Photo 16 (*top*): Student nurses with Sr de Fatima and Sr
Rosario in St Luke's Hospital Anua, 1964.
Photo 17: Anne takes final vows in Drogheda 1993 with
family friends. Front row: Fr Joseph (Anne's brother), Anne,
Bishop McGetterick of Abakaliki, Ogoja Nigeria, Anne's
Mum, Pat Ruane, her best friend.

Photo 18: Anne speaking about the elderly of India at a rotary club in Varanasi, India, 1982.

Photo 19: The Merriman Tavern in Co Clare. The Merriman Festival is held in alternate years in memory of Brian Merriman,* the honoured Gaelic 18th-century poet who wrote the famous poem 'The Midnight Court', essential for good Gaelic speakers!

* https://www.merriman.ie/en/an-cumann/

Photo 20: Pope John Paul I meets Anne with disabled pilgrims in Rome, 1975.
Photo 21: Anne's visit to the Lake District, 1973.

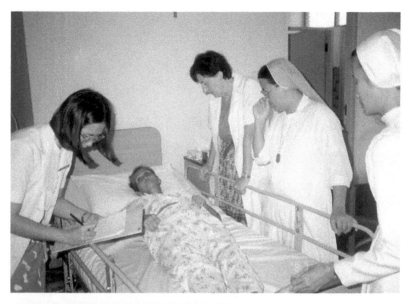

Photo 22: Ward round in St Joseph's, 1985.

Photo 23: Team Party in Department of COFMed (Community, Occupational Health and Family Medicine) at NUS (National University of Singapore), where we needed to wear the traditional dress of the country we represented. For me it was Malaysia with my partner.

PART II

THE STUDENT BECOMES THE TEACHER

20
New Beginnings

New beginnings are often disguised as painful endings.
Lao Tzu

I BEGAN the MMMs as a bright-eyed girl. Nineteen years later, I had an MD with nearly two decades of medical and worldly experience. My time with the MMMs left an indelible mark on shaping who I was and who I'd continue to become. I developed fortitude, discipline and saw first-hand the effects of compassionate action. Despite my father's initial misgivings when I was a young girl, I'm sure he'd be proud of the woman I had become. But the wild girl that entered the MMMs had not disappeared. My sense of individuality and my outspoken nature and passion, although dormant for years, were ready to be reawakened. The love I shared with John gave me the courage and final push to make the decision that would forever change my life's current trajectory – leading outside the confines and rules of the MMMs.

I think most lives are not meant to be travelled in a straight, uninterrupted, linear line; and I don't think mine would be an exception. In reflection, the adversity and metamorphosis I would encounter as a lay person, was exactly what I'd need to continue to evolve and grow into something beyond who I was with the MMMs. Indeed, the next few months would be another great pinnacle of change and transformation in my life. Sometimes, it's best not to know what lies ahead, for rarely does life unfold in the way you had envisioned or expected.

*

I returned to Queen's Drive, Liverpool to live with my mother.

Everything had changed. The Swinging Sixties had transformed Britain. An increase in recreational drug use triggered the rise of hippies, or was it the other way around? Liverpool had suddenly become the centre of the universe as the birthplace of The Beatles. Feminism, a movement close to my heart, had started to take a stronger hold in the collective conscious as more jobs became available to female workers. And then there was sixties fashion, exemplifying the liberated cultural movement. The entire world seemed to be changing rapidly but as I walked back into my home, it stopped.

It felt like I had been transported back into my childhood. Memories of my father and little Bernie came flooding back as I glanced around the living room. The nostalgia of returning home felt wonderful and terrifying. Would I fit into this new world and be accepted the way I had been with the MMMs? Despite an undercurrent of anxiety, I also felt free and excited.

Both Mum and I knew that we could not stay at 313 Queen's Drive. Although the times were changing, we knew that the Catholic community had not changed fast enough to gracefully accept my homecoming. I was very conscious of how Mum would be affected by the fall in my social status. The transition from 'Sister to civilian' would most likely not be kind nor comfortable.

My first attendance at Mass proved to be a rather chilly reception. The service itself was lovely and surreal in the old building of my childhood memories. The smells of church evoked memories of Bernie, dressed in his altar-boy robes, standing in the front. Mum and I took a seat together and waited for the service to begin. A few of our old friends greeted my mother and me with warm smiles and small waves as they walked past us to find their seats. While the priest launched into his sermon, I began to notice the glances in my direction and muffled whispers. The visceral sensation of isolation descended on my shoulders.

As a Sister, the Catholic community had adorned me with respect and love, almost as if I were untouchable, a true servant of God. My Catholic lineage ran strong; a priest or nun had served the Catholic Church in every generation of my family since the Blessed Oliver Plunkett was martyred for his faith in Drogheda, Ireland and beheaded in the seventeenth century!

But the past held no sway to the judgements of today. The respect I was once given left as swiftly with my new civilian status as it had arrived with my habit and veil.

As Mum and I walked out of the church, an older gentleman who had been casting particularly long, cold stares in my direction walked up to me.

'I can't believe you took all the money from us,' he said, 'and now you've left! You ought to be ashamed!'

Before I could respond he snarled and shuffled away.

I knew he was referring to the money I had helped raise for the starving children after the Nigerian Civil War. Before I left for my second tour in Nigeria I had given a talk during Mass about the severe malnutrition occurring in Nigeria. The congregation was incredibly generous and raised a considerable amount for the cause. Didn't he know that the money still went to those in need and I was merely an ambassador for those people? Despite feeling indignant, the heat of shame welled up as I watched the hurt and embarrassment spread across Mum's face.

She and I returned home and had a quiet cup of tea. The interaction with the old man disturbed me more than I let on. Why did I care so much about what these people thought of me? As the old man's words reverberated in my mind, the shame I had felt dissipated and turned into anger. Even though I half expected these types of interactions and knew that his comment was made from ignorance, it still hurt and the hurt doubled seeing those I loved suffer from my decisions. Moving was becoming a top priority.

As a qualified physician, it didn't take long to find a job. I held my first civilian post as a locum consultant in south Wales. But in order to get to Wales from Liverpool, and do the work of a consutant in a rural area, I'd need a car. With no other place to turn, I contacted the MMMs for assistance. Sympathetic to my situation, they agreed to loan me a £1000 with the expectation that it would be repaid at the end of the year. I can still vividly recall that used gold Ford Escort at the car dealers and the excitement I felt as I made the largest purchase of my life. Although it was one of the cheapest cars on the lot it felt like I was driving away with a prized Range Rover.

There were bumps along the way, but things were falling into place more easily than I had expected. I had the love of my mother, a roof over my head, a new car, an amazing new job and a seriously upgraded closet. However, the part of my life that I knew would be the greatest change, and which I was secretly looking forward to above everything else, had yet to occur.

John was still in Nigeria and was expected to arrive back in Liverpool in a few months' time. At night, I would re-read the letters we had written to each other in Nigeria – lingering on his words and imagining what it would be like see him again and feel his touch.

I had settled into my job and was becoming accustomed to my new routine. I enjoyed the work along with the long drive between Liverpool and Wales that allowed me to breathe and reflect on the whirlwind of recent changes. On that particular evening, I specifically remember feeling a lightness as I drove home. I parked my Ford and the cool air stung my eyes as I made my way inside. As I took off my coat, I noticed a dirty envelope in the pile of post on the entryway table. I immediately recognised his handwriting. I discreetly placed the letter into my pocket so Mum wouldn't notice, if she hadn't already.

The post burned through my pocket as I ate dinner with Mum that evening. I barely managed to have a coherent conversation with her before I excused myself early under the pretence of being tired. This was of course the exact opposite of what I was feeling: my heart pounded through my chest as I made my way upstairs. I closed the bedroom door and sat down on the bed, tearing open the envelope.

John always began his letters the same, recalling his daily life in Nigeria with his typical wit and charm.

And then the world stopped.

A quiet ringing hit my ears and my body froze. The writing became distorted as my eyes filled with tears. I wiped my blurring eyes while frantically re-reading the last part of the letter. I choked down a rising lump in my throat as I stared numbly at the wall.

It was over.

The marriage was off.

I felt like someone had given me a swift kick to the gut. Unable to process the meaning of the words written on the smudged paper, I collapsed onto the bed. After years of secretly hiding our feelings, we were finally free to truly express them. Finally, I was free to be with the man I had grown to love and now … he no longer wanted me! The numbness transformed into waves of raw emotion: shock, disbelief, anger, unworthiness, shame, grief, deep loss, loneliness, vulnerability, and abandonment.

I lay crumpled on my bed, gasping for air as sobs began to rack my body. I buried by face in the pillow, muffling my cries so Mum wouldn't hear. Telling her about our love would have been difficult enough, but this? This was something she would never find out about.

Unable to undress, I lay, sleepless in bed, running through the scenarios of what may have happened. But why? There was no specific reason in the letter. No emotional anguish revealed. He had just decided to end it without cause or explanation. He was the one who had persistently talked of marriage and even set a wedding date. Had he confided in someone only to be talked out of it? 'Marry an ex-nun?' they might have said. 'Only if you want to go straight to hell!'

Or was it the strange psychology that he only wanted me when he knew I was unattainable and unavailable. A paralysing sadness flooded my entire body. I felt, quite literally, tossed aside.

As the moon shone through my window on this unusually clear night, the darkness began to creep in. The broken pieces of the puzzle seemed to outweigh anything that made sense. My mother's initial disowning. Leaving my Catholic Sisterhood that had provided me with unspeakable support to re-enter a community that branded me as an outcast.

And now this?

It was a long, dark night at 313 Queen's Drive.

*

Not a whisper of this lost love would cross my lips for decades. At the time, I felt like I had no one I could really confide in. Leaving the order in and of itself was change enough – hard change. The majority of my close friends were mostly Sisters and they were the last ones I wanted to tell. The few friends that I had in Liverpool, like Pat, nearly twenty years had gone by! I still couldn't if she'd judge me or not for leaving the order. I didn't dare risk our relationship and couldn't bear the uncertainty of her reaction if I also told her about John. Besides, there was always this horrible (quite negative) suspicion that I had left for a man!

My mother's friend reiterated a conversation she had with our old piano teacher who taught us how to play jazz.

'I bet she left because she's after a man now!' he had retorted. I felt the anger in my chest when I heard her repeat his words. Although this was mostly true, hearing negative gossip was hard to bear.

*

I would be lying if I said my heart mended quickly. The love and grief I experienced didn't just go away like it had with previous crushes in my younger years. This love almost felt like it had been a gift from God. My heart effortlessly opened. It felt beyond me. It felt like it was something I didn't have a say in.

I appreciated the distraction of my work. Not only did it give me a place to direct my attention, but it also provided a sense of routine, belonging and place where I could still serve those in need. The ethos that I learned while with the MMMs, the way we were taught to care for others, provided my heart with a familiar and comforting outlet.

But there were still tears. Miles and miles of tears. The only place I felt safe to express my sadness was on my way home from work – the drive from south Wales to Liverpool. During those hours, I could be present and honest with my emotions and myself. Sometimes the hardest, darkest stretches in life are the times when we learn of our own humanity and experience our shadow self. I think these moments provide a springboard of compassion for experiences later down the road.

Of course, those weren't the thoughts I was having while I was in the thick of it! I can see God's plan now, but it was very hard to reconcile at the time. In the moment, it felt like dangling off a cliff, holding onto the sanity of life by one's fingernails.

*

It's so easy for people to throw shame at other people's choices, especially women. Why would the path someone chose at the age of eighteen still be the right decision for them twenty years later? It almost felt like it was far worse to have left the order than if I had decided not to join at all! In the hallways of my mind, I could hear the murmurs. 'How dare a women decide she wants to be with a man!' To make the issue more convoluted, traditional society loves to slap criticism and shame on women who decide not to get married or not have kids – or who do get married, have kids and then get divorced!

As I write this, I find myself staunchly opposed to the Catholic tradition of celibacy amongst priests and Sisters. Some of the brightest minds in our community didn't get a chance to procreate. Let them marry and still serve God in all his glory! But maybe in generations to come, love and acceptance will truly be honoured over conformity and outdated traditions that no longer serve our community.

21

Renewal and Rewards

Everything in nature invites us constantly to be what we are.
Gretel Ehrlich

As I DO, I threw my entire self into my work. It provided a needed distraction from my inner, hidden world. However, the locum position I held in Wales only lasted for six weeks. As I sat at home that weekend it occurred to me that I should check my bank balance so I could plan accordingly. On Monday morning I took a leisurely stroll to the bank and asked to see my balance. I glanced down at the number the nice gentleman handed to me behind the booth. Shocked, I looked at a number that I had never seen before. I had acquired more money during that short time than I had ever had in my entire life! God knows, I was not about to be practical with it. As soon as I got home, I informed Mum we were heading to the Lake District as soon as arrangements could be made for our lodging. I wanted to go back to the same area we had always visited in the summers as a family.

I drove with Mum up to a bed and breakfast in Glenridding, close to Ullswater Lake. For the first time since coming home, I could feel myself let go and relax. Surrounded by nature, I could take a deep breath and have faith that everything was going to be fine. Lovely tea shops and bars were a short walk from our b&b. Sparing no expense, we ate fluffy scones with beautiful whipped cream and jam with our tea, overlooking the lakes in the mornings and ended the evening with lamb shanks in the evenings. Every day we'd take a drive to the beautiful surrounding areas and even had a chance to visit the old haunts as far away as Windermere and the cottage in Far Sawrey. The vast green landscape and open sky reminded me of God's mystery. Liverpool was home but I was finding reintegration into my local community more difficult than I originally thought it might be. But out here, there was just Mum, me, the green rolling hills and God. And of course, amazing food.

The Lake District proved to be just what I needed. Fresh air, open space and walking on the best foot trails Britain had to offer seemed to quiet and assuage my tattered spirit and unspoken pain. Sister Brigid had just finished her Membership in the UK and reached out to me before we had left on our trip to the Lake District. We agreed that she must come and stay with Mum and me for a few days while on holiday. Out of everyone, she was the person I had remained closest to after my departure. She joined us just in time for the weekend.

Brigid brought the warmth, familiarity, and friendship I so deeply needed at that time. Her reaction to my decision to leave only solidified and deepened our friendship. She was incredibly sad yet understood that I needed to forge my own path forward. I felt no judgement, or if there had been any, she concealed it quite well! The two of us stayed up talking like schoolgirls late into the night. Tears streamed down our faces followed by bouts of laughter as we reminisced about our time together as postulants and in medical school.

We also had so much to share about our experiences working as doctors in Africa. Brigid had been in East Africa when I was in Nigeria and although we had experienced very different cultures there were many similarities. It was therapeutic to be able to share with someone who could relate to what I had experienced. Despite our incredible connection and trust, I decided to keep my secret about John hidden. I didn't want to risk our friendship with the chance she'd be aghast. That would have been the final blow to my fragile state. Things were good. I wanted to keep them that way and just enjoy our time together.

Brigid – a friend in a million – said goodbye on the Sunday after the three of us attended mass at the local church. Unknowingly, that would be the last time we would see each other until we met again in Uganda in 1993.

22

Life's Next Mentor

It's strange when a stranger completely changes your life.
Anne Merriman

I WAS working in a locum position in Cardiff, Wales, when I received a call from Dr John Munro, the consultant I had worked with in the Eastern Hospital in Edinburgh, Scotland, while I was studying for my Membership. I had contacted him upon arriving to Liverpool in search of a job.

'Anne! Do you remember Dr Jimmy Williamson in Edinburgh? He worked at Eastern Hospital as the consultant in geriatric medicine.'

I remembered Jimmy as I prepared for my membership before returning to Obudo, Nigeria. Although I worked mostly with Munro, I remembered the elderly, dignified gentleman I'd pass in the halls. His work seemed fascinating, and he was highly respected amongst his colleagues.

'I talked with him and he's taken up a position in Liverpool at David Lewis Northern Hospital as the first Professor in Geriatric Medicine in the UK. He is looking for dedicated doctors to join him. You did so well with the elderly patients in our ward at Eastern, I think you'd be really good in geriatric medicine.' He paused for a little before continuing, 'I think he's going to start a special programme down there and it's something you might want to consider being a part of.'

I was pleased that Dr Munro had thought of me for the position, but I knew I'd need some time to think about it before I committed to anything. My first love had always been paediatric medicine. Not only did I enjoy the medical aspect, but I found that caring for sick children was a deep spiritual blessing and it had created some of my most profound memories in Nigeria. The experience of working in paediatrics also went beyond the children, and often involved caring for the mothers, many of whom ended up losing their child, because they came to the hospital to get help too late. I had already applied to a post with Professor Hendrikse, at the Alder Hey Children's Hospital.

I thanked Dr Munro profusely and briefly relayed my current interest at Alder Hey in the paediatric department but that I would think about his suggestion.

In the upcoming week, I had the opportunity to accompany Professor Hendrikse on a ward round at Alder Hey's Children Hospital. Built in a park and catering to the needs and research of childhood illnesses, the operation was impressive and smoothly run. As I neared the end of the tour, I noticed that I kept contrasting the difference between what I saw here and the children I had helped in Nigeria. The children in Nigeria had been *critically* ill and suffered from malaria, meningitis and other infectious diseases. Although the children at Alder Hey needed true medical care and help, they seemed to suffer from a completely different fate, one that involved higher levels of social neglect and injury. I knew it didn't feel right to compare the two places, but regardless, it wasn't what I had expected. Before I walked into the hospital, I had been prepared to accept an offer, now I hesitated. Maybe I should at least have a conversation with Dr Jimmy Williamson, I thought to myself as I drove home.

I contacted Dr Munro and asked if Dr Williamson was still recruiting doctors for his unit. It wasn't long before I got a call from Professor Williamson himself.

'Anne, I heard from John that you were still available and might be considering coming over to geriatrics. John said that you were so good with the elderly patients during your time in Edinburgh.'

'Thank you,' I replied. 'It was very kind of him to say so and to think of me when he heard about the work you're doing here in Liverpool.'

'Well, I think you'll find a lot of value doing this work. I know you have spent a lot of time working for the underprivileged and neglected in Nigeria. It might surprise you, but in Liverpool, the neglected are the elderly.'

He continued to talk about the need to improve elderly care and advance related operations and policies in the community. He envisioned a model that could provide much better support to Liverpool's most vulnerable. As he finished discussing his vision and mission of the work, he asked if I'd join him on a few rounds to better understand the work. I agreed.

I instantly liked Jimmy and his contagious passion for his work quickly infected me. By the end of the day, I found myself accepting a position at David Lewis Northern Hospital in the department of Geriatic Medicine.

Geriatrics was not thought of as a 'prestigious' field, yet the passion Jimmy imbued as he talked about it and introduced me to the patients was undeniable and made me want to be a part of it. Whatever it was.

I find it interesting how so quickly my career swung from one side of the pendulum to the other – the beginning of life to caring for those at the very end of life. Just like that, I set off on a path that I had never planned or expected. And, maybe, that always was the plan. And so it was that Professor Dr Jimmy Williamson became an essential mentor and would have a tremendous impact on the trajectory of my life's work.

23

Geriatric Medicine

In the moment, life feels like a maze.
Upon reflection, it couldn't have been more perfectly guided.
Anne Merriman

Success is not about inventing the wheel, but learning,
mastering and improving upon someone else's wheel.
Jared Fielding

I N 1973, I started working in the geriatric unit at David Lewis Northern Hospital. I agreed to come in as a senior registrar and if all things went well, I'd be promoted to a consultant at the end of the first year. Professor Williamson had set up two geriatric wards in the Northern Hospital. One of the oldest hospitals in Liverpool, it remained a teaching hospital. Jimmy had hired Dr Powell as a senior lecturer, younger than me, but had received excellent geriatric training and was a good physician and teacher. I would join as the team's third doctor.

Jimmy, tall and slender with white wavy hair, held himself in a dignified manner. His broad Edinburgh-Scottish accent combined with his humour and revolutionary ideas added to his mystique. For the next three years, it was an absolute honour to work with Professor Williamson. He was one of the best. The degree to which he cared for his patients felt like the holistic approach we strove for in the MMMs. He approached his practice and patients with such heart and care – a special trait in the world of medicine.

In my short time out of the MMMs, I realised how easy it was to get bogged down in the paperwork, bureaucracy and politics surrounding work. It was too easy to make 'career choices' and forget about your 'why'. Jimmy led our department with a fresh perspective and helped us all remember our why. His primary objective was always to give his patients the best quality of life. In our area of speciality, a high quality of life did not occur in a hospital ward but at home, surrounded by a familiar environment and loved ones. Although I only had three years under his mentorship, his methodology and philosophy to patient care would be one of the greatest influencing factors in my future approach to medicine and patient care.

*

An elderly person, living alone, struck with influenza, has limited options. They were either completely stuck or they had to go to the hospital and the change to a foreign environment often led to increased confusion and an early grave. Professor Williamson promoted high quality home care and had devised a new system that incorporated home visits from a multi-disciplinary team who coordinated with district nurses and other social services to ensure the patient received follow-up care and support.

Initially, a doctor and social worker worked together to assess a patient's situation and make further recommendations of care. Very often, elderly persons suffered from a bad flu bug going around. We'd prescribe drugs and mobilise local community services that provided homecare and meals on wheels. (These community services were later cut due to political changes and policies.)

For home visits, they paired a medical doctor with a senior social worker. Lesley Phipps' petite frame and innocent, bright face made her look quite a bit younger than she really was. However, her girlish features starkly contrasted her calm, level-headed demeanour and paired well with my outgoing nature. Smart and incredibly intuitive, her background and experience helped her brilliantly navigate the different sub-cultures inside of Liverpool. Her practical experience became invaluable as she taught me about the dire situation that many of the elderly in Liverpool found themselves in.

My eyes opened to the hidden poverty and vulnerability that existed in our home city. We entered flea-infested flats, whose inhabitants subsisted with only gas lights for heat and light. Places where the bugs had grown bold and lived out in the open. Our typical patient had little social support and given their declining mobility and mental capacity, their lot in life looked set.

I heard Professor Williamson's words ring in my head, 'In Liverpool, it is the elderly that are the most vulnerable.' This was in marked contrast to Nigeria, where the highly respected elderly were treated with much more care and support. Although it was a field I didn't expect to find myself working in, I found the work highly rewarding.

Lesley and I developed a formidable bond as we worked together on a daily basis in Liverpool's desperate areas. This bond extended outside of work and we'd often spend time on the weekends together at social engagements.

'Anne was incredibly friendly, fun and outgoing.' Lesley recalls. 'She worked hard, enjoyed the challenges we faced and had a team outlook on resolving issues.' Lesley and her husband David Phipps, a researcher in chemistry at the John Moore's University, would both later play a key role in our future work together.

Our team had a great spirit and activities outside of work were held that strengthened our personal rapport with each other. Jimmy held lovely parties for the team at his home a few times a year. His wife, a most excellent hostess, and five children always joined in the celebration. Jimmy did not believe in God and often joked with me about religion, challenging my beliefs in great humour. Having a professional background in proselytising, I always had a great answer for him. We had good fun together and got on well, embracing our differences. Even though he did not believe in God, his humanistic values, kindness, and dedication to helping others embodied my Christian faith. Throughout my life, I've found that people's actions typically stem from their values and not necessarily their theistic beliefs. God works in wondrous ways; often his greatest servants may not necessarily be believers.

Mum and I had moved to a home in Rocky Lane. It soon became a popular place for less formal gatherings. Mum was an amazing hostess and often cooked a large meal for the extra guests that often appeared. To everyone's delight, the highlight became Mum's hostess trolley that kept the food hot for second helpings and any latecomers. I picked up playing the guitar again from my time in Anua, Nigeria and the piano from my childhood. After dinner, friends and colleagues sat around the piano and sang rounds and rounds of songs. It reminded me of when Dad would play the piano in the evening when we were kids. Relationships that would have normally stayed professional expanded to deeper, personal connections. Lesley would later recall it as a special and unique time due to the personal connections made outside of work.

When in Doubt, Laugh It Out

One day Jimmy came into the hospital roaring with laughter. He had just returned from a home visit where he visited an elderly lady with heart failure. She stayed in a very small bedroom, barely big enough to house her double bed. Jimmy could barely fit into the room to conduct his assessment, squeezed between her bed and the wall.

'So how many pillas (Scottish accent for pillows) do you sleep with at night?' Jimmy asked,

The woman looked wide-eyed at his question. Jimmy, unsure if she had understood him tried again.

'How many pillas do you sleep with?'

The elderly woman became quite indignant and looked him directly in the eyes.

'Doctor! I'm a good Catholic and I have no fellas in my bed at night!'

It took some back and forth before either of them had a clue what the other was saying. Jimmy's good spirit and humour, in all situations, spread to the rest of the team.

*

South Liverpool had a mix of many cultures. Often, older immigrants only spoke their native language and never learned English. I found many situations in which sailors married foreign women and the wives, once citizens, brought over her elderly relatives. One of these elderly gentlemen found himself in the geriatric ward at Northern. He was a tall Nigerian with soft eyes. I began to hear whispers amongst the staff about the increasing difficulty they were having with the elderly Nigerian man. During the nurses' routine rounds, they'd find urine all over the floor next to this gentlemen's toilet. Appalled, they brought him over to the toilet like a poorly trained puppy and began lecturing him.

'You need to use the loo!' Angry, the nurses talked loudly and slowly, attempting to get their message across. But their anger and pleas were to no avail: day after day, they'd come in to find urine on the floor.

I became aware of this issue when I overheard one of the janitors venting to another. 'He refuses to use the loo! Do they pee on their floor in Nigeria?' They whispered in disgust as they went to fetch the bucket to clean urine.

'Maybe he's not familiar with a modern toilet.' I asked, breaking into their private conversation. 'Do you know if he speaks pidgin English?' Due to the numerous tribes and diverse dialects and languages within countries, I learned during my time in Nigeria that pidgin served as a bridge of communication.

News got around that I was going to attempt pidgin with our Nigerian friend. A group of hospital nurses and cleaning staff gathered around the Nigerian and me.

'Come here, ma friend. Make you no piss on de floor. You go da piss in da toi-lett.' I did my best to remember the rhythm of the language as words came tumbling out of my mouth in chaos and disorder. My non-verbal communication was as colourful and dramatic as the words coming out of my mouth. In reality, I had no idea what I said or how I said it but I was fairly certain that parts of the message had gone through. Fits of laughter broke out amongst the gathered crowd as I finished my garble. Everyone looked at the Nigerian, hoping he too might respond in a similar fashion. Instead, the tall Nigerian responded by just looking at me with his quiet eyes and a slight smile on his lips. I attempted several more times to convey the needed message but with no assurance that he was understanding me in any way, I had to give up.

But the next morning the ward nurse burst in. 'Anne, you won't believe it! He went pee in the toilet!'

Somehow, the Nigerian had understood the message. The news spread like wildfire amongst the staff but especially amongst the janitors. From that point on my expertise of pidgin talk became highly valued.

*

Mrs Brown was a very sweet old lady in her nineties had a horrible flu and was admitted on a short-term basis. She had always cared for her mentally disabled daughter, Miss Jenny, who was now seventy years old. Although, Mrs Brown was the one admitted for care, Miss Jenny also needed to come to the hospital and receive the oversight and assistance that her mother usually provided. Jenny had a lovely outgoing personality and soon became the ward's social butterfly, participating in the different events, talking to the patients, and bringing a little life to the place. Although she had a knack for being unpredictable and keeping the nursing staff on their toes, the patients and staff grew very fond of her.

In the ward, the elderly patients with dentures, would place their teeth in cups beside their bed every night. After 9.00 pm they turned to lips and gums. The lights turned off at 9.30 pm and the dark stillness slowly became infiltrated with snoring. But not everyone slept that night. Little bunny slippers approached each bedside table in the dark. The sun began filtering in through the windows the next morning and concern spread through the ward like an epidemic.

'Where are my teeth!' one of the patients shouted. 'Mine are gone too!' another patient quipped looking at their empty bedside cup. Shouts of anger arose through muffled lips and gums. It soon became apparent that everyone's dentures had gone missing and it also became apparent that the mystery needed to be solved before breakfast!

Miss Jenny slowly stirred and sleepily pulled herself out of bed and began to change into her clothing. One of the staff walked by and noticed that something was not quite right with Miss Jenny's knickers. Bumps and bulges stretched her knickers in strange ways and then with a small twist, Miss Jenny reached for her shirt and four dentures fell loose and smashed on the floor. To everyone's amazement – or more accurately, abhorrence – Jenny had managed not only to steal everyone's teeth in the middle of the night, but to also stuff the majority of them up the legs of her knickers! After a thorough cleaning of all the missing teeth, they were returned to their owner, although that process took quite a lot of trial and error.

This would not be a one-time occurrence. Jenny had become the official infamous nightly tooth fairy. Unable to control Miss Jenny, every patient wrote their names on the pink part of their dentures with a diamond pen so they could find their teeth, if so be it, it happened the next evening. It got to the point that many patients began stuffing their teeth up their own knickers to keep them safe from Miss Jenny's nightly escapades.

As soon as Mrs Brown felt better, the pair were allowed to go home as quickly as possible.

24

The Smoking Nun

Oh, the places you'll go.
Dr. Seuss

'It's a dangerous business, Frodo, going out your door.
You step onto the road, and if you don't keep your feet,
there's no knowing where you might be swept off to.'
J.R.R Tolkien

People don't take trips, trips take people.
John Steinbeck

I T WAS a quiet but very peaceful time in my life. I was settling into my second year at Northern Hospital and both Mum and I loved our new home and surrounding neighbourhood in Rocky Lane. I found our neighbours to be exceptionally kind – maybe because they didn't know I was an ex-nun! Or maybe it was because I no longer projected my fears and insecurities onto others like I had when I first came home. My emotional situation was also on the mend. I'd have stretches of weeks without *him* wondering into my mind.

It hadn't been a quick process, but I'm not sure one ever really gets over a true love, which John had been for me. But I was healing. I was able to wake up in the morning with a clear mind, work with an amazing mentor in a fulfilling job and go to sleep at night with a still mind. We were financially comfortable and always had a house filled with warm friends. I had little to want and nothing to complain about.

So inevitably, there came an itch. There always comes an itch. The itch when something else awaits you. Maybe things were too good, too familiar, too easy. The call to adventure began to creep into my consciousness.

*

Father Michael O'Leary had become an incredible organiser. Having worked to set up hospice services in South America, local donors asked for a small office in the Liverpool area. As a result, he established Jospice, a hospice type facility, in Thorton near Liverpool. Meanwhile his first cousin, Sean O'Leary, who had been working with him, had driven overland donating cars to the southernmost state, Awassa in Ethiopia, for the Comboni Fathers.[13] The Comboni Fathers are a missionary branch of the Catholic Church dedicated to serving the poorest of the poor and had a huge presence under Archbishop Gasparini.

As Sean drove these cars across the Ethiopian landscape he was overtaken by the need for medical assistance in the more rural areas. Ethiopia was in the midst of a drought: widespread famine began there in 1972 and would grip the country for another two years. With the support of his cousin's connections and the Comboni Fathers, Sean founded the charity Survive, whose purpose was to provide mobile medical care in Africa, specifically Ethiopia.

When I first learned of the charity at the end of 1974, Ethiopia has just broken into civil war. Unrest emerged as the populace felt Emperor Haile Selassie had been complacent in his wealth and palace, as his country folk died in hordes around him. The Marxist Derg, the Provisional Military Government of Socialist Ethiopia, staged a coup d'état and overthrew the Ethiopian Emperor and government and established a Marxist-Leninist one-party state claiming itself as the vanguard party. Hearing about it reminded me of my time in postwar Nigeria. The charity Survive was offering medical care to the poorest of the poor with the support of the local Catholic missionaries.

---

[13] The Comboni Missionaries were founded by Daniel Comboni with the mission to serve the poorest and most abandoned people around the world.

Volunteers would be based in the Comboni compound, which made the unknown feel a little safer. It looked as if I could help by conducting a study to see how Survive and their partners were utilising the vehicles and other resources and assess viable options for setting up clinics for the hospice mobile medical team. Intrigued to see what this part of Ethiopia was like, I also knew my skill set and knowledge could be very useful to their mission. I received Survive's approval to conduct an assessment and then coordinated with Northern Hospital to take my six-week leave. And just like that, I was headed back to Africa.

As the plane began to descend into Addis Ababa, I lifted my window curtain and was struck by the beauty of the mountains surrounding the growing hilltop capitol. The country, located in high altitude, had over 70 per cent of the continent's mountains. The ember glows of the early morning sun cascaded on the rugged landscape below. The landing, slightly unsettling, left my stomach in my throat. The beauty seen from the sky starkly contrasted the ambience of the airport. The Chinese communist party had recently entered the country and communist soldiers surrounded the airport. I instantly had an unnerving feeling of being watched.

Arrangements had been made for a Camboni Father to pick me up at the airport. I collected my bags from the dusty, humid airport and walked out of the terminal. Leaning next to a jeep was an old Spanish-looking man, puffing on a cigarette. I instantly recognised him by his clerical attire and by the way he looked at me expectantly. Mother of Mary, I thought to myself, they've sent me a geriatric priest for a driver! Let's hope he doesn't keel over and leave me stuck in the bush somewhere, I thought to myself.

Father Pedro gave me a sweet nod, 'Anne Merriman?'

'Yes. You must be Father Pedro.'

'I am indeed. We should make it to Sidamo (Awassa capital) before dusk, but the drive will take nearly the entire day. We better get going.'

Fr Pedro had a mixed accent with a different rise and fall in his rhythm, illustrating he was most likely familiar with some of the local languages. We were heading south to a region near the Kenyan border, and I knew these journeys were typically long and difficult.

Looks can be deceiving. Fr Pedro turned out to be an excellent driver, deftly navigating the potholes and aggressive surges of traffic in the cities and towns. A gorgeous drive took us to the

Sidamo territory in the lower middle region of the country. Once we were out of the city, I rolled my window down and took a deep breath of the fresh warm air. I felt a sense of vibrant aliveness that often accompanies seeing something for the first time. However, while driving through a war-torn and famine-stricken country, it's only a matter of time before a sense of eeriness begins to set in. As we made our way, we drove by Lake Sidamo. The lake, known for its avian beauty, had blossomed into a flourishing tourist area. The colours and sounds that emerged from the local birds were known to transfix newcomers. But that is not what we saw that day. Despite the famine hitting the northern regions of Wollo and Tigre the hardest, civil war had torn a seam in the entire country and had decimated this local attraction. The once elegant huts and swimming pools were in tatters, and it appeared that even the birds had deserted their beautiful home.

It was also apparent that China's Cultural Revolution had infiltrated Ethiopia. It felt like the entire countryside was littered with Ethiopian students, dressed in military uniform, sent to educate the rural areas about Mao's little red book.

It was becoming more and more obvious why Sean had been overwhelmed with compassion and successfully pursued setting up a charity called Survive. After spending the entirety of the day in transit, we arrived safely in Sidamo where I was then shuffled to a nearby Sister's convent.

*

They fed me a modest local dinner consisting of vegetables and lentils. Tired, I retired to the stark guest bedroom with concrete flooring. The single bed, placed in the corner of the room, had a firm mattress and a thin cover sheet. A wooden chair, positioned next to the bed, had a thicker blanket folded on the seat, as the nights were known to drop below freezing. The compound had a dog or two for basic security needs.

Sleep evaded me that night. I awoke in the early morning hours and tiredly found myself in the bathroom. A cold drizzle came out of the spout. Cold enough to take my breath away, I washed quickly, and felt quite invigorated afterwards. The conditions were basic – more basic than what I had experienced in Nigeria. I had great admiration for the women and their ability not only to cope but to operate effectively under such circumstances. Breakfast consisted of an Ethopian black coffee and a piece of bread. Most coffee lovers would have been in heaven. Grown at high altitudes, Ethiopian coffee is among the best coffees in the world. However, I have found that a diluted coffee works best with my constitution. I poured some hot water into the dark brew and sipped at it with my bread.

Fr Pedro picked me up and we went back to the Camboni Fathers to plan out our next few weeks. Between jet lag, a poor night's sleep and a reduced calorie intake, I was ready to end the day and go to sleep! My eyelids drooped heavily, and my mind felt dull and tired. We began by planning a trip to investigate the need of medical services throughout Sidamo and the best places to collect information and stay the night if needed.

Dinner was less than agreeable that night back at the Sisters. These women may have learned to manage a little too well! After another poor night's sleep, I packed my bags and prepared to say goodbye to my hostesses. Although they had learned to survive in such minimal conditions, I had not. Bishop Gasparini had invited me to stay in the Father's house and after last night's dinner, the choice was clear.

By the end of that week, we had planned out the data collecting activities for the next four weeks and the routes and lodging along the way. Father Pedro and I were ready to begin our journey.

*

On the first day, we made a few stops at some of the nearby villages to assess the medical needs. Ethiopians in general are a proud people, with a select, elite part of the population being direct descendants of the Queen of Sheba herself! Initially coming across as shy, cautious and unsure of why we had entered their village, they could quickly transition to arguing passionately about issues that were important to their culture and way of life. Once Fr Pedro translated our mission to them into local pidgin, they even accepted us into their homes.

Many of the people were dressed in simple loincloths and many of the men carried spears for protection. Upon further visits and discussions with multiple tribes, I started to understand the intense local rivalry amongst between them. People who wandered too far beyond their local territory were often never heard from again, maybe killed, and possibly even put in the pot! But despite their differences, there was one thing they had in common: fear. And it wasn't fear of each other. They were afraid of a strange new government with little red books. that flaunted violence. A government that littered the countryside with violent college students, disguised in military uniform, demanding ownership of people's cars! But the tribes were also afraid of the rebel groups who had sprung up in opposition, demanding the tribes' resources and loyalty. The constant danger of outside forces created insidious instability for the locals.

The need for medical services, palliative care and other nutritional supplementation was as high, if not higher, than I had seen in postwar Nigeria. Finding a way to deliver these services was going to be the real challenge.

After a good's day of work, having talked with several tribes, we pulled into a Lutheran guesthouse. I was so relieved to see the amenities and cleanliness of the parlour as we walked into the sensibly furnished room.

'Should I go grab our bags?' I asked Fr Pedro.

He looked over at me in surprise. 'Oh, sorry, Anne, I just need to pick something up from Pastor John. We aren't staying here- this place is Lutheran. But don't worry, there is a Catholic convent just a few miles down the road.'

Rather dejected I went and sat back in the jeep and waited for our departure. Once we were on the road, it became apparent that Father's Pedro memory was not as sharp as we both had hoped. The Catholic convent never appeared. With the blackness of night setting on us, he chose to pull over into a little b&b at the next small town.

You might say that this place was quite a step below that of the Sister's convent! The dodgy receptionist led me through a dark hallway and opened the door to my room. Immediately, my attention shifted to something smeared in strange patterns on the wall. I didn't know what it was and didn't want to find out. If this was the bedroom I could only imagine the condition of the loo! The loo was just big enough for a sink and a deep squat toilet – a small hole in the floor. There was no running water and no electricity. My only wish was not to fall into the toilet if Mother Nature called in the darkness of the night.

Lastly, I prepared myself, and walked back into the room and over to the bed. I could literally see the fleas hopping on the white bedsheets. I stood in the middle of the room, exhausted after our long day, unsure exactly what to do. I finally decided to sleep in the bed resembling a mummy, covering myself from head to toe, and wrapping my head in a scarf to keep the fleas at bay.

After a sleepless night of itching, my need for adventure and the unknown had literally been itched. At the first rays of dawn, I got dressed and practically fled the room and waited in the sitting room for people to awake. Breakfast was a cup of Ethiopian coffee so thick you could have filled a pen with it and written a letter! It did not come with a piece of bread. The smells of a nearby café caught my attention and I prepared myself for the day by having an Ethiopian style omelette and cup of tea. This adventure was just getting started.

We finished another busy day and, absolutely knackered, I made up my mind.

'You know, Father Pedro, you should absolutely stay where you want,' I declared. 'But as for me, I'll be staying with the Lutheran family tonight.'

Without missing a beat, Father Pedro replied, 'Well, if you must, I wouldn't want you to go alone. I suppose I can make a few exceptions for your visit.' I raised my eyebrows in surprise. His stoic behaviour had fooled me, but he must have fared no better than I the night before. The Lutheran Pastor and family graciously accepted us as guests. When they asked where we had stayed the night before, they all burst out laughing.

'You must be a brave lady,' the Pastor said and winked at me.

We used the Lutherans as our post for a week or two as we made treks out into the countryside gathering information. Every night after dinner Father Pedro and the Pastor stepped out onto the patio with their coffee and puffed on their cigarettes. The sweet nostalgic smell of the smoke wafted into the room where I sat by myself thinking about the day's events.

'Would you like a cigarette, Anne?' The Pastor poked his head in through the door, holding out a box. I hadn't smoked since I joined the MMMs – well truth be told, I did sneak one smoke as a nun– but that was early on and it nearly knocked me on my backside. But that was it and it had been decades since I had smoked frequently! More interested in the social aspect of smoking, I couldn't imagine that one would hurt.

'Don't mind if I do,' I said, standing up and joining them outside. The bright moon provided warm light as the three of us, an African Lutheran pastor, one Spanish Catholic father and one ex-Irish nun stood out in the cold fresh air, lighting up, laughing and sipping coffee. Once I had my first smoke, being around a chain smoker didn't really help. Father Pedro constantly lit up as he drove us between the villages. Eventually, on a long drive I succumbed to my second. Before long, I must admit, the two of us were quite the pair. Windows down, driving around the Ethiopian countryside, conducting work for a medical organisation with a constant cigerette attached to our mouths. I became a smoker for the next twenty years of my life and was once jokingly referred to as the 'smoking nun'!

*

At the end of several weeks of touring different regions of Awassa, visiting multiple tribes and assessing available resources, I felt like I had the necessary information to finish my report. Ready to wrap up and go home, I first needed the approval of the local Catholic representative for Health in Sidamo. We arrived at his office and were told he had gone to Addis. Arriving at Addis, we found that he had returned to Sidamo! Incredulous at our fate, we slowly walked back to the jeep.

Snoozing in the front seat, the screech and halt of brakes brought me to my senses. I groggily looked around and noticed the long line of stopped cars in front of us. Clearly, this line had been sitting here for a while from the number of people mulling around outside their cars. Some of them had even stretched themselves out on the shaded ground beneath their vehicles, taking an afternoon siesta.

Fr Pedro turned off the engine and looked over at me, shrugging his shoulders.

'I'll go and see what's going on,' I said opening the jeep door.

'Don't take too long and don't go too far away,' Fr Pedro said in a slightly uneasy manner, saying more with his eyes than he did with his voice.

It's not often you find a traffic jam in the middle of the Southern Highland. As I walked on the side of the road, a few of the people seemed rather distressed and impatient while most of the bystanders looked like they couldn't care less. As I had already learned in Nigeria, the concept of time here is different. You might just say, the mindfulness movement has never caught on in Africa because they don't need to learn how to relax!

I recognised the emblem on a soldier's uniform near the front of the line, symbolising the rebel forces. His face seemed to hold a soft expression that gave me the courage to approach him.

'Excuse me, sir.'

He turned his attention to me with his strong, dark eyes.

'Excuse me, but I have a plane I need to catch,' I continued, smiling at him, trying to earn some special consideration.

A large smile spread across his face. 'Sorry mam, but you have come into our country, and you too must wait. We are holding you hostage as possible leverage against the Deng Government.' His English and manners were impeccable.

'Sir, you seem very educated. I'm conducting work for a medical organisation to help your people. Can't you make an exception and let me and my colleague pass so we can continue with our work?'

The man's eyebrows raised, and the smile faded.

'No,' he said shortly. 'You must stay here with everyone else.'

It was clear that I wasn't going to get anywhere, and I didn't want to turn a neutral ally into an adversary.

'Well, I appreciate your willingness to talk with me,' I said, flashing him a large smile but as soon as I turned away, I felt the collywobbles hit my knees.

The news of a hostage situation on our route must have spread by the indication that no other cars came along behind us. Our jeep remained at the end of the line. Father Pedro would not leave the car. Afraid it might get nabbed by the guards if he left it unoccupied, he lit up another cigerette and squirmed uncomfortably in his seat, trying to settle in for the long wait. It was clear this situation had gone balls-up.

I left him and went to find some shade under a small tree where I could stretch out a little. I surveyed the area to make sure there were no strange reptiles or snakes. Satisfied, I took off my sweaty brimmed hat and threw my scarf on the ground to sit on and leaned up against the trunk of the tree. I kept finding myself gazing at the hired military help – tall Ethiopian men, with loincloth wrapped around their hips to mid-thigh revealing their supple muscles and cream skin tones. They held spears across their chest and took turns in prominent positions so no one tried to escape. I believe these men really *knew* how to use their spears. Their intimidating presence alone was enough to cause fear in us hostages. If only I had a camera I could make my own postcard, I thought to myself. Postcards. I went back to the jeep and pulled out the postcards I had recently bought. Now felt like a meaningful time to write home.

One of the postcards had a picture of an Ethiopian girl, completely starkers, wearing nothing but a big smile. As I thought about who I'd give this one to a better idea popped in my head. On second thought, maybe one of the nearby guards would appreciate this more than any friend would back home. I had no idea how precarious our situation could become and thought it was worth a try to get in the good graces with a few of these guards.

I confidently walked over to one of the guards and gave a sheepish smile as I held up my offering. A few of the men gathered around to see the small gift I had in my palm. I held out the card and put it in one of the men's hands. Looking up smiling, 'This is for you,' I said trying to sound as agreeable as possible.

The men looked down solemnly at the postcard only to look up with big smiles. One of the men broke out in a big hearty laugh. Delighted with their gift, I did a small bow and slowly backed away to my tree. I watched the men's demeanours change as they exchanged laughs with each other. Well, that had to have helped any future cause of mine, I thought to myself satisfactorily.

I rested under the tree, feeling a little more secure. I pulled out my first postcard and started writing to Mum. Contemplating the unknown possibilities of my future, my mind wondered to a possible death scenario. I didn't fear death per se but I'd feel horrible if I left Mum behind. Especially if something happened to me out here. It was not like I could shoot her a quick WhatsApp message and let her know where I was or what had happened. If something happened to me in this Ethiopian wilderness it would be weeks or maybe months before she'd find out. I had seen enough death over the last twenty years, smelled it even, to know it better than most and understand that it would claim me as well. I was comfortable with it, but this isn't how I wanted it to end.

As the sun started to get lower in the sky, the higher altitude brought a refreshing coolness. Although I'd like to have shed my long sleeves, I knew it wouldn't be long before the mosquitos came out in hordes and my sleeves would protect me more during the night than it had against the harsh sun. I thought about going back to the jeep but wanted to stretch my legs a little longer before a long night in the jeep next to Fr Pedro, and I'm pretty sure he snored. Besides, I'd wager he was enjoying a little more space now as well. I'd try to get in a quick kip before heading to the jeep for the night. The coolness from the fading sun provided just enough relief to ease me into a soft sleep.

The gunshots reverberated through my body, instantly releasing a flood of adrenaline. My eyes opened wide as I shot up into a sitting position. Disoriented, I tried to regain my bearings as screams and primal fighting noises shot through darkness in terrifying daggers. The guards to my right to whom I had given my postcard were getting pummeled by an entire group of men in army uniforms.

Through the screams and noises, I registered a few words.

'Move! Move the cars!' came the screaming. I could hear ignitions rev up as gas flooded into the engines with a roar.

Oh my God, I had to get back to the jeep. I jumped up in a frenzy and began sprinting to the jeep. Although it was close, the ensuing chaos, thunderous engines and wobbly legs made it feel leagues away. I tried to open the door only to find it was still locked. I began beating on the window.

'We can go! We need to go!' I screamed through the windows.

Father Pedro who was awake but looked in shambles, started the engine and slammed it into first gear. I jerked back from the car as it lurched forward without me in. Bloody hell! Was he leaving without me?

I started to sprint alongside the jeep as Fr Pedro started cranking through the lower gears.

'Pedro! Let me in the car!' I screamed, terrified.

Father Pedro must have been well on his way into third gear before he realised I wasn't in the seat next to him. The jeep slammed on its breaks in front of me, coming to dusty, abrupt stop. I caught up with the stopped jeep and threw open the door, jumping into the passenger seat. Before I even had a chance to shut the door, Pedro had the jeep roaring again.

Gunshots rang through the air as dust from the other vehicles wrapped us in a blinding cloud. I sat shaking like a leaf in a near panic as Father Pedro wildly slammed the gas pedal down to the floor. It wasn't long before the gunshots began to fade into the distance. I pulled out two cigarettes and lit one for Father Pedro and myself. We both sat in silence, nursing them, as the jeep lurched forward.

We drove through the dark night, only stopping at dawn to add petrol and buy a few snacks for the road. Absolutely knackered, we finally decided to pull over at the next major town and rest for the day. At the local pub, we were given updates about the squirmishes between the government and rebels. The rebels appeared determined not to back down, making future travel precarious.

Father Pedro made it clear that he would not be driving to the capital until things had quietened between the rebels and government. If I was going to make it back any time soon, I'd have to go on my own. Rattled but not deterred, I booked a bus that would be leaving for the capital the next day.

By luck or God's grace, no hostage situation occurred on this trip. The 200-mile road trip had its own adventures. The bus lurched between enormous potholes, loose chickens flew down the bus aisle and I had the constant companionship of fleas. I found it strange, but the fleas clustered around the lining of my pant's waistband in blackish-brown specks. With little to do, except pray for safety, I soon became an expert at picking off the fleas and crushing them between my forefinger and thumb. Twenty hours later, the journey came to an end.

I had made arrangements to be picked up by Sister Dr Shirley, an MMM who was with me in medical school and happened to be serving in Ethiopia. Stepping off the bus, I saw Shirley's smiling face as she waved at me to get my attention. I felt relief and gratitude at finally encountering someone familiar on this never-ending adventure.

Some have asked whether, in instances like this where I felt so strongly supported and grateful for the MMM community, did it make me regret leaving the order? No. The decision I made wasn't rash and although gratitude is an understatement of what I felt and the love I continue to feel for my Sisters, the path was no longer mine to walk. It had only been two short years since I left, but it already felt like another lifetime.

*

I woke up the following morning to some very loud singing coming from a nearby church. I rustled out of bed and the bright sun and clear blue sky could be seen from my bedroom window. The birds sang me awake as I dressed, found some coffee and lazily made my way out to the patio to soak up the early morning rays. The warmth of the sun on my face relaxed my entire body. I had meticulous scrubbed every part of my body the night before during my shower. Shirley was kind enough to give me clean clothes while they washed and mine. Sipping on my coffee the flea bites were hardly noticeable.

'How'd you sleep, Anne?' Shirley said, poking her head out of the door and coming to join me. 'I bet you're still shattered from that brutal journey.' Shirley was only a month older than me yet had really blazed the road for for my generation.

'Slept beautifully but was awaken by that church choir just down the road. Their voices really do carry, don't they!?'

'Yes … they were rather loud today weren't they,' Shirley said breaking into a grin, 'It's the born-again church just up the road. For whatever reason, I'm not sure if it's a cultural thing or just something this local pastor requires, but if they've had sex the previous night they aren't allowed to go inside the church! So, all those who've had "relations" have to stay outside the building and sing from there!'

'Well, that church will surely be blessed with posterity in its future,' I said with a wry smile.

We both laughed heartily when the choir began to sing once again.

*

I had a few days before my flight was scheduled to leave, giving me time to conduct some final meetings. The effects of the civil war could be seen everywhere in the capital city. To save petrol, taxi drivers turned off their engines and let their car's coast downhill. I once rode in a taxi that had a hole in the driver's side floor, and as we slowly approached the end of our downhill descent, he stuck his foot through the gaping hole down to the ground to stop the vehicle. The resilience and resourcefulness of these people amazed me.

My report needed to be given to the Catholic Medical bureau for their approval. I outlined areas of improvement, ways to better utilise resources, the dangerous climate of the war and identified a few ministries that would be wonderful places for potential new hospices. The Catholic Medical Bureau dispersed my report to the organisations or individuals that had been mentioned in it. Sadly, the contents of my report were not received well by everyone, including the Holy Ghost Fathers who had put us up for a night in the southern town of Moyale while we conducted our feasibility study. They had a house on the border of Kenya that we thought could provide a strategic location for a clinic. I did not have time to discuss this with them before inserting it into the report and had included it as a possibility.

I left Ethiopia and flew to Rome to get a papal blessing for Survive. On the plane, I incidentally bumped into two Holy Ghost fathers, who I learned had taken umbrage to the report. Appalled that I hadn't sought their review before I officially sent it in, they accosted me with their anger. 'How dare I make suggestions without letting them see it first.' Still at my wits' end from the hostage situation, I remember crying most of the way to Rome.

Life abroad was not for the faint of heart.

*

Father Paddy, from the Kiltegan order, picked me up and hosted me during my time in Rome. Every morning we'd sit out on the patio, smoking and drinking coffee, while he listened to me vent, cry and laugh about my time in Ethiopia. Sometimes, in life's valleys, lifelong friendships bloom. Fr Paddy and I remained friends for some years. May he rest in peace.

Through the help of the Popes' secretary, also a Kiltegan father, I received the papal blessing for Survive and they hung it up in their office back in the UK office. Sadly, in the end, I had a falling out with Survive because I did something rather stupid – as everyone occasionally does.

In my report, I documented the hostage situation, and stated it was too dangerous in its current climate to send someone out. But they did. They sent out a nurse. Upon hearing about it, I was so upset I wrote to the Catholic paper, which at that time was the *Catholic Pictorial*. I wrote that I had given six weeks of my time to assess the situation and one of my recommendations concluded that sending someone in such a hostile envirnonment could put that person in eminent danger.

Survive immediately wrote a response in the *Catholic Pictorial* claiming I was not their representative and had sent them a random report. I felt betrayed – they had completely twisted our arrangement. I had paid for my trip, that was true, but only because they needed the help and I was willing to offer my services. After I read their reply, I never responded to them again.

My inability to curb my tongue when I strongly disagreed with something had the knack for getting me into trouble. This was not the first time, nor would it be the last. Nor would it always be a bad thing.

*

Survive would later donate one of the first ambulances to Hospice Africa Uganda. Even though the waiting list was 1–2 years, we received the vehicles in a few months! I imagine that the person in charge at the time recognised my name only because it was on the papal blessing!

25

A Step Towards Palliative Care

Life is pleasant. Death is peaceful. It's the transition that's troublesome.

Isaac Asimov

I WORKED at David Lewis Northern Hospital from 1973 to 1977. I received invaluable knowledge and mentorship from Professor Jimmy Williamson and immensely enjoyed our team. But times were changing and I vividly recall the stress of my mentor, facing hostility within the medical bureaucracy and constantly navigating the changing political climate. There appeared to be opposition within the medical establishment as Geriatric Medicine became not only a specialty in the hospital but also within the medical curriculum at the medical schools. Even I noticed the antagonism from other physicians as I conducted work at the hospital.

Further, on the national level, the political leadership began to make cuts that severely disabled our 'in-home' services for the elderly. In the end, Professor Jimmy Williamson became so frustrated he applied for the post of Professor of Geriatric Medicine, in Edinburgh and left. Shortly afterwards I also left to take up the position of Senior Lecturer in Geriatric Medicine at the University of Manchester. Lesley and I, although great friends, would not see each other for years but fate would bring

193

us back together years later to begin an even bigger adventure when, together, we founded Hospice Africa.

Less than a year after starting at the University of Manchester, Mum suffered a severe coronary. I was vacationing in Germany and came rushing home to the Intensive Care at Northern Hospital where she had been taken. By the time I reached her, she had drips and wires coming out of her and looked as white as a sheet. Something about seeing my mother so close to death brought me to the brink. I went back to the Nurses station and flooded the place with my tears. Pulling myself together, I noticed a heavy headache forming. It began to increase in intensity and I just managed to keep going with a compound analgesic. This suddenly turned into an attack of shingles so devastating that I myself became bedbound! I was taken home to recuperate while my mother stayed in the ICU for several more weeks.

I lay in bed as needles stabbed my head. The pain was excrutiating. A red rash spread around my forehead and eye area, turning into painful blisters that ruptured in their own time! I could barely lift my head, let alone stand up on my own.

Thank goodness for good friends at such times. Pat Sadler became good friends with Mum after they met at the Legion of Mary. Younger than me, she engaged people in an authentic and caring way with a certain edge and frankness that only made her more likeable. Pat was a godsend and stayed with me at the house, tending to all my needs and cooked meals for both myself and Joseph, who had come home to visit Mum in the hospital. Father Joseph, regimental and stern, had become quite used to order, timetables and women serving him. I know Pat took on more than she bargained for when she agreed to look after me!

Pat and Joseph provided me with daily updates on Mum's progress in hospital. Although the coronary had been severe, Mum continued to show signs of improvement. It's a strange thing not being able to help someone due to your own helplessness. I sometimes wonder if the panic and anxiety of possibly losing Mum set off a stress reaction so strong that it effected where I now found myself. But as I lay in bed, knowing that Mum was also lying in a bed, fighting her own fight, it made the pain I experienced less significant. In those weeks, we faced a parallel journey together, fighting to recover our health.

Eventually we both recovered. Mum's heart had been significantly damaged and the toll had weakened her overall wellbeing. Old age was setting in and I needed to work closer to home. I decided to fill a vacancy near Liverpool at a general practice. A very old patron ran the practice and the buck stopped with her. I unsuccessfully attempted to implement some of the progressive practices we had applied at Northern. It felt like patients were being pushed through on a conveyer belt where my only duty was to write prescriptions. I had a thick stack of records, but the notes didn't list past illnesses. The process left me feeling helpess to understand the whole picture and I was afraid of killing a patient with the precriptions I was writing.

It wasn't working so I continued to look for work elsewhere.

A post was advertised to revamp a failed geriatric unit at Whiston and St Helens Hospitals. These were also near my home and I applied and was appointed.

Whiston and St Helens

In 1978, I started a position with the National Health Service that oversaw geriatric care in two combined districts east of Liverpool: Whiston and St Helens. Both hospitals had geriatric wards, although Whiston, the larger hospital, had more modern diagnostic tools.

The commute between Whiston and St Helens, filled with green fields and farms, was quite a welcome divergent from the hustle and bustle of working at city hospitals at Northern and Manchester. I'd find myself talking to God as I drove between the two hospitals. I'd ask questions, make jokes, and pray for my mother, family and patients. Nature has this way of opening a space to just be with God. I may have left the religious life, but it's way of life and connecting with God didn't leave me. For as I embarked deeper on my path, it was God that I would need.

St Helens, a single-storey geriatric unit, located directly across the road from the main hospital, had an acute ward and a long-term ward. The long-term ward immediately caught my attention. There were many patients who had been there for months and who were not dying well. Many of the patients had Alzheimer's; others had physical ailments and just stayed in bed all day. How could I apply the lessons I had learned at Northern in this context? How could I help create a better quality of life for them when they were on their way out? I wasn't sure, but I was going to try.

At that time, typically, there were no discussions with the patients about what they wanted and how that should determine the medical approach. If someone came down with pneumonia, they were given antibiotics. Doctors and nurses untrained in geriatric medicine, often gave too high a dose. If the patient lived, they became sicker and endured side effects. This meant they endured their painful existence longer while others without antibiotics either recovered or died peacefully. The elderly sick were being treated as a nuisance, and quite clearly, the entire approach to elderly care and end of life care needed a more thoughtful approach.

St Helens long-term ward is where I became very interested in the way people died. The tools and knowledge of palliative care seemed essential in places like this.

What is palliative care, you might ask? Palliative care is an approach that improves the quality of life with people who face life-threatening illness. It helps to alleviate pain, improve psychosocial elements – improving the overall quality of life. Many people ask, 'If someone is receiving palliative care, are they dying?' Not necessarily. Palliative care is not synonymous with hospice care. Palliative care can occur at any stage of an illness. Hospice care is typically suited for people who have less than six months to live.

At this point in in my career, I had very little experience with palliative care. I started reading books by Robert Twycross, who in the 1970s became a major pioneer in the palliative care world. He was a Clinical Research Fellow at St Christopher's Hospice, founded by Dame Cicely Saunders, the modern founder of the hospice movement. I began learning about symptom management, improving quality of life, addressing the psychosocial element of end of life, drug protocols and relieving pain when there was nothing else to be done. Palliative care advocated developing multidisciplinary teams that assessed patient care together, in a comprehensive, collaborative and problem-solving approach with the end goal of improving the quality of life in a holistic manner.

Palliative care in a geriatric population often transforms into end-of-life care. And any time death is involved, ethics becomes *the primary* driver in decision making. Open conversations between patient, family and health workers determine the choices and care pursued. There is no such thing as one-size-fits-all. Everyone is different and needs a different approach.

Many patients welcome their deaths. Although euthanasia, a hot topic, was never considered, we ensured patients were as comfortable as possible, regardless of what disease or the level of cerebral impairment. Sometimes, after discussing options with the patient and family, we stopped using antibiotics with pneumonia, allowing it to be the 'old man's friend'. But on many occasions, the patients lived and had a higher remaining quality of life than if we had given them antibiotics, only serving to weaken their frail systems.

There is no denying that the progression of medicine is marvellous. Advanced drugs and antibiotics have saved millions of lives that would needlessly have been cut too short. However, the questions and conversations regarding how to apply our new advances, new drugs – to whom and when – is a vastly unchartered territory. How much should be done to save a person's life? If that person fully recovers, will they have a full, healthy life – or will it result in a poor quality of life? What does the individual want? Do they want to keep struggling and fight for life? Or are they ready to let go? The answers to such questions will vary as widely as the people that populate this earth. There will never be a correct answer, and sometimes it changes along the way as patients and their families progress through the process.

My oversight at St Helens provided an excellent opportunity and experience to learn about palliative and hospice care and find ways to improve patients' lives. Clearly, my interest in this field intersected directly with my own life as I watched Mum decline. I felt a deeper attachment to, and understanding of, my patients and their needs, knowing that they too were someone's father or mother, brother or sister. Death and dying, is sacred. My faith in God and the spiritual nature of life became more profound and rich: I was honoured to be a part of this journey in other's lives.

26

The Student Becomes the Teacher

I'm not trying to turn you into me. I'm trying to turn you into you.
Master Shifu, Kung Fu Panda

When you know your WHY, you can endure any HOW.
Victor Frankl

THE CHALLENGES of work invigorated me. I began providing lectures on palliative care, not only to my own team but also to other surgical and medical staff. Palliative care infiltrates every facet of medicine and people were interested.

My team, consisting of both nurses and doctors, changed on a semi-annual basis due to the rotating shifts of the young doctors temporarily assigned to my department. Although I usually only had junior doctors assigned to my team, I had some excellent ones.

Paul Tan, a quiet but charming doctor of Chinese descent was most diligent and attentive in his duties, and really embraced the spirit and ethics I tried to imbue in the doctors rotating through. As we got to know each other better he encouraged me to visit his home in Penang, Malaysia, where his father, a doctor in general practice, had increasingly become interested in geriatric medicine and palliative care.

'It's called the "Pearl of Asia", you must come and visit!' he'd exclaim. 'It's on the west coast of the western side of Malaysia. Beautiful country. Plus you'll get some sunshine! A far cry from this rainy country.' This comment would be long forgotten until years later, when I found myself meeting his father, in the 'Pearl of Asia'.

My nursing staff, more permanent and consistent, provided the essential base and fluidity in caring for the patients. However, learning the new method of collaborative problem-solving did not come easy to everyone. Every structure has its pecking orders, its entrenched hierarchy. Although doctors are known for having more cut-throat and competitive attitudes, I found the structure I tried to teach really challenging to the nursing staff. It took a while to peel through the existing bureaucracy and create a safe and collaborative space for my teams to openly discuss patients' care. Listening to and valuing everyone's ideas is not easy concept to accept, especially, when you've been trained in a completely different system of decision-making. On a few occasions, I had to take the senior nurses aside and ask them not to talk to the younger nurses in such an abrupt and rude manner; unknowingly shutting down their willingness to speak up and voice their ideas or concerns.

The junior nurses were of great value and were often the ones assigned to home visits in the community. Home visits allowed patients to return home sooner and still receive medical care, ensuring a higher quality of life at home in a familiar setting. The previous Geriatric Director, whose position I had replaced, had visited our team at Northern and had begun to implement some of Jimmy's ideas, which included home visits. But there was a gap in hiring, and by the time I arrived, they had stopped. After seeing the patients in the long-term wards at Peasley Cross at St Helens, I immediately restarted the home visits.

I also began conducting multi-disciplinary meeting that resolved the underlying issues that kept the patient from making it back home. It's not only better for the health of the patient to go home, but most people want to go home! Home is where the heart is. It's not found in an overcrowded hospital ward. No one wants to spend their final months or days in a hospital.

We didn't have the robust community support we had at Northern. But that didn't matter. I had seen far worse in Nigeria. Everywhere you go, you make the best with what you have.

I had a more senior doctor do just that.

Tall and lean, soft-spoken with intelligent eyes, Ged Faulks exhibited exceptional potential. At twenty-six years of age, he joined my geriatric team at Whiston as a senior house officer in training for general practice. Most of the doctors at that time did not intend on going into geriatrics or palliative care, and he was no exception. Yet, he had something special. He connected with the elderly in such a kind and gentle way, and they mirrored his compassion, opening up about their concerns and fears, wants and desires. His ability to assess their needs in a holistic way allowed him to come up with novel approaches that really improved the patients' quality of life.

At one point, I asked him if he'd consider changing specialties. He had a gift. Alas, he and his wife, a psychiatrist already in training in the Royal Hospital in Liverpool, had already made plans to live in a country village where they'd both start a practice. I am nothing if not persistent and tried a few more times but eventually eased up, knowing he'd be excellent at whatever he chose to do. His future village would have a great doctor.

Ged Faulks, Senior House Officer

'I was assigned to Anne's team for six months, as part of the training rotation required to get a GP (e.g. paediatrics, geriatrics, obstetrics, psychiatry). I entered Anne's programme, young but already pretty damn cynical of the medical profession. Medicine had a culture of ladder-climbers, focused on making a name for themselves. Everyone seemed to be writing and conducting research that they thought would get them "the best jobs".

'I had heard rumours of Anne before I joined her team. She had been a nun, or maybe even a nurse. Nobody was sure. She knew how to get things done. If you have to you do it yourself, and chase it. She never needed assertive training. There's an Irish element to that. As a female consultant with an assertive nature, Anne was already an outlier, and was gaining a reputation for her medical eccentricities. 'In medical school, we were taught to diagnosis and treat. The process was rather sterile. But when I joined Anne's team, I realised she operated quite differently – in culture and method. She really was interested in patients, as people, and developing ways to help them. Here was someone who was much more interested in understanding and caring for patients than developing her career. I watched her, absolutely intent on improving the patients' lot in life, figuring out the aspects impeding their wellness, and dealing with that. She never wrote anyone off. She was determined to do something that actually helped them recover. Very patient centred. It was incredible.

'The multi-disciplinary meetings were unheard of at that time. Anne brought doctors of various specialties and backgrounds together to discuss patient care. The multiple perspectives from these meetings and combined expertise elicited insight, spawning innovative approaches of care.

'Many patients got "dumped" at the long-term ward because no one else had any bright ideas on what to do with these people. They'd have a fall and end up in the hospital. Unsure of what to do with them, the doctors sent them to the long-term ward. They didn't have a disease that could be treated. They were old, finding life difficult. Some had the potential to go back home, but they needed additional help that no one else had managed to provide. Anne encouraged practical solutions and deputised me to identify these patients. We'd get the team together and try to find ways to help the "impossible patients". We got many of these patients back on their feet who still had years left, saving many from dying unnecessarily.

'Anne also emphasised the psychosocial element of care. It wasn't something I was familiar with or had been taught, but it became quite important after working with her and was rather stimulating. Although Anne taught new methods and approaches, I also remember her not only for what she taught, but the way in which she taught. Modest and intense, she was like no consultant I had met before. Nurturing, compassionate, and a great teacher – she never humiliated me. She listened to everyone and valued their experiences and levels of expertise. Anne tried to cultivate the culture where everyone felt safe to speak openly. She taught by example. Listening to others but also giving her views. She was revered by the team.

'Going into general practice, I needed to be able to look at patients from a holistic perspective – their environment and needs. Not to merely make diagnosis, investigate, treat, which were the elements of medicine that I had been taught. She knew there was more to medicine than that. Working with her allowed me to see a way of practising medicine that didn't entail being a git. Even the most hardened individuals couldn't have been unaffected by their time with her.

'Anne has been the single most motivating person I've ever met in my life. If you'd forgotten your "why", she'd remind you of your purpose. If ever you needed to know why you were doing what you were doing – she was it. Even though I was there for a short time, to be so influenced was incredible. It basically shaped the way I continued to practise medicine.

'She turned on a light that at that time was so close to being turned off forever. I could have floated through my career doing far less good. I wanted to chase that light. She provided the model on which I wanted to base myself and my practice.'

*

I relied on Ged more than the others. He took to the approach like a duck in the water. One morning in February, Ged didn't show up. He was normally punctual and reliable and not one to come in late. He had left no message, and no one had heard from him. It wasn't until that afternoon that we heard he was sick and wasn't coming into work. I didn't think anything of it other than he must have been hit hard by the 'flu.

It wasn't until the next day that we heard what had really happened. Ged and his wife had climbed Mount Snowden (in North Wales) over the weekend and had both suffered a terrible fall from a ledge. As Ged recovered from the disorientation of the fall and found where his wife had landed it became immediately clear that she hadn't made it. The dark was setting in and Ged didn't want to call the emergency service because he knew there was nothing they could do and it would only put more lives at risk. The next morning, he was rescued, along with his wife's body. Ged took leave for a few months and when he came back was transferred to another department. We continued to stay in touch, and he'd come over and have dinner with Mum and I on a monthly basis. I knew that he had suffered a terrible loss and as an atheist, Ged didn't have a consoling God in his life. At first, I found it difficult to talk to him in a way that conveyed the hope and faith I had for him, without pushing my beliefs on him.

Each time we met, I tried to be sensitive to the language I used, deriving words and symbols from his repertoire and worldview, not mine. There's a mastery to conveying words and emotions in a way that crosses boundaries and differences but allows you to maintain the substance of your message in a way that is appropriate for the receiver. I made many mistakes along the way. I am grateful to have learned this with Ged, who I'm sure used patience as I developed this new practice. I cherished this time, and learned an invaluable lesson from a great friend, a lesson that would be of great value in my future work. Ged, came through it and eventually remarried Natalie and they had two children, Eleanor and Nicholas. He also became the first person to give a donation for Hospice Africa, later becoming a member of the board, and chairman.

27

Death, the Final Suitor

Yet you do not know what tomorrow will bring. What is your life? For
you are a mist that appears for a little time and then vanishes.
James 4:14

There is a voice that doesn't use words. Listen.
Rumi

I HAD BEEN working at Whiston and St Helens for about three
years. The short, easy commute allowed me to spend more time
with Mum, even making it home for lunch. She was slowly
becoming weaker and weaker and had asked me to start
cooking. Weeds had sprung up in her immaculate garden and I
knew the end was drawing near.

Mum, the greatest inspiration of my life, and a hearth to those
who knew her. Her life, far from easy, became the symbol of her
deeply held values and faith. She faced the sticky and dirty
challenges of life with such grace and temperance, picking herself
up and patiently wiping life's ever accumulating dirt off her
knees. She deftly navigated raising and shepherding four young
children through a desperate war that literally landed in her
backyard, only to bear the loss of her youngest child a few years
later during peacetime. A few years after her remaining three
children left the nest, her husband passed away at an early age,
leaving her in financial poverty and alone in the world. Yet, her
external poverty did not leave her impoverished. It only seemed

to reveal her deeper nature. Despite the difficulty in which life unfolded for her, her kind spirit and warm heart remained soft.

I know not everyone who reads this will believe in God or have the type of faith that guided my mother's life, but to you I say: have faith in something great! Have faith in something that inspires you, regardless of what it is. Let the beliefs that shape your life make you strong and resilient, kind and empathetic and most of all joyful. Our beliefs have the power to shape the quality of our lives, likely to a greater degree than anything else.

After Dad passed away, Mum had begun volunteer work with the Legion of Mary, a Catholic charity that helped care for the poorest of the poor in Liverpool and surrounding areas. This is where my mother met John – yes, that John. I'm often mystified that the actions of my mother, so far away, triggered a series of events that forever changed the direction of my life. Life is strange and mysterious, far beyond what we know.

At the Legions of Mary, Mum also became good friends with Pat Sadler. Mum, Pat Sadler and Pat Ruane all became great friends and often shared their Sunday evening meal together. I'm so grateful that Mum had such an amazing support group and second family while the rest of her children were all away.

When I returned home, having officially left the MMMs, Mum had aged. Away in Nigeria on my second tour, she suffered a silent coronary that made it difficult to walk unassisted and her doctor advised her not to leave the house by herself. In the 1970s, surgeries were not as progressive as they are today and the only thing she could do to improve her situation was to shed a few pounds. This had been recommended by Jimmy Williamson while I was working with him. Determined to improve her condition, she followed Jimmy's dietary advice with zeal and dropped down to her ideal weight, greatly improving her health. Rarely venturing out on her own, her independence at home and passion for gardening and cooking kept her active. Her mind remained lively, and she strongly wanted to keep participating in life. Mum loved life to the very end. I'd come home and find her out in the garden working with her roses on sunny days, or curled up with a book and Suki, our lovely Siamese kitten, when the rains persisted.

Mum never let me cook growing up, and initially upon coming home, things would be no different. Although I offered to help, she refused it at first and only acquiesced in her final years. I have fond memories of our dinners together and watching our favourite programmes like *Coronation Street* while I knitted. It's the mundane, everyday activities that are the ones you miss later on, not realising how special they were during the moment.

Joseph had retired and was living in the Salesian house in Battersea, London. Although, he continued to visit London's prisons, he had the flexibility to visit Liverpool and spend time with Mum. Oonagh and her husband, having lived all over the world, had finally returned to Britain and lived in Maidstone. Busy raising her own children, she still tried to visit Liverpool. Scattered to the wind, all her children and grandchildren had returned to the UK in her final years, visiting on weekends and holidays.

Mum began to slow down and became exhausted from simple tasks. As she came to grips with her declining abilities, she eventually handed over all the cooking responsibilities and sat at the kitchen table, chatting with me while I cooked. We also hired the help of Mrs O'Brien, a wonderful woman who had cleaned our home during my childhood. Not only did she help take care of the home but her and Mum had a special, nurturing friendship and it was a great relief to know someone checked in on Mum during the day. I tried to come home at lunch and join her and Suki for tea and biscuits.

When you spend time with someone every day, you don't always notice the slight changes. The slow decline that takes them closer to their final suitor. Slowly dying from heart failure, Mum remained intrepid in her day-to-day life. Her sense of humour only seemed to expand as she dealt with the cruel way the dying process robs one of their basic dignities.

Mum's bedroom was located up the stairs and down the hall to the right. Her climb up the stairs began to get more and more difficult. A few times I tried to mention relocating the bed downstairs, but she refused to hear of it. To make sure she didn't fall down the stairs, I followed behind and gave her a steady, supportive push from her backside.

'Get on with ya, Mum!' I said pushing her up the stairs. She clung to the rail and tried to take a step up the next stair.

'Don't get me laughing, I need to focus!'

I continued to support her and gave her a gentle push as she took her next step. 'By God, Mum, it's a good thing you lost a few stones!'

'Watch that cheeky tongue of yours!' she said laughing.

Mum and I were the greatest of friends. Her love for others came through in the consistent way she always asked about others. Although she was approaching her end, she continued to be the lighthouse in my storms.

But time doesn't stop. There weren't many days left that she decided to make the journey up and down the stairs again. We made the house comfortable and changed things around the home that would better accommodate her condition.

Life emerges in small mundane tasks and interactions. The hundreds of cups of tea, hearing Mum's laugh over a trivial comment from the telly and seeing her smile in the garden on a sunny day. I wasn't even aware that I had been wrapped in an invisible shield of belonging, through Mum's love, until she left.

Small moments of regret pierce my memories, thinking about the times I snapped at her when I came home, tired from work. It was an adjustment for both of us as she slowly declined. Yet her kindness and patience with me during those moments have created a deeper imprint in my memory. My small failings became precious opportunities to learn more about love. Mum continued to be my greatest teacher about life and love, to the very end.

As that end approached, I took leave from work. I sat with her throughout the day and often slept in a chair by her side during the evenings. Occasionally, I'd go back to my bed to catch a little better quality of sleep. Pat Ruane spent a lot of time at the house, and we'd all sit around Mum's bed, joking together, reading different books and softly singing while I played the guitar.

After weeks of being at Mum's side, she decided to leave after I briefly stepped out of the room.

I walked back into the room and instantly felt the difference.

My mother had passed away. It was 3 June 1981.

28

The Void

We mould clay into a pot,
but it is the emptiness inside
that makes the vessel useful.
Lao Tzu

I CONTINUED to dive deeper into palliative care at Whiston and
St Helens. Learning about palliative care and the struggles my
patients and families faced became very real and meaningful
to me as I cared for Mum in her final stages. Bearing witness
to her final months, weeks and days impacted how I approached
the importance of my work.

As autumn approached and deep reds and oranges shaded the
trees in Sefton Park, I organised a palliative care conference with
the hope of getting Dame Cicely Saunders as a speaker. Dame
Cicely, later referred to as the 'founder of the modern hospice
movement', greatly influenced the culture and discipline of
palliative care. Word of her work spread around the world as
people saw the need and benefits of palliative care and hospice.
With great luck and by coincidence, Liverpool was only a two-
hour train ride from St Christopher's Hospice in South London.
Although, considered far by UK standards, in all relative terms it
was less than a day ride away and increased the odds of her
attendance. In the end, she agreed to come speak at Whiston.

Word spread quickly and on the day of the conference every
seat was taken. People stood packed together like sardines, lining

the outside of the room, interested to hear Dame's message in this emerging new field. The conference was a success. Dame secured grants for two nurses to begin working at Whiston as palliative care specialists. It was clear, that people in Liverpool wanted palliative care. I knew that thousands of people in our country needed help navigating end-of-life care and the United Kingdom was taking the steps to get there.

*

I felt slightly untethered after Mum passed. She had been my grounding anchor, the invisible cord that drew me back home to Liverpool. Now that she was gone, I didn't know where I belonged or where I was supposed to be. I had left Liverpool as a child and gone straight into the life of a nun. Upon leaving the MMMs I was drawn back to Mum. Once it was clear that my relationship with John had ended, continuing to stay with Mum was the right and natural thing to do. It did not feel like a choice but if it had been and I wouldn't have made any other.

Although I originally felt like I was there to care for her, in reality, she was the one that watched over me. She provided a natural bridge from the MMMs into the civilian life. Things hadn't gone as expected when I returned. Yet, having the luck to be able to reflect on things at an old age, sometimes it's life's curve balls, the perceived failures and heartbreak, that turn into life's greatest blessings. The love, companionship, kindness, and joy I shared with Mum during the final eight years of her life are some of my warmest memories.

Again, I was at a crossroad. As a forty-five-year-old female doctor, I was a rarity in that time. Single and successful, I had never seriously considered dating again after my experience with John. Although there may have been a few potential suitors, I believe my background as a nun and my profession as a medical doctor created a wall between myself and most men. Dating an ex-nun was already a reach for most, but add my prominent role practising medicine... Let's just say it ended many possibilities before they even started. Unbound to the duties of marriage and released from the responsibilities of daughterhood, I began to contemplate if I wanted to participate in the world differently.

I felt open to all the possibilities that lay before me. Did I want to do something different? Would I stay in Liverpool? Would I continue to pursue geriatrics or palliative care? Mum told others that she knew I'd go back to work in Africa once she passed away. She had never said that to me directly and I only heard of her words through Pat Ruane after she passed. But Africa was not calling to me. Not yet anyway.

I sat in my big house, alone, for the first time in years. The darkness and rain seemed to close in on me as I sat on my sofa contemplating life and the options that lay ahead. I imagined what it would be like to be somewhere, anywhere. Where would I go? Would it be safe? If I died, would anyone care? A quiet and unrecognisable feeling slowly drifted up from my subconsciousness. The more I thought about life without Mum, the stronger the feeling became. I couldn't shake it.

It took me a while to identify the feeling. 'Alone in the world' is the closest I can come to describing how I felt. I guess I can consider myself lucky, if at the age of forty-five this was the first time the depths of that emotion washed over me. The sense of fear was far greater than anything I felt in Nigeria's postwar chaos, or even when I had been taken hostage in Ethiopia. You might be able to logically convince yourself that you're fine, but that doesn't mean your emotions follow suit. I was raised in a loving family where I knew I belonged. Abroad, I always knew I had the full support of the MMM Sisterhood and the reverent authority the Catholic Church commanded from others. I knew it provided a sense of comfort and community, I just didn't know how much, until it was gone. Returning home, I always knew I had Mum's love. Even though I had wonderful friends and colleagues in Liverpool and all over the world, my place in the world shifted with Mum's passing. Something felt different, I was different.

The fear and loneliness hit me in soft waves as I sat in the dark room. I listened to the rain caress the roof as I snuggled under my blanket on the couch, the steam from my hot cup of tea rised in swirling cascades. But with the loneliness also came an expansion. Infinite and boundless possibilities awoke. I could go anywhere and do anything.

That night, I slept in deep, rich sea of darkness. I awoke the next morning with perfect clarity. If I were to ever leave Liverpool and be completely on my own, I would need more confidence to venture out into the world by myself. So, I went all in. I took my entire life savings (well, eight years of it) and enrolled in the Diploma in International Community Health Care in Liverpool's

School of Tropical Medicine. The course would equip me with the knowledge and skills to better navigate working abroad and the dissertation required data collection in another country for three months. What better way to get my feet wet after being home for eight years and experiencing one unnerving hostage situation abroad? I began the course in January 1982.

29

India's Paradox

God, grant me the serenity to accept the things I cannot change,
Courage to change the things I can, and the
Wisdom to know the difference.
Reinhold Niebuhr

HE COURSE had international students from all over the world- India, Africa, Turkey and Asia. Not surprisingly, I instantly hit it off with the Nigerians and an Ethiopian. The schoolwork, difficult as it was, came natural to me. I enjoyed the university culture in the comfort of my hometown. I continued to have gatherings at my house where many of the students in my programme came together for meals and a good laugh.

I have the gift of the gab, as the Irish would say. I was a social butterfly that easily made friends, which is in fact the reason I had the opportunity to become a doctor in the first place! However, in med school I was surrounded by the structure and the culture of the convent. I must admit, without the rules and social construct of the order, my younger self re-emerged in classic form. I found myself on occasion in poor graces with some of the professors. But this time, I was an adult, and I wasn't going to take the abuse lying down.

'I don't want any talking in this class. There is too much talking in this class,' our teacher said, trying to regain control of his class. He walked over to my side of the room and turned his full attention on me. In front of the entire class, he let me have it. I don't remember what he said, but I remember being gobsmacked. 'What a hokey pokey,' I thought, sitting there and taking it, red faced and boiling over, I somehow kept my mouth shut. I waited till class finished, collected my books and marched up to the front of class. Not one to premeditate my words, I let him have it. After enough shots had been fired to draw a crowd I finished, 'You do not talk to adults that way!'

In general, I got on well with my professors and really enjoyed my time in school. After months of classroom work, it was time to get ready for our dissertation travels. I was to be sent to India, not my choice but I accepted the decision from the lecturers. I decided to do my thesis on the interconnection of culture, religion and medicine for the elderly in India. After a few months of preparation, three others, including two African men and a lady from the West Indies and myself, set off to India for three months.

India

India was an explosion of colour, multiple religious traditions, indigestion and hardship. On my first morning in this country, I watched the deep orange sun rise above the sacred Ganges River. In Hinduism, bathing in the sanctified river causes the remission of sins and liberates a person from the cycle of reincarnation. The water is considered pure because it personifies the Hindu Goddess Gaṅgā. I watched the golden light of morning reach out and touch all the people that bathed at her shores. As the sun moved higher in the sky, the initial beauty and festivity of colour and spiritual devotion was assailed by the surrounding pollution and filth. Muggy, diseased waters splashed young children and the sick elderly. It was common practice to be cremated in India. Unless, that is, you had died from cancer or TB, or happened to be a cow – in those instances, your body was tossed in the Ganges. As I continued to watch the display of centuries of tradition, I saw a rotting corpse floating at the edge of a distant bank in the frothy bubbles.

The paradox I witnessed that first morning would continually reemerge in different events and situations during my time in India.

Out of four of us that to India, I would be the only one to venture beyond Benares (Varanasi). My research needed to go beyond scholarly materials and penetrate the culture. I got on a train and travelled to the northeast of Calcutta (Kolkata), and then onto the southwest of Kerala. Everywhere I went I read the local newspapers and talked with people in cafes to gain insight into the culture and social infrastructure. A great deal of information was also gleaned from spending time with the elderly and having conversations with them about their lives and the issues they were facing.

I had seen suffering in Nigeria, Ethiopia and Britain – but India – this was something entirely different. It appeared to me, an inequitable amount of hardship landed on the women and girls. Nigeria and Britain were a far cry from being model egalitarian societies, but the plight of India's women took my breath away and left me raw. On more than one occasion, I read an article in the newspaper of a new bride burnt to death in a kitchen from an 'unknown cause'. Upon investigating further with the locals, the entire community knew it was an accepted form of murder if the bride price had been too low. As a widower, the husband was free to remarry and receive another dowry.

On one occasion, I was helping a family care for a sick three-year- old child. Alone in the house with the grandmother and sick child I asked her to take the little girl to a nearby clinic.

'Why? The clinic only has paracetamol which won't be enough." She responded. She was right of course. I then offered to give her money and she could get an antibiotic at the pharmacy. The grandmother caressed her granddaughter's cheek with care.

'Just let her die. She is a girl, she will have a very hard life.' Her eyes were filled with love for her little granddaughter. It was impossible to truly comprehend the life this woman must have gone through, what she had experienced and seen. Clearly, for her, letting her granddaughter die was the compassionate choice.

The food in India was as colourful as the markets you'd buy it from. The rainbow of vegetables and spices painted nearly every dish and the taste index matched the vibrant display. The sun was hot and the food was hotter. At the beginning of the trip when I was adventurous, I'd take only a few bites before perspiration swept across my forehead and nose. By the end of the meal, sweat dripped out of every pore, leaving me soggy and uncomfortable.

I continued to explore new foods and eat at new restaurants. I found the spice levels tolerable but ended up losing my appetite and sense of adventure over the hygiene practices I witnessed.

On one occasion, I watched a cook working hard. Sweat spilled out him and he had a towel wrapped around his forehead to catch it. From where I was sitting the towel looked thoroughly soaked. After glancing back at him a few moments later he had taken the towel off his head to dry the clean plates. On another occasion, I watched a guy scoop chips out of the bin with his bare hand (I assumed they were short on spoons) and then turn around and use the same hand to scoop out ice cream.

But the time that really did me in, had been a lovely dinner out with my colleagues. With only a few bites left on my plate I came across a rather large, dirty fingernail. Soon after, I resorted to eating packaged biscuits and cheese, and still, on many occasions, the worms would beat me to the punch. When I returned to Liverpool, I had lost so much weight people thought I had been severely ill!

Mother Theresa and the Missionaries of Charity

For research, I travelled to Calcutta in the northeast region of India. I had heard about Mother Theresa and the great care her missionary order provided to the impoverished. Mother Theresa founded an order with the mission to care for the blind, leprosy afflicted, elderly and dying in the poorest parts of the cities. These women were easy to identify with their white sarees lined with three stripes of blue trim. Having recently come from a relatively advanced geriatric team in Liverpool, I was intrigued to see the type of patients they helped and the type of models and methods they were employing in caring. After all, how many chances would I get?

I found a very dedicated team of women working in very difficult conditions. There were two large rooms divided by gender. The majority of the patients were very elderly and very sick. Immediately, I noticed some strange practices I didn't understand. Only the men were allowed to go outside and get fresh air and direct sunlight. I also noticed that many of the women were dressed in western clothing. In the Indian culture, once women came of age, they wore sarees. Putting them back in western clothing was a cultural sign of regression to childhood. But maybe the western clothing were the only clothes being donated?

I couldn't help but contrast the noticeable differences between the MMMs and the Missionaries of Charity (MoC). The education varied by quite a degree. The MMMs, a medical based order, provided all levels of professional education based on the nun's placement of work. However, even though the MoC provided medical treatment and care, these nuns would never receive professional training. One reason, I heard, was to ensure the Sisters didn't become too proud. Receiving no training would keep them 'spiritually humble'.

Wonderful girls would come into this order, most with no previous training, and never advance beyond being able to provide basic levels of care. I was also told it was the same reason they weren't allowed to buy washing machines. 'That kind of work keeps one humble,' one of the nuns had responded when I enquired.

I had spent an entire summer washing clothes as a postulant and knew how difficult and arduous that type of work could be. No doubt it was difficult, but wouldn't caring for sick, dying people also make you humble? Why would you spend so much time washing clothes when you could be helping people? I wondered. I couldn't help but hypothesise that the decision to provide no education went beyond the need to 'stay humble', and more accurately reflected the founder's culture and customary 'place of women'.

When the word spread that I was a doctor, the nuns began constantly requesting medical advice. Although they did not speak good English, I was able to demonstrate basic medical tasks like putting up a drip for a patient. It was inspiring to see them master new skills that would be helpful to patients. Yet, when it was time for prayer and rest, usually a time block of a few hours in the afternoon, they'd take the drips out of the patients and scoot all volunteers out of the wards. I had to leave during that time and heard the patient's cry as the nuns went to pray to God. I found it difficult not to judge their practices. During my time with the MMMs we were told, 'Your work is your prayer.' Every hour and minute that we were serving others became an ongoing prayer with Jesus. Although I had been so intrigued to see the practices of this world-renowned order, seeing the reality of the situation left me more than conflicted.

I volunteered with the Missionaries of Charity for about a week. During my stay I watched the last days of a lovely relationship unfold between a young boy and an elderly gentleman. The boy, most likely his grandson, would be the first person waiting in the morning to be let in. He'd sit on the doorsteps in the dark, waiting for the Sisters to unlock the ward and let in the volunteers and visitors. He'd sweetly greet a few of the other patients he grew to know and make his way to the bedside of his frail grandfather. They would talk, laugh, and read together. One day, I came across both crying together, wrapped in each other's arms.

It was nearing the end of the week, and the old man was becoming weaker. It was clear to me that he no longer had weeks or days left to live, but hours or minutes. His time was short. His breathing had become shallow, and his skin began to turn a murky grey colour. Night was drawing near, and it was time for visitors and volunteers to leave. I watched as the boy begged to stay. Tears covered his face as he frantically fought to stay near the bed. But despite the passionate show, the Sisters insisted that he must leave and slowly pulled the boy away.

I walked home that night feeling utterly gutted and could only imagine how the young boy felt that night. Would Jesus have turned away the boy? Was this not a Catholic guided missionary? I felt absolutely mystified by the strict adherence to the rules in such circumstances.

I showed up early the next morning to see how the boy was doing. He was of course sitting at the gates, anxiously waiting to be let in. His eyes were swollen, the dirty clothes hung on his skinny frame, his hair matted against his scalp. The keys clanged against the bars as the Sister unlocked the gates and the boy anxiously rushed into the ward to find his grandfather. I followed closely behind, worried about the old man but even more worried about the boy and what he might find. It was instantly clear that his grandfather had died: the body lay listless and cold underneath the sheets, having turned pale from the lack of circulation. I watched the boy break into sobs as he threw himself on the corpse.

No longer being a nun, I no longer had to hold my tongue when I found myself in situations I did not agree with. It was difficult to communicate my concerns with the Sisters in Calcutta and I wanted to speak directly with Mother Theresa. Would God not want His servants properly trained in the work they had chosen to give their life to? Or was 'staying humble' another strange way that society and religion masqueraded under the pretences of God, to control the power and contributions of women? I couldn't help but wonder and didn't know of any orders to which men belonged that forbidded professional training, especially when it pertained to the mission of the order. And why would any medical organisation or charity leave patients unattended? The practice seemed backwards, arrogant and pious not to mention unethical.

It became clear after talking with a Sister for a period of time that Mother Theresa had gone to Rome and I would not be able to talk with her about my concerns. It felt like the Sister was trying to appease me with her nods and smiles. It was time for me to go.

As I walked back to my lodging and began to cool down, I reflected on the bureaucracy of how orders are run. I knew local leadership greatly influenced the day-to-day running of the missions. Rules were rules and joining an order didn't leave a lot of room for free thought and personal choice. These Sisters were bonded to the rules whether they agreed with them or not. I knew that from direct experience, which is one of the reasons why I had left.

Strangely, this experience deepened my appreciation for my time as an MMM. Despite the Catholic origin of both orders, I felt lucky to have joined a truly progressive mission. The MMMs valued education, practicality and quality of care. Although, I knew it was a truly noble mission to serve the sick and dying in the poorest parts of Calcutta, I couldn't help but feel saddened. Chafed and perplexed, I left Calcutta.

Returning to Banares, I prepared for my long trip to Kerala in the southwest region of India. Excited, I'd reunite with Sister Dr Annie whom I went to medical school with and was now the Mother General of the order in Kerala. I'd also get to see Sister Rosie and Sister Mary who had graduated in nursing at the same time as us. They had a wonderful hospital in Trivandrum, similar to the MMM hospital in Drogheda, Ireland. While I visited, Sr Annie invited me to take the train with her to Cape Comerin, the southern most tip of India where the two oceans met. The Arabian Sea and the Indian Ocean came together in a wonderful scene while on the other side of the Bay of Bengal housed Sri Lanka.

*

It was now time to return to Banares. I stared at the train wondering how it would carry the extra weight. People spilled off the top and sides of the railroad cars. Although I had a ticket it was unnecessary for passage. Anyone willing to face various weather conditions and secure a foothold on the outer surfaces could also hitch a ride. I was one of the fortunate few that had reserved a sleeper unit.

'Excuse me, mam. There is no space for you in the female section,' announced the train serviceman after he checked my ticket. 'It's been booked.'

'What do you mean? I have my ticket right here!' I said pushing it back towards him.

The man, looking disgruntled, made some grumblings into the radio.

'Sorry, mam, it's been booked. But we do have room in the male bunker. Would you like that?' He said staring at me blankly. Well, it was one of the worst ideas I had heard that day, possibly that week. It was, however, a two-day journey and I needed a place to stretch out and rest. After my continual futile attempts to protest, I finally agreed.

I walked back to the men's section and found my sleeper-seat. It was midday, which meant I had time to get a feel of the situation and the people near me before the railcar became dark. Sweat dripped off my face and everyone around me. Human body odour – well, it was something you got used to.

Little children wandered the aisles attempting to raise money, thumping their hands on their stomachs like drums and singing a local tune. I always found a few extra rupees for the children that stopped near me. I had packed a few boxes of biscuits to eat on the long train ride. As I peeled open the sealed container my hand jerked back in instinct as movement brushed against my fingers. Little worms wiggled around the white crumbs. I put the lid back on and shoved the container back in my bag.

As the sun fell, my anxiety levels began to rise. Surrounded by hundreds of men, I lay in my little sleeper cart as stiff as a board. I pushed the sleep away and stayed alert to the noises in the railcar. To sleep during the day might be the way to go. Every so often I could hear an occasional creak above my head, which I assumed came from bodies pressing themselves close on the roof of the railcar. If I was scared, I could only imagine what the people above me felt like, the wind and darkness pressing into their faces. Criky! They couldn't get to sleep, I realised, for if they did they'd most likely fall off the train and die! As the morning sunlight flooded through the windows a drowsy sense of relief washed over me. That day I made friends with a few of the men around me and passed the second night with a little more ease.

I awoke the next day as the train screeched to a slow grinding halt. I sat up and stared out of the window. Had we arrived early? It appeared that we were in the middle of nowhere out in the rural countryside. Before the train reached a full stop, people started jumping off the sides of the train and fleeing to the cover of the bush. I gave a nearby passenger a puzzled glance.

'They make their own stops so they don't have to spend an entire day trekking back out here,' he said, clarifying the situation.

Each pulls the cord when near their own home, so the train stops. Prepare yourself. The next eighty miles will take a loooong time." He said in his Indian accent.

The guards had just as much luck stopping people from pulling the communication cords as they had keeping people off the train's roof. The train was chaos on wheels. The alarm chain is placed in multiple locations in every coach. Once pulled the train's brakes are automatically activated. Identifying the culprit would be near impossible. The next eighty miles proved to be a slow trek indeed, with guards pacing the aisles, attempting to stop the cords from being pulled. Interestingly, it seemed to be a train-wide coordinated effort. Every ten miles or so, the cord would get pulled, the wheels would scream and the train would slowly screech to a slow enough speed that bodies could start hurling themselves off. Women, children and even old men would go tumbling and summersaulting into the dirt and rocks. Miraculously, they'd gathered themselves upright with bloodied lips and knees and flee as if unscathed. By the time we reached Benares, the train had lost over a third of its passengers.

*

From beginning to end, India was an experience of paradox. The country burgeoned with enterprise, commerce and energy; and yet, struggled with the severest of poverty. The women were gorgeous, clothed in intricate wraps, and bejewelled with bangles and gold piercings in their ears and noses; and yet, misogyny suffused the culture and daily acts of violence were carried out against the adorned gender.

Spirituality was woven into the fabric of everyday life, seen in the traditions and devotional rituals practised by nearly everyone; yet the caste system seemed to naturally tear the seams of society apart by division, hate and constantly identifying the haves and have-nots. Complex artistry and engineering were seen in the rugs to the ornamental temples, yet the city's infrastructure lacked basic sanitation design from the sewer system to regulatory policies, leaving it filthy and foetid.

Maybe it was the paradox of the hope and potential juxtaposed next to the clashing reality that left me feeling raw and hopeless. Or maybe the hardest aspect for me to swallow was witnessing how a 'great spiritual nation' could degrade and objectify women to such an extent that even murder became common and condoned by the majority. I knew a white foreign women would have little impact in this country.

As my plane I departed, I looked down on the bustling city from the sky; I knew I'd never return to work there.

30

Lourdes
The Place of Miracles

There are only two ways to live your life. One is as though nothing is a
miracle. The other is as though everything is a miracle.
Albert Einstein

Jesus replied 'What is imposible with man, is possible with God.'
Luke 18:27

W HEN I got back to Liverpool, a letter was waiting for
me in the post requesting me to be the advisory doctor
on an upcoming pilgrimage to Lourdes, France. The
place of miracles.

In 1858, apparitions of Mary, Mother of Jesus, were seen on
over 17 occasions. A girl had conversations with Mary over a
period of weeks. At one point, Mary instructed the girl to dig in a
specific location and a spring appeared. After an investigation, the
Church declared that Mother Mary had appeared at Lourdes,
constructed a church, and built a Marian shrine near the spring.
This spring has become a recognised healing source for people
with a variety of ailments and illnesses. Since 1858, the Catholic
Church has officially declared 69 miracles at Lourdes, through
vigorous standards. As many as four to six million pilgrims visit
Lourdes annually. As such, it has more hotels than all of France's
cities, except Paris!

Since I had returned to Liverpool after being released by the MMMs, I volunteered for several different missionary groups that took sick and disabled people to different sacred sites across Europe. The people that wanted to make the pilgrimage were very sick and needed the support of volunteers and the oversight of a doctor. The Cross typically took people from the poverty-stricken side of town, who didn't have the means and resources to privately take the trip with their own families.

There was that one time I went to Rome with the Across Jumbulance, where I reported a misbehaving priest who kept young disabled girls awake late into the night. Although I never saw anything explicit, his behaviour was incredibly inappropriate, and I had to say something. (I would later receive a letter from Across saying to the effect 'How dare I criticise a priest of the Holy Church'!)

I also took a few trips with a missionary group to visit Lourdes. The journey took two full days of travel. Travelling by bus day and night, the bus was fitted with all basic necessities: beds, a toilet and a microwave. I formed lifelong friendships with some of the other volunteers.

Having recently returned from India, I received a letter asking if I'd be the accompanying doctor on a trip to Lourdes. I received permission from the university to work on my dissertation remotely and got ready to leave Liverpool again!

I always enjoyed these mission trips. The people were always so appreciative and grateful for the opportunity to make the pilgrimage. When I began in 1973, I thought I was providing this great service to others. These people were lucky indeed to have a medical consultant take a week or two of unpaid leave be with them on their journey. But after my first trip, I realised what a blessing it was for me. I have come to believe the volunteer receives just as much as they give.

We began our journey with a stop in London to pick up an elderly gentleman. After the man got settled on the bus, his two sons approached me in private and told me that he had cancer but had not been told. They knew I needed to know as the consulting physician and asked if I would keep it secret as well.

'If he asks me what's wrong, I have an obligation to tell him,' I said empathetically, yet with assertion. 'It's not only my duty, but he has a right to know.' I explained my experience and how I had met many family members who felt uncomfortable discussing the topic of illness and death with their loved ones. 'However, in my experience, I always found it was better to have an honest conversation with them, especially if the person asks about it and wants to know.' I also stressed that my relationship with their Dad would be based on honesty.

The sons agreed that if he asked, I could tell him. Despite not knowing of his cancer, he still made it known that he wished to die in Lourdes. Lourdes now has a special cemetery for the Pilgrims that die while there or on ther journey.

This group had a lovely connection and flow. When we arrived in Lourdes we settled into a cheap hostel. I spent long hours working on my dissertation, while still making time to attend to the needs of my patients. When time made itself available, I'd even go into the hospital and see what else could be done. The volunteers on that trip formed a strong bond and you'd always find us socialising together in the evenings.

On one such occasion, I even tried my first shandy! A heavy smoker, yes, but when it came to the booze I was three sheets to the wind. My friends graciously helped me arrive safely in my bed that evening. The next morning, my friends greeted me with hoots and hollers.

'If she just looks at wine gum, she's anybody's!' one of my close friends cat-called. I can't say for sure exactly what happened that night, or what I said, but that would be my last drink for decades.

We had been in Lourdes for about two weeks. I was helping work a shift at the hospital one evening and went to help a patient out of their car. As I reached in the car to help the lady stand up, my back made that horrible familiar crunch noise and pain screamed up my back and down my legs. I almost dropped the patient on the pavement as I went tumbling to the ground myself.

From the first time my back went out in Nigeria, it continued to be an ongoing problem. It had 'gone out' on me at least five times during my twenty years with the MMMs, landing me on my back for at least six weeks each time. A serious liability, never knowing when or where it might render me completely helpless. What if I was out in the middle of nowhere? What if it had happened in India? Luckily for me, this time, I literally lay at the entrance of a hospital.

As I lay in a hospital bed that night, the pain kept sleep at bay. Finishing my dissertation seemed nearly impossible now. The pain pulsed through my consciousness, leaving parts of my right arm numb. The French beds were 'lumpy', far too soft. I couldn't tell if the bed was making my pain worse, so I decided to take a chance and lie on the floor.

Getting to the floor was another story. I slowly rolled upright in bed and decided to take some more painkillers and muscle relaxers that sat on the bedside table. I tossed my pillow on the ground and managed to lumber down to the floor. I yanked a blanket down and tried to relax on the hard floor as my back screamed in protest. The medicine began to work, calming my nerves. I slowly felt the warmth of sleep quieten my mind.

It was the sound that woke me up. That strange, horrible, crunching noise. It was only after I heard the noise that I felt the sensation – the movement of disks as they slipped back into place. I lay there, stunned. What the blimey? Had the disks in my back…? The pain had disappeared. I lay there for several minutes, shifting ever so slightly, waiting for the pain to re-emerge.

But it didn't.

With no struggle or cries, I sat straight up.

Holy Mother Mary.

I sat dazed and pain-free on the hospital floor.

*

The staff couldn't believe their eyes when they found me walking the next morning. But it was I who was truly gobsmacked. My back felt a hundred per cent better. There were no aches or muscle spasms that typically accompanied this injury for the months following recovery. Had I just had a miraculous healing at Lourdes? Goodness! I thought, maybe next time I can be cured of my smoking addiction! I never again experienced another back injury until in old age.

A few days later, the old man in our group had a haemorrhage. Earlier on our trip, the conversation had come up and he learned of his cnacer. He seemed at peace with the diagnosis. It looked like he might get his wish after all. I sat by his bedside for hours as he seemed to be passing between the veil and coming back. In one moment, he looked over at me with misty eyes.

'Doc, is this the big sea?'

'I think it is,' I said, gently squeezing his hand. But miracles don't always work out the way we hope. Despite his wishes, he lived.

The entire group made it back to England that year, which wasn't always the case. The little old man was happily reunited with his sons. He later wrote to me thanking me for being so open with him about his diagnosis. Surprisingly, more than not, honesty is often welcomed, and not feared like so many expect. In the end, he was just grateful he knew of the cancer and knew he was reay to pass to the other side when it was time, but it wasn't time yet.

*

Miracles are different for everyone. I had been cured of the greatest physical ailment of my life at Lourdes. I'd never again suffer another back injury. It doesn't really matter if you believe in miracles or don't. What matters is that having a healthy back directly impacted where I'd be able to go and what I'd able to do, directly influencing the projection of my life, and the confidence with which I could pursue it.

Photo 24: Pat Sadler and Anne, 2017.
Photo 25: Anne and Singapore friends, 2017.

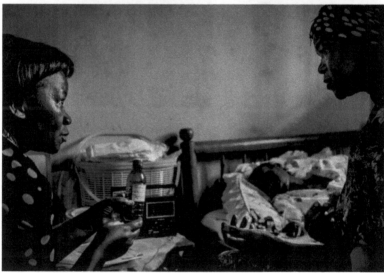

Photo 26 (*top*): Patients of HAU, Uganda.
Photo 27 (*bottom*): Nurse Josephine shows
relative of child how to give oral morphine.

Photo 28: Children with Burkett's lymphoma in the old cancer ward receiving toys made by friends in Liverpool.

Photo 29: Eddie Mwebesa (served with HAU for 20 years) and Anne.

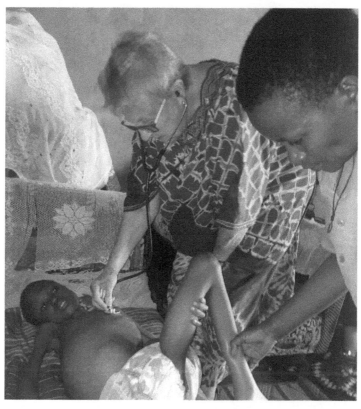

Photo 30: Anne examines a girl child at home.

Photo 31: Anne with her puppies from Adam and Eve!

Photo 32: Anne with volunteers at Merseyside HAU charity shop, 2017.

Photo 33: Anne dances with the students who have just collected their Diploma in Palliative Care at the Institute of Hospice and Palliative Care in Africa (IHPCA), the education arm of HAU.

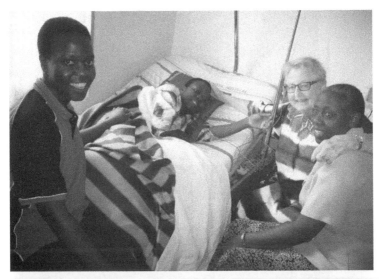

Photo 34 (*top*): Anne, Martha Rabwoni, and Dianah Basirika
visiting Rose Kiwanuka in hospital.
Photo 35 (*bottom*): Students promise to carry their candle of
palliative care to their countries and the world after completing
their Diploma in Palliative Care, allowing the nurses to prescribe
oral morphine in Uganda, 2017.

Photo 36: Anne and her Ugandan family: Mary, Margaret, Ryan, Victoria, little Anne, Anne, Frankie, Alice and Joseph.
Photo 37: Rose Kiwanuka (first HAU nurse) and Anne, 2017.

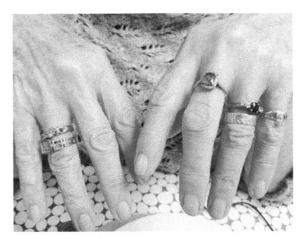

Photo 38: Anne's rings, in remembrance of God and patients.
Photo 39: The President of Ireland, Michael D. Higgins, awards Anne with the Presidential Award for her work in Developing Countries.

Photo 40: The Queen of Buganda Sylvia Naginda with Anne and Fazal at Christmas 2022, at a visit to her at home in Andrew Kaggwa House, Buziga, Kampala.

Photo 41: Autumn Fielding-Monson and Anne in Clifden,
   Ireland, starting work on book, 2016.

Photo 42: Anne celebrating her 88th birthday.
Photo 43: Anne in Clifton, Ireland, 2016.

PART III

THAT'S HOW THE LIGHT GOT IN

31

Into the Darkness

There is no way around it. Dharma always involves, at some point,
a leap off a cliff in the dark.
Stephen Cope

When you walk to the edge of the light, and take that first step into
the darkness of the unknown, you must believe that one of two
things will happen. There will be something solid for you to stand
upon or you will be taught to fly.
Patrick Overton

I T WAS TIME. I was ready.

This was not the first time I had taken a step into the darkness, guided by faith. Nor would it be my last. Many traditions discuss being guided by light, but often you find yourself being guided beyond the light and into the darkness, beyond the pale, into the unknown. It is in the darkness that God's wisdom manifests and we are made stronger. The darkness of the unknown is unnerving. Sometimes, I think we have collectively forgotten that happiness is not derived from constantly seeking pursuits of comfort. The life worth living is the kind that makes us reach deep into our reserves, testing our beliefs, knocking us on the ground, forcing us to regather ourselves, grow, adapt, and try again. It's good to remind ourselves that pain is just another word for opportunity. Obstacles are the fruit of life, and they're typically born in the dark void, often when we feel most lost.

I took my first major step into the dark when I decided to be a nun, foregoing my known life, entering a world of new ways and traditions. The beginning is usually not easy. Well, at least not for me! I felt lost, trying to regain my feet before I drowned. My time as a postulant really challenged my will power and resilience. If not for my father's encouragement – who never really wanted me to go in the first place – I'm not sure I would have seen it through.

Yet, my time as a nun filled my life with irreplaceable opportunities, education, and experiences. I became a doctor (not in my cards back in Liverpool and I had actually wanted to be a nurse because of their close contact with patients), I obtained two MRCP at the Royal Colleges in Edinburgh and Ireland and spent approximately ten years in Nigeria working and assimilating in another culture. Although I had left the MMMs, I still felt connected to this incredible worldwide social network of other like-minded individuals.

The MMMs still graciously accepted me and treated me like one of their own. It would be a network that would continue to provide meaningful connection and assistance throughout my entire life. The kindness and hospitality of these Sisters were top notch and I would feel their gracious acceptance and support throughout my life.

Leaving this network would be one of the most difficult and pivotal decisions in my life. Once again, I found myself in dark, unchartered territories. It took a giant leap of faith. It may have been something that I wouldn't have had the audacity to do on my own. And luckily I didn't, given courage by a bold and blossoming love.

Sometimes, life only makes sense when you have the ability to look back and see how it has unfolded perfectly. Returning to the civilian life was not easy. A broken heart was hard to overcome. But now, I can see that I was given just what I needed to overcome my struggles. Coming home gave me time to reground and reconnect with my family and friends. Nights of laughter and joy, sitting around the fire, playing the guitar and singing. I cherish those final sacred years spent with my mum. Career wise, key opportunities unfolded, and amazing mentors manifested. I grew personally and professionally and gained the confidence and worldly savvy to try travelling again out in the world on my own.

Again, the unknown beckoned. I heard its faint whisper calling to me, summoning me into the dark abyss.

32

When It Rains, It Pours

Everything you've ever wanted, is on the other side of fear.
George Addair

Before something great happens, everything falls apart.
Keith Sweat

I DIDN'T foresee myself going back to Africa. I knew I wanted to leave Britain and go somewhere where I thought my experience and knowledge was needed, and somewhere that was reasonably safe. I hadn't thought seriously of returning to Africa since my time in Ethiopia.

I asked my friend, the Dean of the Liverpool School of Tropical Medicine, if he had suggestions of where I should job search. He suggested positions with universities in both Penang, Malaysia and NUS, Singapore. He knew I had been a nun and suggested places that he considered safe for a woman. I immediately applied to both. A new University in Penang, Malaysia responded first and offered me the position. The University Sains Malaysia, located on Peninsular Malaysia to the west, was a newer institution and had only begun its second year of a medical school. They were looking for teachers and employed me as a senior lecturer in the Department of Public Health (fortunately, I was promptly promoted to Associate Professor). With little money in the bank, I quickly accepted the position.

The farewell parties began in earnest! I had made some incredible friendships during my time in school. All of us were sad to say goodbye to each other, knowing we'd never see each other again. I rented out my lovely home in Rocky Lane and packed up my life. I knew I'd be taking quite a pay cut in Malaysia compared to a consultant position with the NHS in the UK, but Mum's death had changed things for me. I felt ready to leave again.

I arrived in Penang, Malaysia in May of 1983. The security guards at the airport ravaged my luggage before letting me pass. Later, I'd come to find out that Penang was a known hotspot for trafficking drugs across Southeast Asia. A Chinese-Malaysian driver stood outside luggage collection, holding my name on a large paper. Upon introduction he collected my bags and began to lead me back to the car. Once we were in the car, he asked what had brought me to Malaysia.

'Ah, you're just another one who has come to make money in Malaysia,' his voice tinged with disdain.

Absolutely taken aback, and not one to hold my tongue, I replied, 'Excuse me, but I have taken quite a reduced salary to come out here.'

He looked at me in disbelief. We sat in silence for the rest of the drive. Despite my anger, I knew his reaction had merit. Many people began the expat road with well-intentioned hearts, only to have their 'reasons' change over time. I would try to prove him wrong.

Coming in as an outsider rarely made things easier, although, I do have to admit that wearing a habit and a veil had made things easier in the past. It often evoked immediate respect and kindness from others. But that agency was gone. I sat in the taxi, ready to make it on my own.

After being driven around in circles to increase the taxi cost, I finally arrived at my destination. I would be living in a hotel near the city centre, where I would stay until I found a place to rent.

The man at the front desk greeted me with a flashing smile. 'Hi, mam. Welcome to Penang.'

He took my luggage and showed me to my room. 'And, ah, one more thing, mam. There has recently been a murder here, so please be sure to lock your door and secure the metal latch before you sleep. Have a wonderful stay and please let us know if you have any questions.'

I promptly locked every bolt I could find. Exhausted, I sat on my bed and took in the room's inventory. Stuffy and humid, the air stuck to my face, reminding me of my first tour in Nigeria. I had a large bed and dressing table with a glass top. The bathroom was clean. Although it was a far cry from a nice hotel, it would do just fine.

The setting sun indicated the end to the day. I got ready for bed, staring at the ceiling from under the covers. Liverpool felt worlds away. In reality, no one in the world knew where I was. I had told Pat where I'd be staying, but this was not a world of cellphones, emails and WhatsApp. I reached over and turned on the air conditioner. The starting motor creaked in protest. The resulting air conditioning was very cold, but very loud. I had better chances of sleeping in the humidity. I turned off the AC, said my prayers, and switched off the lights.

*

Tap-tap-tap.

I awoke in the total darkness, absolutely terrified. Somebody was in the room.

Tap-tap-tap.

I froze. Had someone managed to get through all the locks? I lay rigid in the bed just waiting to get grabbed and strangled in the dark. But nothing happened. With nothing else to do, I reached over and switched on my night lamp. The room looked just as it had before I went to sleep. Empty.

Tap-tap-tap.

My eyes quickly darted around trying to find the source of the noise. The noise originated from the dressing table. I quickly slipped out of bed to investigate what had awoken me. At first, I almost jumped at the sheer size of the insect. The shiny sleek beasty stood ready with an object clenched in its mouth. One of the hardiest creatures on the planet, Malaysia was home to some of the larger species of cockroaches. It hissed as I approached the dressing table. As I looked closer, I realised this bastard was trying to pinch one of my earrings.

Tap-tap-tap. Clinging onto the bright shiny stone, he rather efficiently began to drag it away. I regained my senses and sent that little roach packing. I secured my earrings and tried again to sleep despite the adrenaline still coursing through my blood.

It would be a lie to say things got easier.

*

The university compound sat exquisitely on a cliff, overlooking the ocean on all sides. Previously occupied by the British Military, the location was stunning. The university had constructed large lecture halls with scenic windows. I wondered how the students would be able to focus!

After getting settled in at campus, I'd made friends through Professor Williamson, with an orthopaedic surgeon, fat and jovial he was full of fun. Prof. Williamson helped me find a room to rent in a house with Dr George, a pharmacologist. George had a kind, easy-going personality and we easily hit it off. He was renting from a Malay, Muslim family who had gone abroad. The Muslim landlord was away when I agreed to move in. I had worked with Muslims in Nigeria but my time in Penang taught me a great deal more! I didn't realise we were not allowed to eat or cook pork in our rented apartment! I'd quickly come to regret my decision to stay there.

The medical school had recruited professors from all over the world: America, Australia and West Indies, to name a few. I was primarily an Associate Professor in my new role and only learned upon seeing the curriculum that the position consisted of teaching and research, largely excluding clinical work. Ninety per cent of the students were Malay and the remaining were Indian and Chinese. It was the first time I had been in a Muslim majority community.

Islam was not new to me. Nigeria had the highest levels of Islam in West Africa, with an approximately 50–50 split between Islam and Christianity. But those that travel know the alchemic effect culture has on religion, shifting from country to country and region to region. The Islam I witnessed in Malaysia was quite different from the Islam I had experienced in Nigeria.

In Penang, the women wore burqas, covering their bodies from head to toe with a small open slit for their eyes. I watched as these women entered my classroom, stepping in from the humid climate, body odour arising as they walked by. In the clinical coursework, I learned that Muslim females were not allowed to remove men's clothes while conducting examinations, and instead, had to examine the men through layers of clothing while attempting to accurately provide a diagnosis. This would be impossible with many medical conditions, holding these women back and only confirming their second-class position in society.

As frustrated as I was on behalf of these women and the culture they found themselves in, I also knew that they were trailblazers, and must have wills of steel. They would have to work harder than any of their male counterparts to prove their competence and intelligence. The Dean of the University, a Chinese man, had tried hard to oppose this practice with little success.

USM wanted all the professors to teach in Malay. I took evening language classes but struggled to incorporate it into my teaching. It was really difficult, but the teachers all had a good laugh as we tried to incorporate the anatomy and physiology terms. I would eventually learn enough to engage in polite conversation but that was as far as it went.

Due to my interest and experience in geriatric care, I was introduced to Peter Tan, a general practitioner in Penang, who had become very interested in geriatrics and palliative care. Incidentally, we made the connection that he was Paul Tan's father! Paul worked under me as a senior house officer at Whiston Hospital. Although he had jokingly encouraged me to visit, neither of us imagined that I'd be surprising him at his welcome home party – his jaw practically dropping to the floor with shock when he saw me!

Peter introduced me to the Franciscan nuns, who ran a hospital with a radiotherapy unit and had many cancer patients. When I had free time away from the classroom, I went to the hospital to teach the Sisters about the progressive practices and methods we had implemented back in Liverpool. I focused on how to care for the elderly and patients on the palliative care spectrum. Having never heard of palliative care, the nuns were very interested in learning ways to help their patients who suffered in great pain.

On weekends, I'd take long walks in the gorgeous Malaysian countryside with a tight-knit group of expats. Known as the Pearl of Southeast Asia, the reputation was well-founded. We discovered old maps created during the Japanese occupation, which guided us through unknown trails in the hillsides. The gorgeous countryside felt like you were walking in a postcard.

The Cameroon Highlands in central Malaysia, were also among my favourite places to visit. Large tea plantations covered the rolling hillsides in swathes of bright green colours with extraordinary panoramic views. Reaching the highlands often took over six hours, so we'd make a weekend out of it, exploring gardens, strawberry farms and ancient Buddhist temples. Although I had never pursued athletic endeavours, I loved swimming. Swimming in the Ocean and avoiding the jelly fish was enjoyable, but occasaionally they got you! I loved swimming with the children of the other teachers and teaching them to float so they could build confidence to swim.

After I had been there a few months, the university asked if I would assist the clinical team at the new USM teaching hospital in Kota Bharu. Kota Bharu was on the north-east coast of the island. I jumped at the opportunity to get involved with patients and felt delighted to work in a clinical setting. However, I also partly accepted the change of position because of the difficulty I was having at my current residence.

On one occasion, George left meat in the fridge and forgot to throw it away before leaving on a trip. The landlord, unannounced, entered the apartment and having found the pork meat, turned on me. He yelled, waving his fists in the air in an ominous and threatening way until he seemed to be satisfied that he had scared me – which he had. Feeling threatened and unsafe in my own home, a change of scenery sounded like a good idea.

Kota Bharu, less developed than Penang, consisted of a higher Muslim population, and closer to the heart of the government. The new teaching hospital was beautifully built, several stories high, a symbol of developing progressive healthcare in their country. Unfortunately, instead of being established under the Ministry of Health, the new teaching hospital had been established under the Ministry of Education, which didn't have a lot of experience in the procurement of healthcare.

I began working in the cardiac unit, and although they had places for oxygen to be delivered, they hadn't sorted out getting it delivered. It was rather difficult to help patients in the cardiac unit with no oxygen tanks. Several such conundrums existed around the hospital as the Ministry of Education learned the healthcare business.

They had built several flats on the compound, mainly for nurses, and I was given one of these flats. I was delighted to be back in a clinical setting again and became good friends with several of the nurses.

The life of an expat can mean constantly starting over again. Just as you get to know someone they leave, or you leave. You must adapt to cultures that don't adapt to you and eat food that leaves your digestive system in upheaval. Although the days were full and busy, I found myself unhappy most of the time. I cried a lot, almost as much as when I left the MMMs. I missed my home in Liverpool, my friends and old colleagues, but most of all I missed Mum. I felt the same undertow pulling at me, leaving me unsettled and ungrounded.

The fear I had felt that night in Liverpool kept rising, trying to reach the surface. I couldn't sleep at night. It was the first time in my life that I felt truly alone in the world. I knew I hadn't properly processed Mum's death as a whirlwind of activity followed with my studies and trip to India. However, walking around yet another new city with unfamiliar sights and faces, it finally caught up, leaving an ache in my stomach.

But there still was joy and new adventurous to find. Kota Bharu had some of the most beautiful beaches in the country. One of the beaches, known as the 'Beach of Passionate Love', was a popular nesting place for turtles to lay their eggs. Large, female turtles emerged from the ocean to begin the laborious mission to bring their children into the world.

Early one morning, I watched a beautiful green turtle, over a metre long, begin digging her nest with her large flipper. Once the nest fit the needed dimensions, it wasn't long before she began laying dozens of eggs into the hole, resembling delicate white ping pong balls.

Counting anywhere from fifty to a hundred, these eggs would hatch in about two months' time. Vulnerable to the conditions – to predators or drowning from high tides and monsoons – they'd be lucky to make it back to the ocean. With barely the strength to break through their eggshells, and small enough to fit into the palm of your hand, these delicate creatures held the intrinsic knowledge that guided them back into the foreboding ocean. Hearing the calls of their destinies, swarms of little green hatchlings would forge forward into the thrashing waves. Surviving would seem impossible for these little mortals, dangers too great to overcome, yet many would learn to navigate the unknown waters, avoid predators and learn how to thrive. Some might even renew the cycle, laying their very own eggs on this beach some day.

I watched the enormous turtle begin to cover her newly laid eggs with her back flipper, broad sweeping motions sprinkled sand over the fresh eggs. Undeterred, by myself and a few other onlookers, she diligently continued the task before her. After finishing her work, she sat with her nest for a little while. Alas, came the moment for her to return home into the ocean. I couldn't help but sympathise with this large mammal and imagined if she had feelings of sadness and loss. As she turned, she began making these strange heart-wracking noises. This large turtle cried her way back into the waves. Her weeping jarred my inner landcape, as I watched how torturous the ways of life could be.

It seemed that final goodbyes are never easy, for anyone.

*

'Dr Anne! Don't ever dress like that again!' scolded a Malay nurse, pulling me to the side. I knew she meant well because we'd recently established a warm friendship with each other.

Bewildered, I looked down at what I was wearing – beige trousers with a red striped button up blouse, long sleeved, neatly tucked into my pants. I generally wore neutral shades of makeup with a soft pink lipstick. I was completely covered and looked rather fasionable. What had I done wrong?

'Dressed like what? I'm covered! I've got everything covered,' I said quite indignant.

'Yes, but your buttocks are showing.'

Astonished, 'What do you mean?" I exclaimed, "My buttocks aren't showing! I've got trousers on.'

'Yes – but you can see your buttocks. You shouldn't be on duty showing your buttocks!'

My confused look elicited a greater response from her.

'Wear a longer shirt! It must go below your buttocks!'

I looked around, realising all the other nurses wore a suit trouser but all of their shirts were untucked and draped to their mid-thighs.

Later that day I had a good laugh about it – but really had nobody to share my laughter with. I went out and bought a few longer shirts that afternoon. Although I tried to be considerate of the culture, I often felt very misunderstood by the people. Assimilating to Malaysia was proving much more difficult than I had imagined.

And when it rains, it literally pours. A biblical style flood hit Kota Bharu.

I had been in Kota Bharu for about a month and people began to get really excited.

'Let's look for the rain!' the children could be heard laughing, 'When will it be time to play in the rain!'

Even though I had only been there a short time, it was clear that the rain monsoon was an important season. People's livelihoods depended on the rain for their crops and survival. However, the approaching storm clouds also felt ominous. Many people lived along the rivers and the rain brought flooding affecting large portions of the population on a yearly basis.

The billowing dark grey-blue clouds above heralded the change of season. I walked out of the hospital doors and felt the first drop on my nose. I reached for my umbrella in my briefcase and before I had a chance to pull it out, I stood soaked to my under-britches. This was no rain I had ever seen, and I was no stranger to rain, having grown up in England and Ireland. It was as if God had turned on a tap and the water poured from the heavens above. The people began dancing and singing in the streets, grateful for the free water that fell from the sky. But even though the people around me rejoiced with laughing and dancing, I felt dread as the heavens poured down on us.

After the first day of rain, I drove by the hotel that had become a popular tourist destination for the people who came to see the 'beach of passionate love'. The beach had turned into anything but its name. The waves thrashed the and the water had risen past the turtle nests! The turtle eggs, defenseless and vulnerable, if not hatched, had no doubt been killed.

But the rains didn't stop. Within a few days the city literally became swamped in chaos. It was difficult to move anywhere as the water began to rise in the streets. It soon became obvious that this was no ordinary monsoon. It didn't take long before the city's grid quickly transformed into raging tributaries, flooding homes and shops. Broken tree limbs, garbage and dead animals got swept down the streets.

Fortunately, the new teaching hospital was on top of a hill and avoided the type of damage inflicted on the lower parts of the village. The older general hospital, however, was not so auspiciously located and took on terrible damage. I managed to make it down to the hospital and got out of the car. As I stepped into the water, it ripped my shoe right off! I didn't dare make an attempt to grab it but focused on keeping my footing. The water came up to my knees and I had to steady myself to maintain my balance in the water's current.

We carefully made our way into the hospital. There was hardly a difference between outside and the first floor. The water levels rose just beneath the beds. Attempting to escape the ever-rising water, patients and their family members all huddled closely together on the patients' beds. They clung to each other as they helplessly watched the water continue to rise. Efforts were made to take as many people as possible to the upper floors, but not everyone could be evacuated. It was hard to imagine how people survived, let alone those who were terribly sick.

The floods continued for over a month. The lower part of the city was demolished. People died. Animals died. I have never seen anything like it.

I felt isolated, ineffective and unappreciated at work. I continued to process the loss of my mother with waves of loneliness.

When God sends you a lifeboat, you take it. I received a letter from Singapore requesting a job interview for the position I had applied to eight months earlier. I interviewed for the job, got it, and immediately left.

33
Keep Moving: Singapore

You can't start the next chapter of your life, if you keep re-reading the last one.
Anon

But while we bend, we don't break. This is no dark hour;
this is the dawn before we remember who we are.
Arthur Davis

A T THE START of 1984, I found myself travelling to yet another country. Tired but hopeful, this time at least, I wouldn't need to travel far. Located at the southern tip of Western Malaysia, Singapore was less than a day's drive from my current residence. I signed a three-year contract with the Department of Public Health at the National University of Singapore (NUS) with Prof. Poon Wai On, who demanded respect and oversaw many areas. I was employed as an Associate Professor, but as an expat given the title of Senior Teaching Fellow (not a 'Fella' as the Scousers would say!).

Sometimes in life, you just need different. I had no idea what Singapore would have in store for me, but I was ready to try something new. I've learned that life is about not only embracing and overcoming the hard, the challenges, and the unexpected; but learning to bend, adapt, and catch the next wave that comes our way.

*

A true melting pot of the world, Singapore was home to diverse ethnic groups and religions. Singaporean children were taught to accept the diversity of different customs and practices as seen by the Taoists, Muslims, Hindus, Christians, and Buddhists living together in harmony and respect. The wealthy city-state consisted primarily of an ethnic blend of Chinese, Malay, and Indians. Yet the predominant Chinese culture infused every Chinese household. Almost every home I'd walk into had enshrined alters for their ancestors, with tinkling bells and chimes to honor the memory of the departed souls.

Up until 1965, when Singapore was a part of Malaysia, the population had been mainly Malay. However, the Chinese had moved in from different parts of Malaysia and were mainly Hokien but Cantonese and others were also present, though in the minority. The Chinese had become the largest part of the population and the Government and the Malays were now the minority. The Malay often exceeded the 'two-child' rule and were often quite poor. They took the menial jobs, and the women were often working as house cleaners to the richer population. The Indian population were now the second largest and their temples, vibrant markets and wonderful food brought a vivid, colourful change to the city as well. Domestic workers were also brought from the Philippines, India and Sri Lanka. Although the Government had strict rules about importing 'maids', many expats and Chinese managed to have a live-in maid to look after their children and do the housework and cooking while both parents were professionals and working.

Despite the convergence of different ethnicities, religions, and socio-economic backgrounds, Singapore enjoyed peace, stability, and great economic prosperity. After Singapore gained independence in 1965, unemployment rates fell to 3 per cent, public housing and development bourgeoned, and the success of international trade could be seen by its bustling port. The country evolved quickly from a developing nation into a competitive economy, surpassing a few European states in GDP per capita.

Incredibly clean, safe and newly renovated, Singapore's character and history could still be found in the bustling vendors, street food markets, the unrestored shop houses in Bugi Street and, of course, there was Chinatown. An explosion of flavours and mix of chaos and order, the exploration of Chinatown filled many of my weekends. Luckily, a local friend of mine carefully helped me select the most delicious food dishes that would also keep me from rushing to the bathroom. And as much as I loved the city, if at any time I needed a reprieve from the bustling city, the lush countryside of Malaysia was only a short boat ride away.

I adapted much quicker to my new life in Singapore. I settled into a fourth-floor flat on MacAlister Road – an older building built by the British. Luckily, I furnished most of my apartment through an expat who was moving back home to Sweden. High-quality pieces made in Japan, I bought her rattan suite of furniture, tables and two beds and mattresses. I still sleep on the same mattress over thirty years later! One of my colleagues and his wife helped me get settled and gave me a short course on some of the important cues imbedded in the local customs and traditions. Fortunately, I also had help navigating the local shops from a lovely couple living in my building. A young couple with a child on the way, they were very generous to me, inviting me for meals and sharing their roof balcony with me. The wife, Looi, is still my friend and a talented Chinese artist. She now lives in London with her son Edward. Her husband has passed on.

My flat was situated across from the Singapore General Hospital (SGH), a teaching hospital for the Medical School of NUS. The Department of Public Health, where I worked, was located perpendicular to SGH in Tiong Bahru on Outram Road. Constructed years ago, by the British Empire, the red brick building had a slight musty smell and was a rarity, given nothing old lasted in Singapore, except, perhaps, the growing elderly population. The proximity of my flat from the SGH and NUS allowed me to walk to work every day in the sunshine, a special treat for a British gal. However, living off the main University campus meant I'd still need a car. Cars were quite expensive, with a 100 per cent tax. I bought the smallest and cheapest car I could find with help from a university loan. Sometimes, you can't put a price tag on a little freedom!

I was given a kitten early on who I named Sylvester. I put his tray for potty training on the balcony. One day he slipped through the railings and fell to the ground. After coming home from work, I nearly fainted when I saw my little furball lying dead on the pavement. How did he… I looked up at the balcony realising what must have happened. I wrapped him in my arms, and through tears began to make my way back up to my apartment. Suddenly, Sylvester let out a cough! I nearly dropped him again which would have surely done him in if I hadn't regained my senses and caught him. Maybe he had only been unconscious? I later adopted a friend for him, Sylvia, who was begging for food while I ate at a restaurant. Sylvia and Sylvester provided me with great friendship (and even joined me later in Africa).

Within a few short months I began to feel settled into my new Singapore life. I felt incredibly fortunate to have had the support and generosity of others as I learned about the Singaporean culture and its thriving city. That cross-taxi driver in Malaysia now had something to be angry about – for indeed, I now had a great salary.

34
The Summit

It is good to have an end to journey towards;
but it is the journey that matters, in the end.
Ernest Hemingway

Life isn't fun without being a little cheeky.
Anne Merriman

I HAD BEEN living in Singapore for about six months and became well-adjusted to my new accommodation on MacAlister Road and the work at the University.

The sound of my phone at the flat was a rather jarring cacophony of intermittent rings. Not a common occurrence, I enjoyed it. I had slowly started to become better acquainted with some of my colleagues and the couple that lived on the floor above, but nobody ever called me at home.

'Hello?' I answered, wondering who it might be.

'Anne? Is that you! This is Debbie from Liverpool!' Delighted to hear her voice from across the world, we caught up and she explained that her friend, a young doctor, was coming to Singapore for three weeks to explore South East Asia and asked if I'd be willing to be his base camp while he explored the surrounding area. Hospitality, imprinted into every MMM, is an extension of who I am. I didn't think twice about hosting him and was happy to do my friend a favour.

Matthew arrived in Singapore in great spirits and ready to explore everything the area had to offer. Young, slim, and athletic,

Matthew had a lovely personality and was energising to be around. My hosting responsibilities were quite easy as he was always off on another adventure, never overstaying his welcome. However, one of Matthew's excursions left him worse for wear. Returning from a short hiking trip with extreme fatigue, a high fever and profuse sweating – it didn't take long to diagnose his condition. Malaria was common in the rural areas where the mosquitos came out in hoards when it cooled off in the evenings. I started him on Quinine, and he quickly began to look better. Strong and young, he still looked pale but was regaining his energy quickly.

'Anne, I think I'm going to climb Mount Kinabalu!'

We were sitting at the breakfast table when he announced his next adventure.

'Are you sure? You are barely back from the dead!' I exclaimed. ` However, over breakfast it became quite clear he had his mind set, and there was only one thing I could do. Go with him. There was no way I was going to let someone I was supposed to be looking after, die on my watch.

Despite my total lack of knowledge around anything 'mountaineering', I was committed to climbing the highest mountain in Southeast Asia. My brother Joseph had always been an avid hiker. His passion extended beyond his own personal enjoyment, and he used it as a tool in his ministry as a Salesian priest to help struggling youth find a way to ground and balance out in nature, often in the hills of the Lake District. Not only did the solitude, scenery, exercise, and fresh air help create space for stillness and peace in their lives, it was also good fun. Joseph loved these episodes so much and wrote avidly about them to me. Well, not sure I'd find much peace on this kind of trek, I knew I'd probably find a few blister and sore muscles. While telling Joseph about my plans to summit the mountain, I delighted at hearing undertones of envy in his solemn voice. There was about to be two mountaineers in the Merriman family.

One day in the lunchroom, I mentioned I'd be climbing Mount Kinabalu with Matthew. A colleague, Ken, originally from near Liverpool, perked up.

'I've never climbed that mountain; do you mind if I come along?' He enquired.

Although I didn't know him very well at all, he seemed like good stock to have around on a serious climb.

It took time to collect the gear needed to make the summit. We needed to have proper outfits and leech boots. Yes, leech boots are exactly for the purpose they are named for, keeping the bloody leeches out! Sturdy but flexible, the canvas boots laced up to the knee and were worn over the trousers to keep the blood suckers out while trekking through swamps and streams. Prepared and excited, the three of us caught a two-hour flight to Kota Kinabalu.

*

The coldness stung my eyes as we climbed out of the jeep. Upon landing, we rented a car and drove to the base camp. Coming from warmer terrain, I always found it surprising how a slight rise in altitude drastically dropped the temperature. The round-trip trek would take about two days. We'd begin by hiking 6 km to Laban Rata where we'd have basic lodging for the night. From there, we'd rise in the middle of the night for a 4.5 hour trek up to the summit at sunrise. After a cold breakfast on top, we'd trek all the way back to Laban Rata (six to nine hours).

Ready and needing to get to Laban before nightfall, the three of us set off. Six kilometres may not sound like very far, but when you're going straight up a mountain, the distance appears to elongate exponentially. Each step felt like a rigorous lounge upwards. I summoned all my strength to keep up with the lads. There's always a moment, when attempting do something out of your comfort zone, that your mind strongly questions how the hell you got yourself into this mess. My burning legs and lungs continued to shout out their complaints as I trekked on. Well, the one thing I had going was Joseph would most likely be a little envious. A little sibling rivalry never hurt anyone. Well, maybe Abel.

A few hours into our 6 km of stair climbing, the men appeared just a little too chipper for the lack of oxygen my lungs seemed to be struggling to find. The habit of eight smokes a day was not to my advantage. I began lagging a little behind my group and ended up joining up with a few Singaporean women trekking right behind us. Poh Chan, May Woo, Mei Ken, and Jennifer, all had kind and adventurous spirits. The girls had planned and prepared for their walk diligently, with plenty of hill work, and it showed. Their fun conversation and energy helped me sustain until we reached our evening destination. My bond with these four friends was immediate and would be long lasting. Our two groups joined for camp dinner, and we discovered that Poh Chan lived only a few short blocks from my flat back in Singapore! Little did we know we'd become life-long friends and still stay in touch to this day.

Simultaneously excited and exhausted, sleep came to me quickly.

Climbing out of your sleeping bag in the freezing cold is terrible business. However, once the cold pierced through my clothing, my senses quickly awakened. The six of us and our guides had decided to summit together the night before. We all quickly ate some tin food and biscuits with some hot tea the guide had graciously prepared. With headlights adjusted, the faint light guided our paths as we set off up the trail.

I heard a noise behind me on the path as a scantily dressed lad stepped into the narrow light of my headlamp. Looking at his bare forearms and legs gave me shivers. He muttered something that sounded like an American accent. Plus, I didn't see leech boots strapped to his pack. Climbing alone, he swiftly passed our group. I heard our guides mutter as they shook their heads.

The air was dewy and the silence, touched only by our footsteps and soft breathing, complimented the blackness of the night. The headlamps provided just enough light to feel safe in the eerie dark outdoors. Once you're awake and moving it is amazing how the cold subsides into a delightful adventure. As we trudged up the side of the mountain in single file, the darkness began to grow even more opaque as the mountain mist began to encircle us. The summit trek felt like climbing a large boulder – it technically wasn't too difficult – but the weather and slippery terrain began to rattle my nerves. Not one to announce my feelings of insecurity, I maintained a veneer of bravado.

The encompassing mist made it difficult to see a few feet beyond my next step, yet I could tell the trail had narrowed and based on the guides' movements I knew a precipitous drop lay just beyond visibility. My eyes had adjusted to the darkness and the midst broke over the left side of the trail. As I peered over edge, I realised I couldn't even see the bottom of the drop. I flashed back to the moment in Nigeria when John had been moments away from driving us the side of the cliff. A flash of terror seized my gut. In addition, I also began to develop stomach pain which heralded my monthlies. The fright I felt turned into a queasy faintness. I sat down. Despite the elevation's toll on my lungs, I announced I needed a smoke. The group was kind enough to give in to my request.

After the nicotine softened my nerves, the slow trudge continued onwards and upwards. The higher we went the mist turned into thicker swirling clouds and a damp wetness began to penetrate my clothing.

'I see someone coming down!' Matthew said at the front of the line.

The man was almost on top of us before we saw him. The American came bounding forward with short jerky movements. The summit was no place for his naked skin. He was mad and of course and was visibly shaken. You could tell from his eyes he was happy to see our faces. He trembled uncontrollably and his movements were rigid and slow. My training kicked in and I went over to him and quickly sat him down and conducted a brief examination. Moving into hypothermia, his toes and a few of his fingers were showing signs of frost bite. He clearly needed medical supervision getting back down the mountain.

'I'll go back with him,' I volunteered along with another guide. 'He's in poor shape and needs to be with someone.' However, the reality was, I too was in poor shape and was more than happy to turn around and head back to camp.

'Are you sure?' Matthew inquired, 'we only have about an hour to go?'

'I better get him back. I think he needs medical supervision when we get back to the camp. But I'll be there with you in spirit.' I smiled, secretly relieved to begin the descent.

The American and I started back down the hill together with one of the guides.

The descent became rather tricky as the man grew more and more handicapped. Luckily, the guide deftly guided his fumbled movements and managed to chaperon him down the mountain. Although I missed the sunrise at the summit, the view was still magnificent on the way down as the sun inched its way above the horizon. The golden rays of light spread across the mountainous expanse below.

We made it back to Laban Rata. A few of the people at camp donated more clothing to his cause and brewed him some hot tea. When he felt more solid, we were able to descend more carefully to our initial base camp where he could receive proper medical treatment. The way down was harder than the way up and soon the proximal muscles of the legs, worn out from the climb up started to ache. Gratefully, the three of us made it back safely. The American received care and I warmed up with some more hot tea and waited for my group to arrive.

*

As I reflect on this adventure, I realise that in life there will be trips and experiences where despite how badly you wanted it to be about the destination, as cliché as it sounds, it really is all about the journey. It's not so much about what we do and what we achieve, rather who we become, whom we help and the friends we meet along the way. I made lifelong friends with Poh Chan, May Woo, and Mei Ken – all of whom have greatly enriched my life. Although I didn't make the summit, my journey will be forever remembered in the summit sunrise photo that Matthew took, which today hangs proudly on my wall in Andrew Kaggwa House in Uganda.

It's quite possible, my brother – Father Joseph – only received a copy of the summit photo with a dark bold caption that read, 'The Summit of Mt. Kinabalu!' Cheeky enough to let my brother believe he wasn't the only mountaineer in the family, my brother never heard a peep about the mad American that needed help going back down the mountain.

*

Singapore continued to feel more and more like home. The tears had stopped. A group of close friends often came over to my flat at lunch because I lived so close to work. I became dear friends with a younger Irish girl who worked at the University, Lynn Alexander, a loyal and sweet friend with whom I've stayed good friends to this day!

I remained close with my mountaineer friends, Poh Chan, May Woo, Mei Ken and one of their friends Karen, who – although they were 10–15 years younger than me – we got on very well. They were strong ladies, who practised jogging and swimming. Poh Chan lived near to me in Tiong Bahru and we began jogging around our area 2–3 times a week. On Sunday mornings, we'd all meet at 6.00 am and jog around the MacRitchie reservoir, followed by a strong ginger tea at a local café. If I didn't work up a sweat from the exercise, the strong bite from the tea had my pores 'hopping and lepping'! I really enjoyed morning swims in the municipal pool on the weekdays, eventually managing 22 lengths in the Olympic sized pool twice a week! How strong I was then! The five of us shared many experiences together including weekends, vacations to Malaysia and even Poh Chan's wedding. Through the friendships I had with these wonderful women and their families, I learned so much about the Chinese culture.

I really enjoyed social smoking and could not evade the contradiction that I worked for a health department that constantly told people to stop smoking. A of my friend back in Manchester, had even introduced me as the 'smoking nun', which we all got a kick out of. However, in Singapore, the culture took strongly to the change in policy that frowned upon smoking in public areas. I did not smoke at work but could not help but join post meal light-ups with friends. I remember one incident at the Singapore airport when I had a cigarette before a flight. As I sat quietly savouring a sweet smoke, a small little woman came over to me with a concerned look. 'Don't you know you aren't supposed to smoke here!' she said in a rather troubled voice. But becoming emboldened by our age difference, her timidness turned to indignant mothering.

'Besides, it will kill you!'

Singaporean people had no problem giving out to strangers if they thought such a lashing was needed (which might be why I fit in so well!) I felt mortified. My future smokes were confined to private settings after that.

I didn't adapt to everything, but there were aspects of their culture that became automatic. When you give a present to someone, you never gave it with one hand, but with two. Even a sale's assistant would hand our cash back to us with two hands. If you wanted to gesture to have someone to come over the palm of your hands must always be face down and you needed to curl your index finger under. If at a park, people are sitting on the ground for a picnic or such, you can't just walk past them, but you need to bend down and put your arm in between and scoot. I guess, after a while all these little changes became subconscious.

*

Between work, friends and even some dating (I had one episode of falling in love in Singapore with a specialist doctor from a most interesting family... but this book is only long enough for one love story, and it didn't last long), my life was starting to feel easy.

35

Singapore's Elderly

Though people have different status in life, everybody's dignity is the same. *IP Man, Master Martial Artist of Win Chun*

Caregiving calls us to lean into love in ways
we didn't know were possible.
Tia Walker

D UE TO GOVERNMENTAL policies that encouraged lower birth rates, Singapore faced an inverted population pyramid. The elderly population began to outnumber the younger population. On a policy level, there became an awareness and growing concern that the shrinking 'younger' population would not have the time or money to care for the elderly population. For the previous twenty-five years, families were not allowed to have more than two children, and if they did, they had to pay the school fees for the child. This was particularly difficult for the Malay families, who were family-centred but were often too poor often to pay school fees and struggled to educate their children.

Early on Professor Pwo called me to his office and told me, in no uncertain terms, that any research or writings I did from his department had to be seen to have come from a Singaporean. I was employed to research the needs of the elderly and what policies might mitigate the current trajectory that would inevitably overwhelm the system.

Singapore was still considered an underdeveloped country, yet as my time unfolded, I realised that it was far more developed in many areas, particularly in the health sector, than the UK and parts of US. The University hospital, equipped with the latest state of the art diagnosis and treatment devices, had me excited to get involved with patients again. Holding a teaching position, yet a clinician at heart, I soon found an outlet midway through my first year. My latest research project, Parkinson's disease and incontinence in the elderly, had me visiting private and religious organisations for data collection where I was able to interact and get involved in patient care again. This led to writing a book for families of Parkinson's patients in conjunction with our Occupational Therapist.

One evening after work, I planned to visit an elderly care facility with a reporter. Having received permission from the administration to observe a few of the patients, we walked around the facility independently. Still dressed in my white lab coat, my presence must have passed as an on-site physician. In most facilities, if a staff spots a visitor, they present their best behaviour. Or that's what I'm going to assume based on what happened next. Clearly overwhelmed with too many responsibilities, I walked into a room where a janitor or low-level staff quickly mopped a patient's room. He looked hurried and frustrated and paid me little attention as I walked into the room. In a language I did not understand, he said something to the patient in a rough and abrupt way. The young man, diagnosed with brain damage had spastic movements that kept him confined to bed. I stood in the corner of the room jotting down a few notes when the janitor went over to the side of his bed and began undressing him. Not particularly gentle with him, given his limited mobility, he quickly pulled his clothes off. What happened next is forever seared in my memory. The janitor went over to the mop bucket, plunged his mop into the muddy water and began to mop the patient while he laid in bed. He rubbed the dirty mop water on his frail chest, with swipes down his leg. The brown water pooled on the sheets of the bed next to his body.

My jaw must have nearly dropped to the ground. There have been few moments in my life where I've been left speechless. Instead of stepping in to stop the mop-bath, I watched, frozen. A few more exchanges took place, and the janitor rolled the man over onto his stomach. He pumped the mop back in the water and began scrubbing his back. It ended as abruptly as it started. By the time I had regained my senses, it was over. He had flipped him back over, tugged his clothes back on and wheeled out of the room. Presumably onto the next room and next poor soul. I looked around for a towel, finding one in some cupboards next to the bathroom. I went over to his bed and tried to dry him and soak up any of the remaining water on his bedsheets. We exchanged a few words in English, with little success, as I tried to assess his state of well-being after experiencing such a demeaning act. Given, the janitor didn't flinch in my presence, and that man didn't put up a fight, mop-baths must have been a common practice. I left his room, found my voice, and asked to speak to the manager. The reporter I was with also found her voice and wrote an article in the newspaper which was taken up by the authorities and after further inspection the home was closed.

Although, I witnessed some of the most grotesque practices towards the elderly in some institutions, I also saw some of the very best.

St Joseph's, headed by Sister Geraldine and Mary Tan, was such an organisation. St Joseph's, which was Catholic based, provided exemplary care not only on a medical level but also in the way they cared for their patients. The staff, nurses and doctors spoke softly, with kindness and patience, helping each person to adapt to the changes in their lives. Getting older is hard. The loss of independence and change in physical and mental function is only amplified if the caretakers don't show compassion for the transition. However, the reverse is also true, and the transition can be very hard for family caretaker. To watch someone you love lose their ability to move, make unsafe decisions and even lose their connection and remembrance of close family members and friends, can cause deep grief even before their death. Compassion for self and others on this journey is key. We are all on different paths yet going through the same journey.

I visited St Joseph's often and developed a close relationship with some of the nurses that later developed into innovative ventures in elderly and palliative care.

I continued to learn about Singapore's customs and traditions. Very progressive and very diverse, I knew it had so much potential to overcome the challenges it faced in public health, geriatric, and palliative care sectors. This became highlighted by Singapore's very own president.

The *Straits Times* was an informative newspaper that kept a pulse on ongoing local and national issues. It even published citizens' responses and commentary to its articles creating a national conversation on key issues. Sometimes, I took advantage of this, highlighting the plights of the elderly, much to the chagrin of the University's administrators. Unmalleable to authority, I never was the teacher's favourite.

The President of Singapore changed several times during my time there. Interestingly, the coming and going presidents came from different ethnic and age groups. One of the presidents, an elderly Indian gentleman, was very well respected but often experienced poor health. On a visit to United States, he saw a geriatrician and came back full of the wonder. How could one physician assist someone with all his different diseases? Whereas in Singapore he saw several specialists for his diabetes, GIT problems, urinary issues, and other problems. The combination of medications was sometimes overlooked, creating an unintended host of side effects. He wrote to the *Straits Times* asking why Singapore did not have 'geriatricians', specialised doctors for the elderly. I immediately responded by writing a letter back to the paper supporting his request for geriatric specialisations. I couldn't have asked for a better spokesperson to highlight this need!

I find that the tide can turn in slow, subtle ways. There is always hope. Not only did the President's personal experiences nationally highlight the need for better elderly care but I also began to find local clubs and organisations that focused on elderly wellbeing. There was a wonderful Chinese cultural club run by an elderly doctor which included social evenings for the elderly with musicians, dancing, and games. It brought so much joy to this community in which isolation and lack of social connection can be a major issue.

Many cared. Many were trying in their own way. I needed to find them. I also needed to find how my experiences, expertise, and talents could help too.

36

Bravehearts

When the establishment doesn't know what to do and sends
people away hopeless, that doesn't mean nothing can be done. It
only presents you with an opportunity to do something different.
The darkness in which we find ourselves, is always rich with
potential and possibilities.

Anne Merriman

Respond to every call that excites your spirit.
Rumi

IN 1985, after doing weekly rounds with the elderly patients at
The Franciscan Sisters Home and St Joseph's, I began giving
occasional short classes on hospice etiquette that the nurses
and Sisters could try to utilise with their patients. After one of
these classes, a few dedicated Sisters and Nurses gathered around
me and spoke up in rapid concession. It was clear they had
something important they wanted to tell me, which had them all
quite upset. They had followed a poor man home from the hospital
who had been discharged. Still very sick, the hospital had sent him
home because there was nothing left they could do for him. He
had cancer and was sent home to die without medical care or
supervision. I had enough experience in the hospital to realise that
patients were being sent home while still frail and very much in
pain, with no analgesics and just being informed there was

nothing else the medical world could do for them or their cancer! I listened to these brave nurses who wanted to do something.

His story was not special. Many have a story like his. The hospital could do no more for him. Even though he was given moderate pain medicine, it did little to quell his screams. Unbearable pain, for months, is not only a horrible way to go, but also a horrible experience for the loved ones to watch, leaving an indelible mark on the living.

I had been living in Singapore for about a year and a half when a group of us decided to do something. Or at least we decided to begin having serious discussions about doing something. A growing number of distraught nurses began talking about how uncomfortable they were with what they saw. They could no longer bear seeing patients turned away from the hospital, sent home to face painful deaths, with no answer to control the suffering. The problem was not well known because people were hidden away from the community in the confines of their homes and there were no survivors in this game. The survivors – family member and close friends – rarely had the reserves to take up advocating for reform after their loved ones had passed away.

We wanted to convene a meeting that gave people the space to talk about what they had seen and to brainstorm options and survey the support and energy levels there were to do something about it. The medical community may have decided there was nothing left to do but I had a feeling we'd come to a different conclusion. We advertised the meeting and put little flyers up throughout the Singapore General Hospital. The news spread by word of mouth, and I was happily surprised with the turnout. A few doctors attended, but not surprisingly, the seats were filled by the nurses. It has always been the nurses that connect with the humanity and suffering of their patients. Not only did we have a good turnout of nurses from SGH, but we also had nurses from other surrounding hospitals.

The meeting was lively, and people shared stories of family, friends and patients they knew that were discharged from the hospital and sent home to face a bleak, destined ending. The stories painted a clear picture of the agony and pain these people endured, hidden away in their homes. I listened, impressed by the passion and heart these women expressed when they shared their stories and searched for other possibilities.

Lynn Alexander

'My boss worked in the same building as Anne. Anne always had her door open and would talk to me and everyone. Despite our twenty-year age gap and difference in position, she seemed genuinely interested in who I was and we developed a lifelong friendship. She came to my wedding, snuck my mum into the delivery room after I had my first child, even though normally only the husbands were allowed, and often smoked with my husband after meals!

'Anne didn't stop. She was always on the go – "How can I connect this person with that person?" Anne was unique, open to differences. She had an edge to her and could be polarising. She wouldn't blindly go along with something if she didn't agree with it. People could be shocked by her, especially if she shook things up too much or they felt threatened. They wouldn't confront her directly but would air their grievances with others. Anne would get hurt. It felt personal to her. But she was so passionate about what she did. She'd always rise back up and wouldn't let it deter her from her mission.

'Anne had a charismatic personality. Very friendly, cheerful, committed and caring, with a wonderful sense of humour and mischief! She won a lot of people over and really connected with her students. But it must have required a leap of courage to support this unconventional doctor in her cause. Those who joined her were adventurous and really believed in the mission. They shared Anne's spirit and heart.'

*

Sitting in the meeting, in a country far away from home, I knew I was exactly where I was supposed to be. This was not a mystical calling, like what I had experienced in the Lake District when I *knew* I would give my life to Christ. This time I knew something needed to be done and I knew I had been given the experience and knowledge to do something about it. My background in Liverpool while working with Prof. Jimmy Williamson and my time at Whiston and St Helens had prepared me for the type of home care service we needed to create in Singapore. We discussed the possibility of starting a home care team that would travel to people's homes and provide hospice assistance. A few dedicated nurses with myself, formed a small team of volunteers that would visit patients outside of working hours and on weekends.

At the end of the meeting, two Sisters from St Joseph's Home for the Elderly approached me. Sister Geraldine, who previously trained in palliative care in London at the Royal Marsden, and Sister Mary Tan were both very interested in the positive outcome of the meeting and offered to be a part of the initiative. The Canossian Sisters offered to provide 16 beds for hospice care for those who needed intermittent relief. Although we'd be developing a palliative home care service that visited people in their homes, beds were occasionally needed for temporary admission in case things in the home were not right. Again, I felt amazed by these Sisters. Powerful in action and driven by compassion, they had the gall to do more than talk about what needed to be done.

Unsure of where it would lead didn't matter, they had the courage to begin. These ladies are the unknown, unsung heroes, the Bravehearts, that quietly led Singapore to a higher path. And so it was, a group of volunteers formed the 'Hospice Care Group' and later to become Home Care Association (HCA).

37

The Seed Is Planted

Don't despise these small beginnings,
for the lord rejoices to see the work begin.
Zechariah, 4:10

From a small seed a mighty trunk may grow.
Aeschylus

IN 1985, the volunteer operation began out of my little flat on McAllister Road. We had no money. Three nurses and myself were working in our spare time as volunteers. We used my car and petrol to see the patients. Anything extra we needed also came out of my salary. Anyone who has pursued a labour of love knows your bank account will also bear the marks.

We started putting flyers all over the hospital and talking with SGH staff about potential discharges that might need palliative care in their homes. The networking required to learn of potential patients was critical. When I was advised about a potential patient, I'd notify the nurses to see who could be available and most of the time we'd make visits as a team and kept case sheets for each patient. The nurses, new to palliative care, learned quickly. We were all learning, all the time, from one patient to the next. Their difficulties helped us learn how to better help the next individual and their family. When people think about hospice work, they often think about the elderly. But death is a suitor to all.

There are always patients that leave a deep-seated mark on your memory. Clare had large soft brown eyes that twinkled as she'd laugh with her little brother. Just nine years of age, unaware of what it meant to feel sorry for herself, she embodied a joy for life. This girl had a sarcoma in her rectum which had metastasised to her spine and threatened paraplegia. We managed to avoid paraplegia in the beginning by giving her steroids. However, the effects only lasted so long, and a second dose of steroids was no longer effective.

'Will I ever be able to walk again or go back to school?' she asked solemnly one evening during a visit.

I grasped her hand and responded as honestly as I could in a manner that still respected the fragility of such a question.

'It doesn't appear so,' I said softly.

She reacted instantly, letting out a piercing scream that transitioned into sobs. Children cope in such a natural state. Acknowledging the pain and heartbreak and letting it express itself. Giving voice to the pain and emotion. She really cried and let everyone know how torn she was. The entire family enfolded around her, and they all cried together. It was heartbreaking and yet so touching to see the love and compassion. I came back two days later, and she was sitting up in bed smiling with her brothers and sister!

It's always been interesting to watch the difference between adults and children when they receive hard, life-changing news. Adults often find it difficult to even register the scope and related emotions of their new circumstances, let alone demonstrate or express their emotions. This can often lead to suppressed and prolonged grief and sadness. This girl illustrated the depth of the human spirit in a span of a few days, showing such resolute qualities and cycling through grief, heartbreak, vulnerability, resilience, and courage. Her family, in great support, mirrored her emotions, although you could feel their sadness for a much longer time.

I found it truly inspiring to see the compassion and support the families in Singapore gave their sick. I watched husbands crying with and for their wives when they suffered. Not something I witnessed regularly with Indians and Chinese. There were great family bonds amongst these people and culture. When you are doing hard work with those who are suffering, seeing the love, tenderness, and strength amidst the pain, made the work incredibly rewarding.

38

The Game Changer

There are no rules here, we are trying to accomplish something.
Thomas Edison

If challenges exist, so must the solutions.
Rona Mlnarik

O UR SMALL volunteer group felt the wall of pain in Singapore. The people were suffering and based on the trajectory of the population, the situation we faced was only going to grow. As we grew, the Singapore Cancer Society provided strategic shelter for our cause.

My experience in geriatric medicine, palliative care and community medicine gave me a solid foundation to begin exploring solutions to this growing issue. The intravenous morphine that was being used in the hospitals couldn't be used in patient's homes. I was just so upset about what I was seeing in the wards. Intravenous morphine has a ceiling and people kept getting side effects. Plus, you can't go home. Like everyone else, they wanted to die at home. So, they'd send them home to high-rise flats without any care. I scoured the literature and read as many of Dame Cicely Saunders' reports and manuals as I could get my hands on. Based on some of the suggestions she discussed I had a simple idea. To effectively control the pain, pure oral morphine would need to be titrated against the pain, regularly. An oral solution also made it easier for family members to administer it at home.

In Singapore, the only oral solution with morphine was the 'Brompton Cocktail', which contained not only morphine sulphate powder but also a sedative such as chlorpromazine and other doctor-prescribed additives, including alcohol, such as gin or whisky. A true cocktail. The trouble is it led to side effects, making it difficult to understand if the resultant drowsiness was due to the morphine, the sedative or the alcohol! With pure morphine, when the patient becomes drowsy the dose is too high. If the patient is alert and the pain is still there, the doses are too low. The mix of sedatives and alcohol would often mean the patient is aware of pain even if drowsy. It was clear we needed a better solution.

Cynthia Goh, a beautiful Chinese lady in her early thirties, had returned from UK with her husband where she had studied and obtained MRCP. Before going to UK, she had approached the Governmnet about commencing palliative care but this had been refused becaue of the experiences of Sago Lane death houses.

She dressed immaculately and spoke in a perfect Queen's English. She was a go-getter, balancing the responsibilities of a wife and mother of two with work.

Cynthia and I had begun collaborating when we decided to ask the Chief Pharmacist at the new University Hospital (NUH) to develop a pure morphine formula that could be easily titrated against a patients' pain. From this, NUH pharmacy produced the first formula of affordable, pure oral morphine. It consisted of only three ingredients: morphine powder, water, and a preservative. (Later, to differentiate the strength of the morphine by colour, dye was added.) This formula was a game changer for two primary reasons: (1) it was so cheap, and (2) it effectively titrated against the pain without heavy side effects.

There would be no party. No big celebration. But oral morphine changed the game. Not only for those we cared for in Singapore, but for other regions in the world where curative treatment is not an option and events like cancer equate to a death sentence. This formula of reconstituted oral morphine became the only affordable and accessible Step 3 analgesic and would later open the gate to palliative care across Africa.

In 1986, the Universe further conspired to give palliative and elderly care a more public platform in Singapore.

The World Health Organisation sent out the best seller, *Cancer Pain Control* to every national government. Singapore's Minister of Health was very upset because his sister had died the previous year in severe pain and upon reading the findings in this book, he realised it could have been controlled. He called a meeting of all interested parties, of which I attended. There was great opposition to morphine in the meeting, but they all agreed in the end, morphine was needed for end of life care and pain control.

In the United Kingdom, the UK Geriatric Society provided tremendous value. I talked with several of my colleagues, who would have greater insight and understanding of the cultural sensitivities needed for it to be more accepted.

In 1986, in collaboration with my colleagues Phua, Goh Lee Gan and Kua Ee Heok, we spearheaded the formation of the Gerontological Society. Created from a multi-disciplinary group, it served as a platform that gave patients and families a louder voice in patient care, and more resources and knowledge. It also promoted collaboration between organisations, gerontology training and research and organised educational seminars, publications and networking events. It turned out to be very successful, driven by great leadership from the Singaporean nationals.

Greater awareness around caring for the elderly and those dying was gaining national momentum.

39

Bearing Witness

The nature of humanity, its essence, is to feel another's pain as one's own, and to act to take that pain away. There is nobility in compassion, a beauty in empathy, grace in forgiveness.
John Connolly

There is no coming to consciousness without pain.
Carl Jung

IT'S A STRANGE thing. To so many people, so many issues don't really matter until it happens to them. To their life. Or to someone they love. Then the direct experience, often imbued with pain, creates meaning and opens a space for understanding and empathy. It introduces compassion. It creates a crack in the soul, in which God can work miracles. The imperfections of our lives. Our trauma. Pain. That is how the light gets in.

We are all going to die. And most of us don't slip away in our sleep. Something that isn't very nice will probably take the majority of us. And it won't take us immediately. In times and places where there is no access to proper medicine, inadequate economic and social infrastructure, no specialised health care training – what happens? Dying without dignity. Dying with uncontrolled pain. These are just words to most of us. But bearing witness to it, moves the witness.

*

Choon Sin was in her early thirties. She designed jewellery and specialised in gorgeous hand-crafted rings. Choon Sin fell in love with Francis, a younger man and the two got married on 27 December 1987. They decided to take their honeymoon on the Chinese new year. While on honeymoon in Thailand, Choon Sin developed abdominal pain. What began as light cramps turned into more intense and unending pain. Returning to Singapore, she was diagnosed with stomach cancer. After conducting certain tests, it was determined there was nothing that could be done for her. It would be an unbeatable cancer, and she was sent home to die.

Her husband had quit his job to be with her during her final days. But there weren't days. There were months. Twelve months to be precise, of a slow, but not too slow, road to death. He stayed with her and helplessly watched her as the pain got worse. By chance he heard about a voluntary clinical unit that was helping relieve the pain of cancer patients in their homes. We found both Choon Sin and her husband in horrible pain.

Choon Sin had obstruction of the bowels. The resulting cramps had her crumpled up in bed crying and moaning. Disturbing is not quite the right word to use. I could see the exhaustion and panic on both her and her husband's faces when we first arrived. We immediately gave her morphine. I left feeling confident that it would help.

The morphine did very little to soothe Choon Sin's pain. The cancer she faced presented a very difficult case. We continued to increase the morphine dose to no avail. One evening, called my private residence, and I could hear Choon Sin in the background wailing. Unsure of what to do, I knew I needed to seek the advice of a specialist. I immediately called Mary Baines, a dear friend and palliative care specialist in London who was the first doctor to join Dame Cicely Saunders in 1968. Incredibly helpful and knowledgeable, Mary provided ongoing consultation until we eventually worked out a combination of drugs that stopped Choon Sin's pain and let her rest comfortably. Combination drug therapy is used in the most complex of cases.

Now her pain was managed for the first time in months. When our team visited, I could see the indelible mark of grief in Francis' eyes, yet some of the light had returned. To be with a loved one who is unable to escape from the grip of pain, day or night, is its own torture. For the loved ones bearing witness, they are faced with an avalanche of emotional pain and inner crisis. But now, Chu Sin and her husband could be still. Have a conversation with each other again. Smile at each other again. Breathe and sleep again.

Two days before she died, I visited and found them both smiling. I did not know that Choon Sin had been designing jewelry in the shop she worked in. She gave me a beautiful friendship (pinky) ring she tht she had designed and made for me, which I still wear today and use it to tell her story.

She died on 28 December 1988, exactly one year and one day after her wedding. Francis kept in touch with me for years.

I believe my work with my patients helped heal my own soul as much as it has helped theirs. Bearing witness to my patient's struggles and helping them see past the pain has been an honour.

*

(The experience I described above was captured in the writing of *International Geriatric Medicine* my first handbook published by PG Publishers, Singapore, in 1989. I wanted more practitioners to have more available knowledge to deal with complex pain management, especially for the elderly that have multiple underlying conditions. Rosalie Shaw wrote a beautiful book that goes into greater depth about the patients and families she worked with. Rosalie joined Singapore from Perth where she was a specialist in palliative care and continued to spearhead the movement with Cynthia Goh after I left in 1990.)

40

The Shadow Self

In order for us to liberate the energy of our strength, our weakness must
first have a chance to reveal itself.
Paulo Coelho

To be ourselves causes us to be exiled by many others and yet to comply
with what others want causes us to be exiled from ourselves.
Clarissa Pinkola Estés,
Women Who Run with the Wolves

IT'S IMPOSSIBLE to get along and meet the expectations of
everyone, especially if they go against who you are and the
expectations you have for yourself. Deeply seated in my
identity is the need to speak my truth, even at my own
detriment, and often at the offence of those around me. They say
your greatest qualities are also your greatest weaknesses. I can
relate to this saying. My ability to speak my mind forcefully and
say what I believe, often followed by action, has led to many
interesting moments in my life as I may have already alluded to
in previous chapters.

In Singapore, I often found myself using the local newspaper
as a platform for my inner thoughts. Sometimes these thoughts
were related to public and community health issues, sometimes
they were not. Either way, my university superiors were not fond
of my uncensored dialogues on public platforms. Looking back, I
can see how some of the things I wrote and said may have caused
a little whiplash. One time, I managed to get a politically incorrect
diatribe of mine published in the local paper called 'Chinese
Women in Pyjamas'. The piece was about how I had heard many

(post menopausal) women lament about how their husbands stopped paying attention to them. Yet, none of them took good care of themselves and they dressed in pyjamas all day. I went on to write that maybe if they stopped dressing in nightwear during the daylight hours their men might be more interested! At the time, it felt like something that needed to be said. In retrospect, it amazes me they let a white, foreigner publish such remarks in their local papers! But times were different. I can clearly see why the university heads rolled. Not surprisingly, I received a very stern talking to from the university. And not surprisingly, it didn't have that much effect on my future censors.

As I was getting closer to the end of my three-year contract, the head of department, Prof. Poon Wai On, called me in and told me in laymen's terms that he was sold a pup with me. I had come highly recommended and had not performed up to my potential or value. I was patient-centred, and he was result-orientated in public health papers. All this, together with my occasional articles in the local papers, meant that my future contract renewal wasn't looking bright. However, soon after, Prof. Poon Wai moved to Australia. It was rumoured he had looked into running for President against President Lee Kwan Yew and the political climate had become too dicey!

In my good fortune, Prof. Lee Hin Peng took over and renewed my contract for another three years! The department moved into the new medical school National University of Singapore (NUS). I continued to research urinary incontinence and Parkinson's disease in the elderly. I wrote two books, one a handbook on caring for patients with Parkinson's disease and the other was called *International Geriatric Medicine.* The latter provided information on community care of the elderly, international diabetes and palliative care from the public health approach. It also had a chapter on palliative care for the elderly and gave training programmes on how to make and use oral morphine.

Outside of my career at the University, our little volunteer palliative care unit grew. By 1987, over 60 nurses had volunteered their time and we had visited over 50 patients. HCG volunteers also served at St Joseph's Home and All Saints Home. But not only did we continue to get referrals for patients who had been sent home, but we also received requests from the general practitioners who wanted to learn more about geriatric medicine and palliative care. By 1987, I felt like we had gained enough experience to commence training health professionals, including doctors, nurses, pharmacists, and lay people from the community.

We began teaching training courses and seminars for healthcare practitioners on how to provide palliative care for the dying. The courses went beyond medical training and also focused on how to respond to the emotional and spiritual needs of the patient and their families. We taught the need to be respectful of people's different religious and spiritual beliefs, and to be careful not to impose your beliefs on them. The goal is for them to reach peace with themselves and their families. In the early days, I'd provide a series of eight classes, scheduled in the late evening from 8.00 pm to 10.00 pm, so everyone could attend after work. The turnout for these courses was very successful and, based on the content from the classes, we wrote up a curriculum for general practitioners both in geriatric medicine and palliative care.

I remember one night I was particularly tired. I needed to take a nap before I went to teach at 8.00 pm. The phone rang at 9.30 pm. Through my blurry tired consciousness, I could hear a panic-stricken voice. 'Are you OK, Dr Merriman?'

'I was until you woke me up,' I laughed. After he realised I was alright and had just missed my alarm he delivered the news that one of the other GPs had been murdered. Such a tragic event. Maybe I was meant to miss my alarm. However, in Singapore, everything runs like clockwork and the culture is very punctual. It was something I never forgot, and I tried to never take a nap again before I gave a lecture! I continued to conduct seminars and classes until I left Singapore in 1990.

*

I know I am far from perfect. I know my brash and insensitive ways have hurt and offended people over the years. I apologise to all the people to whom I have misspoken or lashed out in anger. I apologise to colleagues I have coarsely disagreed with about the direction of mission, ethos and policy work. Yet, I find it amazing that God has used this blemish as one of my greatest strengths for his purpose. It has allowed me to be a forceful and obstinate advocate in the hospice/palliative care world where most of the advocates perish. It has allowed me to bullheadedly push against governments and ministers who did not yet understand the importance of morphine and pain control for those who are dying. It has allowed me to hold sway in cultures where women did not take positions of leadership.

When open to providence's path, this blemish has been transformed into strength and power to act on behalf of my patients who no longer had that ability to fight for their rights, tell their stories and the need for reform. Embracing this aspect of who I am has been an important part of my journey, and yet, it has definitely been a challenge to moderate this quality when the occasion didn't call for it. It has clearly got me into trouble and hurt people. Part of my inner work has not only been accepting this part of myself as a great tool and blessing but also learning when it is not needed and not appropriate. I believe everyone has qualities and parts of themselves they must boldly embrace, parts of themselves that you might want to repress, parts that are counterculture and may get them in trouble. These parts, if accepted and embraced by ourselves, provide the fire of creation and the fuel to be something greater. Yet, if the fire is not moderated it can needlessly blaze out of control, burning those around us and counteracting our purpose. This is work we all must learn on providence's path. I am still learning it.

41
The Call Back

Coincidences mean you're on the right path.
Simon Van Booy

THROUGH ONGOING immersion and constant interaction with patients and their families, I slowly became more sensitised to Singapore's culture and how a medical home care system could be adapted to fit their needs. I was amazed at how my previous work had prepared me for what we saw and gave practical insight and ideas on how to respond.

HCG (Home Care Group) continued to grow beyond our capacity. We continued to get busier and busier. We had already cared for over 130 terminally ill patients. When a distressed family member came to us, it was impossible to turn anyone away. We knew the dismal reality they were facing at home behind closed doors. The evenings and weekends did not hold enough time to see everyone that needed help.

Yet, we needed more resources not only to respond to our current workload but to cast a greater net. We fit under the umbrella of the Singapore Cancer Society.

They gave us a little desk but we were 100 per cent volunteer powered. However, through providence, Lady Percy McNiece, daughter of Loke Cheng-Kim, wrote to the Singapore Cancer Society and said she wanted to donate money directly to HCG. The Loke Cheng-Kim Foundation pledged to give HCG $40,000 for three years to pay for a full-time nurse! By December 1987, Nurse Leekiang Chua began working for the Hospice Care Group as our first paid nurse coordinator (and continued with Hospice Care Association until 2000!). Not only did she conduct home visits, but she also helped coordinate all the volunteers including nurses, doctors and lay people as well as schedule meetings and network with religious groups and other related organisations and individuals. She also played a major role in organising several conferences we held.

'Anne was the loveliest doctor anyone could ever work with. She was so warm with her patients. She gave them her phone number, and if they called in the middle of the night, she'd pick up and go. Sometimes, she'd stay with them for hours, especially if they were dying. There are a lot of poor people in Singapore... Anne would write a prescription for someone, and if they couldn't pay, she'd go pay for it herself and bring it back to them. That's just how Anne is.

'But Anne would also step on people's toes and push and push if she felt right about something. There are people that can't stand her because she pushed them. But without Anne, there would be no palliative care in Singapore.' – *Nurse Leekiang Chua, first salaried nurse for HCG*

*

With the help of early donors, including the Loke Cheng-Kim Foundation, the British Association of Singapore and the Reuben Meyer Trust Fund, this movement continued to gain steam. By the end of 1988, we were looking after 130 patients. Overstretched, even with Nurse Chua, it was time to contemplate transitioning Hospice Care Group to Hospice Care Association, a legally registered society, that would be able to receive more government sanctioned funds and monetary funds from other donors. Many people came together to help in this effort including Cynthia Goh, Dr Vijay Sethi, Sister Geraldine, Teddy Lim and many more. We applied in early 1989 and waited for approval.

In 1989, the world was changing rapidly. *Time* magazine heralded 1989 as the Year that Changed the World. The collapse of the Berlin Wall had most of the world in cheers and yet the Tiananmen Square Massacre and World Series Earthquake in San Francisco left the world in shock. My life would once again dramatically shift course. I was coming to the end of my second three-year contract and unsure what my next move would be.

While we waited our new status, the Hospice Care Group, in partnership with the Minister of Health, Singapore General Hospital, National University Hospital and Mount Elizabeth Medical Centre, facilitated the first regional hospice conference in October 1989. We wanted to raise awareness and educate countries on the importance of this work and the work and progress that we had made in Singapore as well as what other countries were doing. An astounding success, the conference was attended by 250 delegates from ten countries. I've been told that this conference led Malaysia to start its first palliative care unit under the National Cancer Society of Malaysia. The ripples continued.

At the conference, Robert Twycross, a British pioneer in palliative care, attended. I have always considered Robert 'the first son' of Dame Cicely Saunders. His research, training and publications have been jewels to us working in palliative care, bringing knowledge, inspiration and care to so many countries in the world. At the conference, I met Robert's personal assistant, a wonderful British lady, who was a member of the Board of a new venture in palliative care in Nairobi, Kenya. She urged me to apply for their post in Nairobi Hospice, as their first Medical Director.

I knew I eventually wanted to return to Africa. The timing of God always amazes me. I agreed to fly to Kenya for an interview.

A system can work wonderfully in a certain culture with a certain economic and social infrastructure and fall flat on its face in another. Yet, a small tweak or missing puzzle piece is all that's needed to shift the calculation of success. I'd realize this all too soon, on a different continent with many different cultures.

42

The Queen of England

It has been women who have breathed gentleness and care into the harsh
progress of mankind.
Queen Elizabeth, 1966 Christmas broadcast

Our modern world places such heavy demands on our time and attention
that the need to remember our responsibilities
to others is greater than ever.
Queen Elizabeth, 2002 Christmas broadcast

Each day is a new beginning, I know that the only way to live my life is to
try to do what is right, to take the long view, to give of my best in all that
the day brings, and to put my trust in God.
Queen Elizabeth, 2002 Christmas broadcast

It's worth remembering that it is often the small steps, not the giant leaps,
that bring about the most lasting change.
Queen Elizabeth, 2019 Christmas broadcast

MY FLIGHT for my interview in Kenya was on the same
night as a party being held by the British High
Commission. I never missed a party, and this would be
no exception. Although it made my logistics a little more
challenging, this party would be worth it. The Queen of England
and the Duke of Edinburgh would both be attending.

Albeit a strange system to outsiders, the British monarchy has
existed over a thousand years and lays entrenched in the British
system, government, culture, and our people. The tradition and

history of William the Conqueror, Richard the Lionheart, Edward I, Henry V, Elizabeth I, Queen Victoria and others makes the monarch in the United Kingdom take on a life of its own. It has stood the test of time and is still active in the twenty-first century. Although in many parts of the worlds this type of system is loathed and considered outdated, we loved our Queen. Or more accurately, I loved our Queen. Only a decade older than myself, I felt like I had watched her whole life unfold. The way she conducted herself and overcame challenges and political snafus, while always bearing such dignity, grace, and consistency, even as a young woman, was commendable to say the least. I deeply admired her journey through life, which gave women of the world a positive and strong role model. Of which there were almost none at her level of status.

Every British person and related family, friend, acquaintance, or colleague tried to get on the guest list for that party. The Queen in Singapore would be the highlight of the year for most people. I wore a beautiful green lace dress that had black jewels beaded into the ruffles. Cars continuously dropped people off at the gates. Dazzling gowns and tuxedos were on display as people wore their closets best. The British High Commission pulled out all the stops – the champagne was flowing, the food was Singapore's best and the décor was fit for a queen – The Queen.

I mingled in and out of conversations. I always enjoyed these occasions. It was a wonderful opportunity to catch up with so many people in one place. I also never missed an opportunity to advocate for the work we were doing. It created a perfect opportunity to network and also raise funds, volunteers, and awareness.

'Anne was incredibly well connected. She would seek out the mover and shakers. Get the things she needed, develop her role, whatever it was she was doing, she'd make it happen. We were visiting Anne on a holiday in Singapore, and she knew someone who got us upgraded. Would you like to go sailing? I know someone who has a boat at the Yatch Club. Anne never lost touch with people. People would become her family wherever she went.' – *Ged Faulks*

*

And then it was time. The music changed to signal the incoming royalty. The Commission tapped his fork on his glass and everyone's attention turned to the opening doors.

The Queen was smaller than I expected – a few inches smaller than myself. I honestly don't remember what she was wearing other than she fit the part and emanated regal authority.

'Thank you for having us here today,' Her Majesty began in her renowned imperial tone and accent. Standing next to her, Prince Philip matched her air and his striking physique and looks made them a striking couple. Her comments were short and sensible, leaving everyone wanting more, yet fully satisfied with having the opportunity to have been in the same room as the Queen and the Duke. It's not every day that us commoners get such opportunities!

After the speech, everyone milled between the different rooms talking and drinking. The truly distinguished and upper class had the opportunity to have a conversation with the Queen and/or the Duke. Lynn and I were talking when I heard my name mentioned above the buzz of conversations. Interestingly, it was coming from the direction of the Queen.

I turned to make eye contact with the British High Commissioner who was standing next to the Queen.

'There she is!' he said waving me over. 'This is the woman who started palliative care in Singapore!' Quite the introduction to the Queen of England if I do say so myself! Humbled and a little embarrassed, I somehow found myself standing next to Queen Elizabeth.

Her erect carriage complimented her dignified manner. Beneath the veneer of polite niceties Her Majesty emanated an endurance and strength required to hold reins in a man's world.

The Queen smiled at me. 'Pleased to meet you,' she said, holding out her hand, gloved in white silk up to her elbow. 'And how on earth did you manage to do that?'

The conversations flowed from Dame Cicely Saunders, to setting up the first volunteer community outreach clinic, to working out of my bedroom and highlighting the amazing spirit of the Singaporean people that would carry this work on. The Queen and Duke were most attentive. The Queen knew Dame Saunders and was impressed that her work had stretched across the globe to Singapore.

I curtsied when our conversation came to a natural ending. The Queen and Duke had been more than generous with their time. And I had lost track of time! Mother of Mary, I had a plane to catch! I frantically glanced down at my watch. It was 7.00 pm and my plane left at 8.00 pm! Goodness! That meant my plane began boarding in thirty minutes!

*

I rushed to the airport, still entranced from my regal encounter. When I checked in for my flight the lady across the counter glared at me. 'But the plane is leaving right now!' she said in a gruff voice. 'This is very irresponsible of you.' I found whenever the cultural codes were broken, everyone found it quite within their right to dress you down. Despite this, the lady still went to exceptional lengths to ensure I made my flight. I may have let it slip I had met the Queen of England and was dreadfully sorry, but what can you do in such situations? The concierge personally escorted me, at a run, to my gate. I sat comfortably on the plane as the wheels lifted from the ground.

Albeit the first, it would not be the last time I had the chance to meet the Queen of England. Twenty years later, I'd get to meet the Queen again in Uganda. There are some conversations that one side will remember but the other side may not. The Queen was delighted to meet me again for the first time, and again we talked about palliative care in Uganda and Africa.

May she rest in peace.

43
Angels by Candlelight

We can deny angels exist, convince ourselves they can't be real. But they
show up anyway, at strange places and at strange times.

Douglas Adams

I FELT AN ALIVENESS stir in me as I stepped off the plane at the
Nairobi airport. The dark air sprinkled rain on my face as I
stepped on the tarmac. The sun would be rising within the next
hour and already you could see the lower horizon turn
luminescent oranges and yellows. Will this be where I go next? I
wondered. I walked towards the airport door filled with
excitement. After being dropped off at my hotel and given time to
rest, I was picked up around noon by one of the Nairobi Hospice
staff. Nairobi Hospice was the first hospice in Africa to be
established with the needs of the African patients in mind. Ruth
Wooldridge, a nurse and wife of BBC correspondent Mike
Wooldridge, witnessed patients leaving the hospital in severe
pain. Deeply struck, she formed the Nairobi Hospice Charitable
Trust in the United Kingdom and began to raise funds for the
hospice movement in Kenya.

Jane Moore, a nurse from the United Kingdom and Brigid
Sirengo, a Kenyan nurse – both employed by Nairobi Hospice –
took me around and showed me the challenging conditions they
were facing. I remember going on a home visit to see a middle-
aged woman who had been discharged after receiving
chemotherapy for her facial tumour. Her face, terribly disfigured
by the cancer, improved little with the chemotherapy. The growth

293

and pain continued after she was discharged. I felt sickened knowing the strongest medication the nurses could give her was codeine. Codeine was not nearly strong enough for these types of cases and it was expensive. Only the rich could afford it, which often meant the Asians. But I was uplifted to see the commitment and heart from Jane and Brigid. One evening, they made time to see an elderly gentleman. I watched as they worked by his side in the darkness of a small wooden hut, reading their case sheets by candlelight. Still to this day, this scene is etched in my mind.

I stayed for about a week. I became more familiar with the local medical facilities and their practices surrounding homecare visits. Aware of the potential and need, it was in these conditions and places where this work was most needed. They offered me the position as medical director before I left. Although I wanted to join this organisation, I could not accept the position if I did not have the tools to be successful. I let them know I would only come if they were able to get and make oral morphine. There needed to be an affordable morphine solution for all the patients in need. It is nearly impossible to holistically look after the patient if the pain is not first stopped. And selfishly, I knew I couldn't bear seeing patients in such pain, for which I could do little for. I departed, leaving the book *International Geriatric Medicine* with the nurses, the formula for oral morphine with the board and the address of where they could get the powder morphine from.

Working in these conditions would be a great challenge. I had seen very hard things throughout my life. But in Kenya, the poverty and lack of socio-economic development heightened the pain crisis. However, I believe God had guided my path, preparing me for this next step with Angels by candlelight showing me the way.

*

There are people all over the world, unseen by the media and the public, doing great things, making great sacrifices. Serving others. Overcoming the 'hard'. Facing insurmountable challenges. Their reward may never manifest in fame or fortune. And beyond the services they provide, the people they help, the systems they implement, the products they create – the real reward is the transformation that is happening in the unseen. For when we die, we are left with only one thing. Our souls. The true reward for life is polishing our greatest eternal jewel.

44

The Master Bedroom

We have a 'strategic' plan it's called doing things.
Herb Kelleher, Southwest Airlines Cofounder

It's not about ideas. It's about making ideas happen.
Scott Belsky, Behance Co-founder

I RETURNED to Singapore with my contract coming to an end. Although my university work was winding down, our little organisation was gaining steam. As we continued to wait for our official status as a society, we needed more space. Although we were given an old clinic on Stevens Road for our community palliative care nurses, it still needed to be renovated. So, like all labours of love, we began the Hospice Care Association out of my flat on Gillman Heights. With my contract finishing at the end of the year, the University of Singapore was incredibly gracious and allowed me to keep my flat until I made arrangements to leave without having to put my things in storage. So, we worked out of my flat for nearly a year, even after my contract had finished.

I had one air-conditioned room in the whole apartment – the master bedroom – so we converted that room into the main office.

Lynn Alexander recalls the kitchen table piled high with documents, papers and books. Nurse Chua comments that it was 'always a mess, but Anne knew where everything was. Once I tidied it up, and then it became a real mess for her!'

I even wrote an article in the *Singapore Medical Journal*, titled 'The Master Bedroom'. The Master Bedroom team consisted of myself, Nurse Chua, Nurse Tye May Lee, Sally Tan who served as an administrator and later we hired Dr Anthony Tham. They came every day to work there. We'd also have committee meetings there and I'd meet regularly with Cynthia Goh and Sr Geraldine.

*

'Anne was deeply involved with HCA at the begining. A small group of us worked out of her flat for over a year. She always made lunch for me. She treated me and my girls like family. She'd have everyone over on Christmas day for lunch, and she cooked everything. My family enjoys a microwaved scrambled eggs now and again and I will remind them that I learned how to do that from Auntie Anne. My daughter became a GP and later volunteered with Anne in Uganda.' – *Nurse Leekiang Chua*

*

The Hospice Care Association was finally approved by the registrar on 4 December 1989. Hospice Care Group transitioned to Hospice Care Association and became the first service provider in Singapore dedicated solely to hospice and palliative care. At the time, St Joseph's Home and Assisi Home were also providing palliative care services under their umbrella. I felt excitement and appreciation for the wonderful leadership and initiative of those around me. As an official society, we received support from the Community Chest of Singapore. The Community Chest was a local donation fund where people donated money from their salaries every month to support the poorer people and to support charities. A fitting symbol for the heart of the Singaporean people. The lady in charge, Winnie, a caring Chinese lady, was so good to us. Knowing we had applied with the registrar, the Chest already budgeted and approved salaries once our status was approved for a medical director, two nurses, a social worker, and an administrative assistant. At this point in time, we had cared for 450 patients, trained 145 nurses, 44 doctors and 140 lay volunteers through our seminars and classes. Dr Cynthia Goh served as the first medical director of HCA, providing tremendous energy, networking, dedication and leadership to HCA.

Shortly after HCA was formed, President Wee Kim Wee organised a garden party for special organisations. President Wee Kim Wee was a lovely man, seen as a grandfather figure and had a strong following. HCA was among one of the organisations invited. I was able to invite many staff and volunteers. I took full advantage to letting those at the top know all about the mission and ethos!

The hospice movement would continue to be spearheaded by Dr Cynthia Goh, Sr Geraldine Tan and Dr Rosalie Shaw. I had planned on leaving when HCA got off the ground. The organisation had air. It was time to find my next journey.

'Word spread fast about the HCG and it grew quite quickly. When the organisation become more formalised and turned into HCA, more doctors and governmental agencies became involved. Anne still wanted to influence its direction and it must have been hard to hand over the reins. But I know she fondly kept in touch with everyone and was deeply proud of Singapore's progress and how her colleagues took up the torch.' – *Lynn Alexander*

Coming Full Circle

Hospice Care Association in Singapore is one of the best in the world. The current (2022) clinical director of HCA was one of my medical students. Twenty years after leaving Singapore I was invited to speak at a palliative care conference in Kinabalu, the town below Mount Kinabalu. Memories from the past made me excited to see the mountain if only from afar and also reconnect with many of my Singapore friends who were also speaking.

After arriving, I got into the lift one morning to go to breakfast, when a tall Singaporean with sweat dripping from his brow got into the lift with me. Wearing athletic gear, he had clearly just finished his workout. He looked at me and then did a quick double take, his eyes lighting up.

'Are you Anne Merriman?'

'I am.' I responded with a smile on my face yet wondering who he was. As if knowing my thoughts he responded, 'You taught me about palliative care when I was a medical student! Word got around that you were visiting patients in their homes. My grandfather was very ill, so I asked if you would come visit him.

You agreed! We went together and you helped take care of him and make him more comfortable.'

Chong Poh Heng, now forty, had been in general practice since qualifying. However, he told me he was contemplating specialising in palliative care. The experience he had with his grandfather and watching how palliative care had really helped him had a strong impact on him. After reconnecting in the lift, we stayed in touch. I learned that Poh Heng applied and was accepted for the special training to become a Consultant in Palliative Medicine! Years later when I visited Singapore, he had become the Medical Director of Hospice Care Association, which had started out of my master bedroom years and years ago. Reflecting on the intricate web God can weave leaves me in awe.

I was recently very sick with Covid in Liverpool, UK. In quarantine all alone, one of the first people to contact me outside of my small circle was Poh Heng. As the news of my illness had spread to Singapore, he called to see how I was doing and if he could do anything to help. I was really touched. A true son!

45
Africa's Elixir

The only trust required is to know that when there is one ending
there will be another beginning.
Clarissa Pinkola Estés
Women Who Run with the Wolves

I HAD KEPT in touch with Nairobi Hospice's board and knew
they were doing everything they could to meet my requests.
Professor E. Kasili, Oncologist and Chairman of the Board,
was having success working with the government to get oral
morphine made in Kenya. Although things looked promising,
they still had a few obstacles to clear.

I had enough in savings to catch my breath and return to
Liverpool for a short holiday. I relished the opportunity to catch
up with friends and family. Although never one to stay idle for
long I began working on a request from Cynthia Goh. Cynthia
asked me to write a practical book on palliative care practice
before I left. I wrote to Dr Derek Doyle, the Medical Director of
St Columba's Hospice in Edinburgh, and asked his permission to
produce a second edition of his book *Pain and Symptom Control
in Terminal Care*. With his permission, I went to work. While
waiting to hear from the board in Kenya, I holed up in the Lake
District and finished editing a version I thought would be
beneficial for Singapore.

I'm not sure why the edited version of Dr Doyle's book was
never published in Singapore. Although I was hurt at the time, it
wasn't completely lost. In future years after additional editing for

Sub-Saharan Africa, it later became known colloquially as the 'Yellow Book' in Nairobi and the 'Blue Book' in Uganda and would be destined for the rest of Africa. I always find it interesting to reflect how painful experiences or events are not always personal and can reveal a higher purpose.

I returned to Singapore and tended to the new blossoms of HCA. Just as I was getting good leads on other jobs, word came from Kenya. For the first time, affordable, oral morphine was coming to Africa. And with it, I also would return.

As part of my original contract with the university, they agreed to help me get repatriated when I left. All my belongings were shipped to Nairobi, and I paid to fly my two cats, Sylvia and Sylvester to follow me. (Although, after I got to Kenya I felt great guilt about the money I had paid to keep my cats with me!)

*

I've had many endings and beginnings and the transition always creates a paradox of emotions. An undercurrent of sadness wells up leaving behind my friends and colleagues, the routine, the familiar food and culture. It's also difficult to walk away from the progress and years of work it took to solidify the success and beginning of the Hospice Care Association. There is fear and anxiety in starting over, yet again, and acclimatising to a different place, culture, people and work politics. Yet amidst this uneasiness, like a fresh spring of water, excitement, hope and the zest of adventure flood through my spirit.

I arrived in Nairobi in June 1990. By the time I arrived, they were already producing oral morphine from Nairobi Hospital Pharmacy (a private hospital where one of the Board members worked as a pharmacist). The work had begun.

46
Kenya

You have enemies? Good. That means you've
stood up for something, sometime in your life,
Winston Churchill

I RENTED a house that the MMMs had found for me. The house
was safe with a wall and locked gate around a small lawn. My
neighbour, Gloria, a delightful, kind woman in her mid-thirties
greeted me and gave me a quick tour of the premise, giving me
a sense of security and kinship. I settled into my new home, later
to be joined by my two furballs, all three of us adjusting quite
quickly to the change of scenery. My furniture, somewhere in the
ocean on a freight, would arrive in the next few weeks. Not a
stranger to minimalist living, I knew I'd be much too busy with
my work and only needed a mattress to sleep on. Gloria, who
seemed to be highly resourceful, spoke to the guards at the gates,
who had a mattress and sheets brought to the compound before
evening!

I arose to the sound of wheels rolling over gravel. I looked out
the window and saw a guard open the gate for a very fancy Range
Rover leaving the premises. (I would later discover Gloria had
many visitors. Turns out she was friends with gentlemen in well-
paid and high-ranking positions. I also later discovered that the
guards did not come with the compound but were there solely for
Gloria's protection, and as such, I too was well protected!)

The breaking dawn outlined the Ngong Hills in the distance. I wondered if I'd ever get around to hiking it one day. I took a quick shower and caught a local motorcycle taxi, referred to as a boda boda, to the hospice premises. Buying a car would be a priority.

From the time I had interviewed with them to the time I arrived, they had been able to change their work location from a small hut without electricity to a prefabricated building on the grounds of Kenyatta Hospital. I had agreed to a much, much lower salary. Compared to Singapore, it felt like a handshake. But I knew that would be the reality of doing this work here. On the upside, and as promised, they were already using morphine. It was time to work.

*

Our hospice team consisted of myself and the two nurses that I had met months earlier, Brigid Sirengo and Jane Moore. We'd collect the morphine from the pharmacy at Nairobi Hospital and use it on home visits. In general, it felt like we were repeating the Singapore process but in a much poorer area. Nairobi Hospice had already begun networking with the hospitals about referrals, but there needed to be much more education and communication about our mission to other health professionals and organisations. I began teaching courses and sharing power points at Nairobi Hospital. We also travelled to Eldoret and gave a course to the new Oncology Unit. The use of morphine spread to Nairobi Hospital and Kenyatta (the Government) Hospital.

I felt a strong connection with my team. We relied heavily on each other for understanding and emotional support. About six months in, we had enough funds and were busy enough to hire another nurse. After a few interviews we came across Fazal Mbaraka. Bright-eyed and bushy tailed, Fazal was full of energy and emanated the hospice ethos. She differentiated herself from the other applicants instantly. Full of ideas and life, she brought a great morale booster to the team. She was a great help to me. She took on the hospice spirit and palliative care approach naturally and with ease. She'd later help me more than I could imagine!

Once I bought a car, we used my car and a car temporarily rented from the Chair of Board, Professor E. Kasili. The work was hard. But good. We spent the majority of our time in slums, but as word spread, we also visited some of the posh areas too. Kenya had a large Asian population and many of them used our services and supported us financially. I know we visited men and women, the young and old, but for me, in Kenya, I remember the women.

*

Through networking with the locals, it came to our attention that a woman living in the slums had terrible pain. Unable to afford a hospital visit, she was confined to her bed. I parked the car and Brigid and I gathered our supplies and were met by a local who started to guide us to where she lived. For those who haven't visited, a white person to children is like a moth to a flame. Some have never seen such white skin before! Children from all over, came running and yelling, laughing and pointing, big smiles on their faces as they shouted 'Mzungu!' (white person). By the time we reached our patient, we had a parade behind us. People and children were cramming in the doorways and faces lined the windows. Despite the fact we were checking on a woman that was laying on a mattress in quiet pain, the people still had exuberance and happiness as they watched with smiles and comments to each other that I could not understand. Death and disease were something even small children were familiar with.

The woman lay on a dirty mattress on the floor with a coloured blanket wrapped around her. She had short, black hair and dark, warm eyes. Her thin arms wrapped around herself in a hug and she lay with her knees tucked up to her chest. Her pain came from her abdominal region, and I believed it was cervical cancer but wanted to do a more in-depth examination to understand the extent of where the cancer had spread. It was dark and to provide some privacy from the onlookers we tried to put a blanket over her while I looked at her closer. The cancer had disfigured the outside of her body, making aspects more difficult to identify. Suddenly, I became acutely aware that I had got lost in the examination, 'Oh God, I'm in the wrong hole!'

'Shhhhhhhhhhh!' Brigid exclaimed to me, slightly horrified, as many of our onlookers could understand English. The mix up, combined with Brigid's horror, incited a burst of small uncontrollable giggles from me. I had not hurt or offended the woman, but sometimes in life, mistakes happen and to react solemnly is not always my nature. It's like the moment in church when you are *not* supposed to laugh, but can barely keep yourself together, mostly because you're not supposed to laugh! Also, I think it's important while conducting serious work to find the joy when you can, otherwise burnout will eventually take hold of you.

I eventually got a hold of myself and finished the examination. The woman's cancer was advanced and would most likely not make it past a few months. We'd make her as comfortable as we could. I was so grateful we now could prescribe morphine for cases like this.

The actions I've seen people take do not always reflect the culture they are a part of, but sometimes they might. I know every case is specific to the choices of the individual, and I try not to label, but I do think a cultural overlay inevitably influences people's choices. We visited a couple in a modest home for the area. They did not have an excess of material goods, but they were not wanting either. The wife had cervical cancer and was in terrible pain.

Many people still refused to go to hospitals as they held a stigma. People would see them go to the hospital sick and come home in a coffin. Many people in Kenya would still see the local medicine men and woman, sometimes referred to as 'witch doctors'. In some instances, these local healers could help some ailments with herbs and other remedies, but many of the times what they offered was not enough. It was possible the chemo could have helped this woman. Even if it did not cure the cancer, it might slow its progression.

After the assessment, I talked with the couple about different options they might pursue. It felt like they were both resigned to the fate of her death. I gave them morphine and described to the husband how to give it to her. Even as cheap as morphine was, he seemed hesitant at the cost.

As he escorted me out of the house, I asked why they hadn't gone to the hospital and attempted chemotherapy. He told me in no uncertain terms that he knew in the end his wife would die, so he was saving all the money he could for his next wife. His comment caught me off guard.

It took me a moment to pull myself together before I could respond. I knew the economic and social constraints affected everyone differently. They had a family. Maybe he felt too overwhelmed to take care of his children by himself and was motivated for their cause. In moments like this, I found it hard to leave my judgements at the door. I know there are individual exceptions to cultural norms. But I also knew I'd struggle in general with the ways women were treated and regarded in Kenya. (I was already facing my own issues with the Board!) However, after experiencing many different cultural norms around the world, I know it's very important to respect the people and their ways, albeit different from your own. You are there to help them, not impose your worldviews on them. Another case I'd work with soon would emphasise this point all too well.

Each patient gives us an opportunity to learn something new if we are open to it. Names often go forgotten with me, but I don't forget faces. Late twenties with midnight skin and ivory teeth, with a stunning smile, most likely Sudanese descent, this young lad was near the end when we heard about him. His pain was severe. After our assessment and administration of oral morphine, you could see the light in his eyes return and his first smile spread across his wide face. I knew we'd be able to make him comfortable for his remaining time on Earth. Grateful for our help, we scheduled to see him again in a week's time.

When we returned you could tell he felt conflicted. Something had changed. He seemed adamant that he no longer wanted to take morphine. His pain was increasing, and he was becoming more incoherent. I couldn't understand what had changed when the week prior, he had seemed so comfortable and grateful for the morphine. We ended up talking with his sister to try to discover if there were any side effects from the morphine that made him uncomfortable. That's when we learned about the visit of his friend. In parts of Africa, it's more common to have 'Born Again Christians'. Although I am a staunch Catholic and have a relationship with Jesus Christ, I am always amused at the Born-Agains that have tried to convert me. Like all new converts, they are zealous proselytisers. Based on what his sister could understand, her brother's friend's faith was not congruent with the morphine we were providing and argued that he only needed to pray to Jesus for help.

Making peace with death is hard enough as it is. Having someone throw out theology questions and debates in your final days when you can barely think straight is less than appropriate in my opinion. This young man, due to the confusion and pushy beliefs of his friend, died in extreme pain, unable to have final conversations and moments with his loved ones.

The ethos of hospice has become very important to me over the years. It is never the position of a hospice caretaker to impose their worldview on their patient. We are there to help our patients and their families find peace – in a holistic manner – physically, mentally, emotionally and spiritually. As caretakers, it is not about us finding peace and being comfortable. Everyone is so different with different worldview paradigms. It is our honour to try to understand what theirs is and how to best support them. My experience with this young man only solidified my perspective and what can happen when an outsider adds fear to an already fearful and difficult situation. Death is a very hard thing for most people to accept and embrace. When I hire someone, I now screen for tolerance. Tolerance of other people's beliefs, albeit different from your own, is paramount at end-of-life care.

*

Our team did excellent work. The board did great work and I'm so grateful they were able to get morphine into the country and fundraise for more nurses. I remember teaching courses again. I used the material I had in Singapore but changed it based on the needs and culture of Kenya. I felt like we had a great team. But God forbid, things stay stable for too long. Maybe it's not my nature, and I can't help but find a little trouble.

It sometimes is hard to write about the challenges that come up in life. I know my perspective is only mine, and I try to do right by what I see, just like I think everyone else. But in these conflicts, we learn about ourselves.

Our main nurse, Brigid, was strong, devoted to our patients and the work, and reliable. She had many qualities that suited the hospice work wonderfully. But her career had started and grew in government services, a more bureaucratic system. She was aware of politics and the people on the board she needed to please. She strongly supported the Chair of the Board, a successful and well-known oncologist, Professor E. Kasili. Our Chair had done wonderful things. He had started one of the first paediatric oncology units at Kenyatta Hospital. He had worked with the Minister of Health to get morphine imported into the country, and he rented his car routinely until we had our own car, for various circumstances. But he was also a 'big man'. He wanted things his way, and I guess I wanted them my way.

In the Kenyan culture, women are typically more subservient and less confrontational than I am. I can imagine that it's rather annoying to have an outsider from the 'lower sex' always disagree with you. Overtime, different issues would come to a head, and I could start to feel the team splinter. On many occasions, he would come in and take his car and our driver, so he could go to a big meeting. I know he rented the car to us in the first place, but he gave us no warning when he needed it. So we'd have made prior arrangements to go on a patient visit, and then he'd come in and take the car, throwing our whole day into shambles! Patients we needed to see and who expected to see us, would wait all day, and we wouldn't be able to come. (A long time before the mobile phone!)

On one occasion, quite upset and unable to control my temper, I went up to him and barked, 'I'm trying to help you! But you're not letting me help you!' I don't think it had the intended effect.

Tensions grew. I could tell that people were being asked to take sides. Outsiders would never know it, but non-profit work can often become more vicious and political than other fields. At one point Ruth Wooldridge, who had started this organisation, visited. I took her to Nairobi Hospital, and one of the doctors said to me, 'You're the one that started palliative care in Kenya!' I immediately put him right by introducing Ruth as the person responsible for Nairobi Hospice and the start of palliative care. His comment made me feel proud. Although inaccurate, it was nice to get recognition for the long hours and dedication I had given. Yet, I knew it was taking many people – near and far – to make it work. I knew I had not started it, but I knew I was boots on the ground making it happen. However, that comment, even when corrected, did not go over well with Ruth. I can understand how she must have felt, given she was the one that had worked so hard to get it started.

The cards felt like they were stacking against me. At our next board meeting I could tell some of the main players were starting to feel hostile towards me. Less smiles, more formality. They decided to make me a medical officer and not a health coordinator which indicated my specialty of palliative medicine. I had last been a medical officer in 1964 in Nigeria.

Shortly after I went and talked to a good friend who was also a lawyer in Kenya. 'This is what happens here. I've seen it before. If someone feels threatened by someone else, upstaged, they turn against them.' He explained there was nothing I could really do and advised me to resign. Deflated and worn out, I agreed this was the best I could do and decided to resign. It was hard enough to swim in the river, it felt nearly impossible when it felt like I was swimming upstream without the board's support. When you're working for peanuts, not being appreciated makes it very difficult. I gave the board my notice.

My team expressed sadness at my decision. Even some of the board members wrote to me and were upset at my decision. It was incredibly painful for me. When I left, they brought in a junior doctor from the UK. He was a man and I felt like he had gained more status in a short time than I had during my year and a half there.

In early 1991, Dame Cicely had asked if I'd write an article about the work we were doing at Nairobi Hospice in Kenya. I based the article on a case study where we had got the patient's pain relieved and she was able to live peacefully with her family before she passed away. The patient, Mary, said, 'Before I met you, I was dying... Now I am living.' The article was published in October 1991, in the journal *Contact*, published by the World Council of Churches in Geneva, which was free of charge in many African countries.[14]

Upon deciding to leave, I could not understand how God could introduce me to such a great need and yet the circumstances had become so untenable as to lead to my departure. But around this time, letters started coming in – from Cameroon, Nigeria, Uganda, Ghana, Senegal, Cote d'Ivoire and Tanzania – asking if I could help them start in their country what we were doing in Kenya. I realised that Africa needed a palliative care service model, suitable for resource-restricted circumstances. The idea of providing a model that was culturally suitable and affordable for all African countries was born.

---

[14] The article is in Appendix A of *Audacity to Love*.

47

The Vision:
Hospice Africa

It's not what you look at that matters, it's what you see.
Henry David Thoreau

The path from dreams to success does exist. May you have the vision to
find it, the courage to get on to it, and the perseverance to follow it.
Kalpana Chawla

I N 1993 I didn't have a plan, but I had a vision. I wanted to
create a hospice model that could be adapted to countries with
limited resources. I had witnessed the need for such a service
and had seen the calls for help from other countries. Even
though my life felt scattered and up in the air, I held the vision in
my heart – asking God for the resources and guidance to make it
come to fruition. But in the meantime I had to deal with reality. I
needed a job. I made arrangements before leaving Kenya in which
I rented my flat to the housekeeper who also took care of my cats. I
knew I'd return to Africa some day soon and it would be easiest
to transfer my belonging at a later date when I knew where I'd be
going.

Arriving back in the United Kingdom, I needed a means of
income preferably in the hospice setting near my home in
Liverpool. I wanted to stay in Liverpool because I felt I had a
community of friends and colleagues that would help with my

vision. However, shockingly, in 1992 Liverpool had no established palliative medicine service. So I decided to commute and ended up taking a locum medical director post initially in Myton Hamlet Hospice in Warwick and later in St Mary's Hospice in Birmingham. Although, the posts were quite far from Liverpool, I would always return on the weekends to further network and meet with people who were supporting the new venture.

The first two people that came seriously on board were Lesley and David Phipps. It had been over twenty years since we first worked together at the University Geriatric Medicine Team in the Northern Hospital in Liverpool. Although Lesley had grown, she still had her girlish charm and was a proud mother of twins, aged eleven. It had been a while since I had seen her, but we immediately reconnected. Perhaps it was the experience in that pioneering development with a wonderful leader, Professor Jimmy Williamson, that gave Lesley and I the courage and vision to dedicate ourselves to this new mission. Lesley's husband, David, was a senior lecturer in the Chemistry Department in John Moore's University. Lesley and David fully supported the mission and gave themselves to it in a way blessed with the spirit. With their great support, Hospice Africa was born.

The objective of Hospice Africa was to create a 'model' hospice in a selected country. This model would be affordable and culturally acceptable and capable of being adapted to other African situations. The initial meetings of the future board were held in Liverpool. We decided that the founding mission of Hospice Africa was to promote the relief of suffering in African countries by: (a) establishing a palliative care service, (b) promoting related research, (c) promoting the teaching or training of doctors, nurses, physiotherapists, students and other persons engaged in any branch of medicine and (d) providing and assisting in the wholistic care for the patients and their families.[15]

*

Travelling up and down the M6 was a way of life that year. I worked long hours and felt the weight of my eye lids on the motorway. One day, while traversing Spaghetti Junction, a police

---

[15] For the full mission statement, see *Audacity to Love,* p. 52.

car pulled me over. A big man climbed out of the car and walked to my window. He had been following me for several miles because I had been zigzagging all over the road. Upon seeing my very awake and sober state upon seeing him, he knew I was not inebriated! Instead of giving me a ticket he offered to follow me to the next service station where I promised I'd drink a cup of coffee. True to his word, he followed me and even came in and joined me! I drank my steamy cup and set off again, arriving home safely. That policeman probably saved my life.

The Feasibility Study

We needed to conduct a feasibility study to assess which location would have the most viability and support in establishing a model hospice service. We began by visiting the countries we had received letters from in response to my article. At that time, it was difficult to reach these countries since there was no email and 'snail' mail was literally snail mail – it travelled very slowly. Now during the latter part of 1992, while locum Medical Director at St Mary's Hospice in Birmingham, I was joined by one of my nurses at Nairobi Hospice, Fazal Mbaraka. Fazal and I had developed a great connection in Kenya and she was deeply committed to helping support the mission to set up the model hospice in Africa. When Fazal gave her notice at Nairobi Hospice they suspected that she was leaving due to my departure. She traversed this problem gracefully.

Fazal was born in Kenya of Pakistan immigrants who came to build the East African railway. Fazal's mother died when she was a young girl, being raised mostly by her older sisters. Their family had a small farm in Eldoret. Although Fazal was raised Muslim, she later converted to Christianity. Dedicated to learning, she constantly read the Bible and attended Church. Her father confided in me how impressed and proud he was of her perseverance and spiritual outlook which enabled her to dedicate her life to the less fortunate.

Fazal flew to the UK. While working at Hospice in Birmingham, Fazal and I stayed in a flat in Coventry lent to me by a friend whom I had met in Penang. There, Fazal and I worked out the logistics of the feasibility study. (In the meantime, she was able to take some higher PC courses at the Hospice.)

So now we had a real plan. But everything needed money. The funding for the feasibility study came from Ireland from the Civil Service Third World Fund. In February 1993, Fazal and I set out from England. We'd start in Kenya (Moi University), then travel to Uganda, followed by flying to Zimbabwe (Island Hospice, to learn from their experiences) and finish in Nigeria (Lagos).

Kenya

Before flying back to Kenya, I had been tipped by someone at Nairobi Hospice that Professor E. Kasili had been so upset with me that he had used his power to block me from arriving back into the country. The airport security guards had been given my passport ID and were to stop my entry because I was a threat to the Nairobi Hospice! Having been tipped off, I changed my passport and somehow got through! We arrived in Kenya, and stayed at my little house in Kileleshwa, Nairobi, which I was still renting. My two darling cats, that had come with me from Singapore were still there being looked after by my former 'live-in lady'. My car was there and moving ... so we were able to make contacts and to go to Moi University in Eldoret, who were very keen to have a palliative care unit attached to them. It seemed auspicious to have a university in Eldoret, Fazal's hometown. However, at some point I was alerted that another hospice in Kenya might compromise Nairobi Hospice, as we would both be competing for funding from the same sources.

Uganda

So we crossed the border at Malaba and went into Uganda. There we met with Celia Stephenson and her friend, who was revisiting the places where she had worked for many years for the VMM (Volunteer Missionary Movement). She and her friend Anne were staying at the convent attached to Nsambya Mission Hospital. This hospital was one of the several mission hospitals that had sought answers to meeting the needs of the AIDS epidemic with the resultant rush of patients to hospital, by providing a home care service for such patients. Funding was coming into Uganda for the support of these patients not only with health provision but also with food, school fees and the support of widows and orphans. All of these services were being run from this wonderful hospital.

Nsambya Hospital was founded in 1903 by Mother Kevin, an Irish teacher, who started a chain of services as well as the hospital. Their first service to the local people was under a tree. Gradually they got help to build a hospital which, in 1993, was the chosen hospital for most of the medical specialties and also as a training school for nurses. From the pictures of Mother Kevin and her helpers early on, Nsambya Hill was then fields. In 1993, it was the Catholic Hill of Kampala along with Rubaga Hill which has the cathedral. We found that Nsambya had its own cathedral then with many Catholic activities attached, including the Joint Medical Store (Catholic and Protestant Mission procurement of medications for the Mission hospitals), which we still use for the procurement of our morphine powder and other medications for palliative care.

Sister Rosemary Needham, FMM (Franciscan Missionary of Mary), was the accountant at the hospital, and welcomed us with open arms. 'You are coming for cancer patients? You are so welcome. All our activities are having to go to the AIDS patients and the cancer and other patients are being left out.' Apparently there was so much available if you were HIV positive that some patients, after being given the good news that they were negative, were going away crying because now they could not have school fees for their children!

Fazal and I were invited to stay in their convent. We were so relieved as we had nowhere to lay our heads and were living on a shoestring. So we worked out of Nsambya and travelled to other countries on the feasibility study from there.

In Uganda we met with the Minister of Health, Dr James Makumbi. He was delighted to hear of palliative care and how it could assist the many who were dying at all ages. His response, at the height of the HIV epidemic, touched our hearts. He said 'My people are suffering! Please bring your morhine and palliative care and relieve their pain.' He was so supportive and agreed to upport the importation of morphine powder.

Zimbabwe

Fazal and I could not believe we were still in Africa when we arrived in Harare. At that time the population was ten million. Wide tarmacked streets, dual carriageways, traffic lights and no potholes! The children were going to school in beautiful uniforms walking along the streets. The shops were full of amazing things not available in post-war Uganda. We noted in the report that this country was more akin to Scandinavia than Africa! A tropical, temperate climate made it an easy place to live in.

The team at Island Hospice made us very much at home. They had just been gifted a beautiful little cottage, used for daycare, that was across the road from their active Hospice offices. It had two bedrooms, tastefully furnished with pretty, flowered curtains and bedspreads to match. We were invited to stay there while we met and worked with different members of the hospice team.

The first official palliative care unit in Africa, Island Hospice, commenced services in 1979. The service used St Anne's Hospital for relief admissions and for terminal care of those unable to die in their own homes. The cost of admission was covered by private insurance for wealthier paitients and Government for the poorer patients, up to $400 per month.

The team consisted of the Senior Administrator, Dave McElvaine, who was born in Zimbabwe, had a social work background and as such had a wonderful understanding of the local needs. He was supported by a part-time medical director, eight social workers and nine nurses, all able to drive, so therefore no drivers were employed. There were also five support staff including a cashier and part-time secretaries. The team was supported by many volunteers.

Each car had five safety devices against theft, and the hospice guards at the gate did an excellent job at surveying who came and went. They also had a donated ambulance. Once week patients were collected from home and brought to the daycare centre in the ambulance.

The team had great coordination in patient care and worked well with each other if someone's workload became too heavy. There was a special bereavement coordinator who worked four days a week. They accepted bereavement referrals from not only their own patients but also from suicides, road accidents and coronary heart deaths. They provided a group counselling session that supported bereaved parents and grandparents. Education was mainly volunteer training at that time. Medical students had lectures and clinical placements with Island Hospice. Nurses came for three-day programmes. Local fundraising was well organised.

The computer operator doubled up for M&E (monitoring and evaluation). Morphine powder was available, and an oral solution was made up and was available throughout the country from the Government store. Tablets of 10 mgs were also being made by a local firm, CAPS, in Harare. The local brand cost $40 for 100 tablets compared to the same tablet imported which cost $100 for 56 tablets.

The hospice was serving all ethnic groups but the ratio of white to black in 1993 was 3:2. However this was moving rapidly towards more Africans benefiting as their needs were increasing with the HIV epidemic.

The white bereaved relatives took more time to work through bereavement than the African families. In reality, the average age of death was in the seventies for Caucasian decent, as compared with 20–40s for the Africans. Most Africans have seen death since childhood, and often must return to working hard to provide for the rest of the family, which in a strange way, protects them from severe and protracted bereavement. We have so much to learn from Africa.

Island Hospice was the best in Africa at the time. We learned a great deal during our time there.

Nigeria

Nigeria was the first African country I had worked in from 1964 to 1973, and this was my first time back to Nigeria since I had left. Having worked there for ten years with intervals to Ireland, I had a special leaning towards it as the site for the 'model'.

However, Fazal and I were in for a culture shock. Since the Biafran war, two generations had been raised on raw survival. Thieving was rife and Nigeria had earned a reputation as having one of the highest levels of corruption in the world. Even the airport felt unsafe. Hands grabbed at us from all directions, wanting to exchange money, get us a taxi, and sell us water. The heat and humidity were familiar but no less a shock. I was (and still am) afraid of arriving in Lagos without someone to meet me.

We got into a taxi and asked to be driven to the Catholic Mission in Maryland. The taxi car had no shocks and on occasion we weren't sure if the driver wasn't running the car via his legs through a hole under the driver's seat! Riding downhill, the engine was turned off to preserve petrol and we cruised down to the bottom when the engine was put on again. We dangerously screeched to a halt many times as we tried to move through the Lagos 'jam'. Inching along in the traffic jam, through the windows we were offered everything from a fridge to a fur coat!

I vaguely remembered Lagos and knew that Maryland was close to the airport. After an hour and a half, I told the driver he must be going the wrong way. We had passed signs for Maryland but the driver kept on going. Eventually we arrived at the Mission and were met by a Nigerian Sister. The driver demanded $100. Fazal and I started to bargain him down when the Sister took charge. She told him in pidgin English, in no uncertain terms, that he was letting down the whole of Nigeria by his behaviour. She gave him a real dressing down until, ashamed, he reduced the fare to $20.

We arrived in Nigeria with the intent of finding the Medical Missionaries of Mary, my own Sisters with whom I had worked as a missionary in the 1960s. But without the internet and emails, we did not actually know where they were. I knew they were in Lagos, but with darkness setting on us we needed a safe place to stay. The Kiltegan Fathers, with whom I had also worked in the 1960s took us in and gave us a bed. They had great stories to share over dinner about what had happened in Nigeria the last twenty years.

The following day we found the MMM house and met with Sr Laurence Hoey. Sr Laurence was doing groundbreaking work in Amukoko, covering health services for 70,000 people within a 2 km area of the centre itself. She welcomed us and gave us hospitality and guidance during our time in Lagos.

We had planned to stay three weeks in Nigeria. Most of our time was spent in Lagos working with Mrs Fatumnbi, the founder of Hospice Nigeria. Mrs Fatumnbi, a retired nurse of the traditional type, felt inspired after meeting Dame Cicely and visiting St Christopher's in 1991. Returning to Lagos, she felt determined to help cancer patients dying in pain. She welcomed us with open arms and got us introductions at the Ministry of Health, the University Hospitals and the British High Commission. We also visited the University of Ibadan, where they were interested in setting up a palliative-care team.

Things were going well. So well in fact that we laid down groundwork and even formed a two-year plan with the Lagos team. The Ministry of Health agreed to the importation of morphine powder and were very keen to have the 'model' in Nigeria.

While we were there, I really wanted to visit the SE region where I had worked, trained and been introduced to Africa in the 1960s. I booked a bus to Uyo, a full day's drive away from Lagos and left at 5.00 am. The driver of the small minibus was named Patrick and I suggested he had been baptised by an Irish Kiltegan Father. Sure enough, he had been born in the MMM hospital at Urua Akpan and given the name Patrick there! We immediately bonded and I was put in the front seat of the bus.

I had been warned not to carry my passport, but a copy. At one point we were stopped, and the police got me to come down. I was the only white on the bus. He asked for my passport, and I gave him the copy. He asked me where the original was, and I told him that I only carried a copy because I was told the police might take the original! He laughed and let me back on the bus. It was true, the police were known to take the passports of visitors and hold them to get bribes.

At one point, we stopped for lunch and all the passengers went in different directions promising to return in time to continue the journey. Now it was only Patrick and I on the bus, so he took me for a meal in his home in Onitsha! The hospitality of some people can be astounding. After we finished we travelled on, arriving in Uyo in the dark. Uyo was the nearest town to St Luke's Hospital in the 1960s and was now a city with a university. The taxi park was full of small private hire taxis trying to get my fare to take me to the hospital. Again, it was very frightening. As the harassing peaked, Patrick took over and told them all to go and put me back on the bus and drove me himself to the convent attached to the hospital where they were expecting me.

I was about to be shell-shocked. When I had arrived in Nigeria in 1964, St Luke's was eclipsed only by UCH Ibadan as the most modern hospital in all of Nigeria. St Luke's had all the departments necessary for a teaching hospital, each department headed by an expatriate who was training Nigerian doctors. We trained doctors and nurses with a firm ethical background. The students respected the teachers and senior doctors we were producing some of the best trained and equipped nurses in the country. Our nurses were recognised as SRN in UK as well as their local qualification.

Yet, now, I could not believe the state of the hospital. Patients lying on beds without sheets, nurses sitting around doing very little for the patients and having absolutely no respect for the Sister doctor who was taking me around, and had been there since 1959! St Luke's had become a government hospital, dismissing the Sister's guidance and influence. The present degradation was a result of the Biafran war and the ensuing lack of support from the Federal Government for the area declared as Biafra.

An expatriate doctor who I knew of, Dr Ann Ward, met us on the hospital tour. She had for years specialised in the repair of vesico vaginal fistula (VVF) and had set up a special clinic and operating area in Uyo with residential accommodation to allow these women to live there and build them up before surgery. Dr Ward's great work has relieved the suffering of so many women and enabled them to regain respect in their families and communities.

Dr Ward brought me a patient. Akpan will remain in my mind forever because although I could do little to help her, I was beginning to realise the terrible agony for my African colleagues when confronted with someone in severe pain that they could not relieve. Akpan had been admitted to the hospital with cancer of the breast. The mass in her right breast had been incised by a traditional healer and the tumour had eroded through the wound, producing the smell of dead tissue, so familiar to us who deal with cancer. In fact, the smell is due to the putrefaction produced by anaerobic bacteria living in the dead tissue so that they produce a smell similar to that of a decomposing dead body.

We knew then and had known for many years that this could be controlled by using metronidazole; a medication found all over Africa as it is used for amoebic dysentery and other intestinal infections common in tropical climates. The tablet is crushed and applied to the area. It dries up the secretions and even stops bleeding if the wound is oozing, but most of all it attacks the anaerobic organisms and the resulting smell. Metronidazole was available in the hospital so now Akpan could join the rest of her family without the smell that had ostracised her.

But Akpan was in severe pain. Her cancer had developed secondaries locally. She had not slept for some time. How helpless I felt! Here I was on a feasibility study, with no doctor's bag, no medications and the only analgesic in the hospital was paracetamol, a Step 1 analgesic! I turned to God to ask, 'Why oh why have I been presented with Akpan when there is nothing I can do for her pain?' It was a desperate feeling of hopelessness. How many years would it take before affordable oral morphine would be available in Nigeria and how many years before it became available in SE State?

I meditated on why ... and suddenly I realised this was so that I could know what my African colleagues who cared would feel. Many left the profession and others became hardened to pain and just turned the other way. How sad for the caring professions in the whole of Africa! But now I could empathise with them as well as with my patients, and, thanks to the terrible burden of suffering of Akpan, this would hold me in good stead when dealing with frustrated trained health workers who were unable to get the medications required for their patients in many countries.

I returned to Lagos and Fazal by bus.

In my heart, I originally believed we'd choose Nigeria. I knew the culture, had a trusted network and there was a familiarity for me. But so much had changed. It felt frightening to be out in public places with the amount of people that would come up to you, tugging at your shirt, harassing you, grabbing your hands and trying to pull you their way. I knew donors would be hesitant to provide contributions with the level of corruption in Nigeria. Corruption and the game of bribes would make the process of building anything 10x slower and more expensive.

The places where the model shouldn't be built were clear. One place in particular had many of the building blocks needed for success. It felt like God shined a beacon of light on where we needed to go.

48

Uganda, the Model

Nothing could have prepared your heart to open like this. Once it began,
you were no longer your own. A new more courageous you, offering itself
In a new way to a presence you can sense But you have not seen or
known.
John O-Donahue

My people are suffering! Please bring your morphine and palliative care
and relieve their pain.
Dr James Makumbi, Minister of Health Uganda, 1993

I N REALITY, Uganda was chosen for many reasons. First, the
Minister of Health, Dr James Makumbi, agreed to accept the
importation of morphine powder into Uganda, which had to be
the first requirement. Pain needed to be controlled. Second,
Uganda had the confidence of the international community for
raising funds. This reflected a lower corruption rate, although it
still existed. Donor confidence and reduced corruption would be
paramount in building an organisation from the ground up. But
there was something more, less tangible, that really drew us in…
Uganda's people emanated hope and kindness although they were
emerging from twenty-five years of war. Poor and struggling
through the AIDS epidemic, they were also in great need of, and
very accepting of, having a hospice service. The AIDS epidemic
had increased the cancer level, and these patients were in terrible
pain. Uganda not only showed the need for a palliative care
service, but the people, government and movement on policies
showed that the soil was fertile for success.

After several discussions, Fazal and I decided to fly straight back to Uganda and get started. We arrived back in Uganda in March of 1993 with very little money. I have always been able to find refuge with my Sisters in Christ. This time would be no different. The Franciscan Sisters at Nsambya Hospital offered us accommodation.

Shortly after arriving back, we were invited to be guest speakers at the Combined Scientific Conference on the Management of Advanced Cancer, held in Lacor Hospital in Gulu. This hospital had the only chemotherapy and radiotherapy in Uganda at that time. This was a very enjoyable meeting for we met many key people who would help us in the future.

The Honourable Minister for Gulu, Mrs Betty Bigombe, answered our address by asking us to start a branch of Hospice Africa Uganda (HAU) in Gulu, promising to donate two acres of land. Despite our intent to follow-through, the horrific fighting in Gulu which soon commenced from the 'Lords Ristnce Army' made it too dangerous. However, Mrs Bigombe, a very brave lady with the courage of her convictions, continued to fight for her community. She even attempted to negotiate with leaders of the Lords Resistance Army to release the sixth formers of a convent school who had been kidnapped to be wives of his senior officers. The LRA had instigated horrific fighting and suffering, stealing children – both boys and girls – from the surrounding areas to serve as child soldiers and mistresses to the Leader. The terrible fighting in the north went on for decades.

*

The meeting was a good start but we needed more money. Following the Lacor meeting, we decided that Fazal would stay in Uganda making local contacts while I'd travel to the UK, Canada and the US from April to September to raise awareness and funding.

My ventures in UK were greatly supported by Fr Tim Redmond who drove me to London to meet with Dame Cicely and then all the way up to Edinburgh where I would meet again with Dr Derek Doyle. (Dr Doyle, a great supporter, had allowed me to edit his book for Africa, which became known as the 'Blue Book' for Africa.)

The meeting with Dame Cicely stands out in my mind. I remember telling her about my vision for a palliative care model in Africa. I'm not sure if there was tension because I had left the MMMs or simply because she didn't like my idea at first, but she was rather abrupt with me and I remember feeling embarrassed in front of Fr Tim (also a medical doctor). She wondered why I needed to go to Africa to start palliative care when I should leave the Africans to start it themselves. Immediately, I heard Acts 8:31 in my mind, 'Unless some man show me.' I did not feel a need to defend my vision, so I kept silent. Dame Cicely eventually came round to being a dear friend of mine and Hospice Africa. She became encouraging and supportive of all of Hospice Africa's future progress.

Mary Baines told me that when Cicely died in St Christopher's in 2005, she had a picture we had sent to her in bark cloth, showing a patient returning home to her family to be cared for by Hospice Africa.

Although we met roadblocks, there were many who supported us. Fr Tim and I were invited to stay with Margaret Driscoll in her bed and breakfast in the Lake District on our way to Edinburgh. Margaret, already a great family friend, was to become a special friend of Hospice Africa in Uganda. We met with many people and organisations, including, CAFOD (Catholic Association for Overseas Development), SCIAF (Scottish Catholic International Aid Fund), and Sr Dr Maura O'Donohue, MMM, who was on their AIDS desk.

Next, I travelled to the US and visited the Catholic Relief Services in Baltimore. They were covered by government policies which stated they could only help curative services. Saddened, the Chief at CRS put me in contact with Hospice at Hawthorne, on the outskirts of New York. Here, the Rev. Mother was interested in our new organisations which would be working with the poor who could not reach hospitals in Africa. I was given $5,000 and was so grateful as this was the only start-up financing we'd receive in USA.

My visit to Canada proved even less successful. The Canadian Palliative Care Association was not able to assist us but sent us a copy of the new *Oxford Book of Palliative Medicine* and eventually built a small sitting area with a thatch roofed on our grounds for team discussions and mealtimes together. (They continued many years to send us copies of their regular journal on palliative care. Even such small gestures made a difference.)

I returned to UK to find that our organisation had been registered as a UK charity in Liverpool on 12 August 1993. The Mission was 'to support affordable and culturally acceptable palliative care for all in need in Africa'. This would be done by establishing a model in an African country, which could be adapted to the countries in Sub-Saharan Africa. The initial board consisted of Lesley and David Phipps, Celia Stephenson (RIP), Alice Davidson, Paul Hargreaves and Pat Linnell. This group made up the initial Board of Trustees.

Back in the UK, I received a tragic call. Fazal, crying on the other end of the phone, managed to communicate that her father had been murdered. She needed to return to Kenya and help with his funeral and deal with family matters. She had made amazing progress, although I could not say the same about the progress I had made on my goals. With Fazal returning to Kenya and despite having only three months' worth of funding to keep our little shoestring operation going, it was time to go back to Uganda. I prayed we could make a model that would shine for others to see, spreading like wildfire. I'd do everything I could and pray like hell for more support.

Background to Uganda, 1993

The British occupied Uganda from 1894 to 1962. Uganda would see unrest and civil war for the next twenty-five years. In 1962, the British passed power over to President Obote. By 1970, the country was troubled and in 1971 Idi Amin took over in a bloody coup. In 1973, Idi Amin expelled most of the Asians in Uganda, who had been vital in building the economy of the country. Obote came back into power in 1983 but took over a country that had no discipline. Museveni led an army in the bush and overtook Obote in 1986. But a war continued in the north, as the Lord's Resistance Army wreaked havoc for decades.

The twenty-five years of civil war left the economy in ruins and the people in fear. Museveni was declared President and began to rebuild the country. He was the first president in Africa to admit there was an AIDS problem in his country. Out of 22 million people, 52 per cent of the population was younger than fifteen years of age, and many of their parents had been killed by war or the AIDs epidemic. And many of those dying were not dying well. More than 55 per cent of the population was not reaching health services.

HIV had been recognised and was locally called 'slim disease' for obvious reasons. Support organisations began to appear in Uganda in those years because the beds in the hospitals were completely taken up by patients with AIDS. Once the patients were discharged they needed support. Kitovu Hospital in Masaka was the first to provide home care for HIV patients, covering a huge catchment area. TASO, the AIDS support organisation, commenced in 1989.

In 1993, Ugandan's cancer rate was on the increase. Kaposi's sarcoma, a marker for AIDS, was the most common cancer seen at hospice and this continued up to the year 2002. There were no antiretrovirals (ARVs) or antibiotics, and antifungal agents were scarce and expensive. Thus, we were seeing people who were severely ill and often died within a few weeks after we first met them. These people were young and 60 per cent of them were women.

In Uganda, life expectancy was thirty-eight years and HIV prevalence was considered to be 30 per cent. The first few years we saw a lot of very sad cases. Many parents were dying with unfinished business for their children. We saw tragic mothers dying shortly after childbirth and babies dying due to lack of safe breast milk.

Hospice and palliative care was desperately needed.

49

Everything Led Me
to Here

You've always had the power my dear, you just had to learn it for
yourself.
Glinda the Good Witch, The Wizard of Oz

I will not follow where the path may lead,
but I will go where there is no path, and I will leave a trail.
Muriel Strode, 1903

TURKEY Lurkey came bursting through the door, escaping
the snarling teeth of a stray dog. The dog, still in hot pursuit
took one look at me and froze at the door. Waving my arms
and making whooping and hollering noises, I scooted him
back and shut the door. This turkey was becoming more trouble
than he was worth. Maybe he would end up in a pot, I thought to
myself.

I had been in Uganda for few weeks. I booked a flight
immediately upon hearing news of Fazal's father's death. I can
still remember the exhaustion that followed me to Uganda. Fazal
had already left for Kenya and she arranged a friend of hers to
pick me up at the airport and bring me directly to a colleague's
home. While waiting for tea, I fell asleep. I was kindly nudged
awake by the hostess and in mid-sentence, I fell asleep again. It

almost felt like I had developed Narcolepsy! I found it quite embarrassing to have such a lack of control over my consciousness. Shortly, the hostess graciously led me to a bed!

Although Fazal had decided to stay on the 'Asian' side of Kampala, I found comfort being near my Sisters. By grace, the Sisters of Franciscan Missionaries of Mary offered a two bedroom-house (known as the VMM House as it had been built by a VMM volunteer) to work and live free of charge on the Nsambya Hospital compound, while we began our palliative care service. I had been working out of it for the last week, and although I was still in a knackered state from all of my travels, I felt comfort and security.

My dinner with Sister Dr Brigid the previous evening had renewed my spirit. I felt so grateful to still have the support of the MMM community and a trusted kinship of a long-lost friend. Even though I left the MMMs in 1973, I would always have the support of the MMM community for the rest of my life.

I lit a cigarette and finished some case notes as the morning sun got higher. Laying on the corner of my desk, the dirty letter caught my eye. I needed to get to the airport!

I started the motor of the large Land Rover and shifted out of the compound. The sun was warm and vendors and people lined the streets as commerce began. I dodged people and animals alike on the busy side streets as I made my way to Entebbe Road. I reached the main motorway and the air cooled off as I picked up my speed through my open window. I enjoyed driving as it gave me time to reflect, an activity I did not seem to have time for lately. I pulled into the airport, parking in a side area.

My stomach began to flutter as I walked towards entrance. The letter had informed me that a package had arrived. Unsure of where to go, I asked an airport attendant, and she directed me to look in 'unclaimed luggage'.

And there it was, sitting unguarded. A small box labelled 'Dr Anne Merriman' sat with a few other boxes and luggage. (Wow! How things have changed!) If that's what I thought it was, I already had a long list of all the people that would desperately benefit from its contents. I picked it up and decided to open it as soon as I got back to the Land Rover.

Sitting inside with my window rolled up, I carefully began to rip off the tape off the box. Covered by bubble wrap, the contents revealed a white powdery substance sealed in plastic. A great wave of relief washed through my body. This was the first shipment of powdered morphine into the country. We had achieved a major marker to begin the first palliative care service in Uganda.

I drove back to the Nsambya compound with the box tucked safely beside me. Excitement and fire burned through my core. Yet simultaneously, I felt the peace and comfort of thousands radiate through my heart.

Home had always been where I made it. Families blossomed where love and kinship grew. Uganda felt like the start of another great beginning.

Epilogue:
Hospice Africa Uganda

Just as one candle lights another and can light thousands of other candles, so one heart illuminates another heart and can illuminate thousands of other hearts. *Leo Tolstoy*

They allow us to explain everything, and they listen. We don't even call them doctors; we call them family members. The way they treat us is like family.
Patient's daughter to nurse at Hospice Jinja

I N 1993, Hospice Africa Uganda (HAU) was founded with the vision of 'palliative care for all in need in Africa'. It took blood sweat and tears and a village all over the world, but the vision became a reality. HAU's model of palliative care is now being adopted throughout Sub Saharan Africa.

Hospice Africa and Hospice Africa Uganda are having their thirtieth anniversary in 2023! For more information on the last thirty years and the story of Hospice Africa Uganda, please read *Audacity to Love* and see https://www.hospice-africa.org and https://www.annemerrimanfoundation.org.

Thirty Years of Highlights

Uganda has been the forefront of palliative care innovation, spearheaded by collaborative leaders dedicated to eradicating unneeded suffering.

- In 1993, after hearing about my vision of Hospice Africa Uganda, the Ugandan political leadership, spearheaded by Minister of Health (MOH) Dr James Makumbi, allowed the importation of the first stocks of morphine powder. Morphine powder is crucial for the reconstitution of oral liquid opioid, the cornerstone medication for the management of severe pain in life threatening illnesses.

- In 1994, HAU provided tailored education and training programmes at Makerere University to medical and nursing students.

- In 1995, HAU also provided education and training programmes at Mbarara University of Science and Technology (MUST) with clinical training at HAU.

- HAU expanded to three hospice sites in Kampala (1993), Mbarara (1998) and Hoima (1998).

- In 1999, the Palliative Care Association was commenced at HAU.

- In 2000, the International Programs (HAU-IP) commenced visiting, training, and introducing affordable oral morphine to other countries. By 2023, thirty-seven initiatives have occurred in Anglophone and Francophone countries.

- In 2003, as a way to increase the numbers of patients receiving pain control, Uganda became the first country in the world, through meetings led by Dr Jack Jagwe, to change the statute that allows registered nurses trained in palliative care to prescribe morphine. This was prompted by the shortage of doctors in Uganda and other African countries.

- In 2003, the Ugandan Government provided free oral morphine to the entire country, initially through an Italian grant to WHO, followed by funding through MOH, and continuing to this day.

- In 2003, at a meeting in South Africa, Uganda was chosen for a new Continental organisation, African Hospice and Palliative Care Association. I was chosen as the leader of the steering committee.

- In 2003, at the first AHPCA conference in Arusha, AHPCA was officially launched, but renamed APCA to suit a donor.

- In 2009, the Institute of Hospice and Palliative Care in Africa (IHPCA) was officially recognised by the National Council of Higher Education. Prior to that, HAU had been providing short and long courses since 1994. In total, HAU and the IHPCA have trained over 10,000 health and related professionals.

- HAU-IP has also trained over thirty African countries on the Anglophone (2009) and Francophone (2012) initiators course.

- In 2011, HAU entered a private public partnership with National Medical Stores, Minister of Health and the Government of Uganda to become the sole provider of oral liquid morphine to the National Medical Stores. Many thanks to Dr Megan O'Brien (who was then working in Geneva, now with the American Cancer Society) for streamlining this process.

- In 2014, Uganda was internationally recognised as the only country in Africa with comprehensive palliative care by the WHO and WHPCA (World Hospice and Palliative Care Alliance) and published in the Atlas.

- 2014, I was nominated for the Nobel Peace Prize.

- In 2018, due to HAU's International Programmes and partnering organisations, over twenty African countries have affordable oral morphine.

- At the end of 2023, HAU clinical programme has cared for over 37,000 patients, mainly in their own homes.

- In 2018, Uganda is seen as 'a beacon in Africa' in palliative care services. However, much more is still needed. https://www.lienfoundation.org/sites/default/files/qod_index _2.pdf (Lien Foundation).

- 2018–2023 HAU constantly struggles with funding, but keeps fighting the fight.

The Ethos of Hospice Africa

At the age of eighty-eight, I cannot believe I am still alive! I continue to provide lectures and presentations but the message I am most compelled to share with others relates to the 'spirit of hospice' and our guiding 'ethos'.

Hospitality

Here in Uganda, my relationship with Jesus is still guiding me to learn more about Ubuntu, the original expression of their love for each other and their God through Hospitality to the stranger and each other! Hospitality and compassion are how we express our love to patients and families at our Hospice premises as well as in each home. Our hospitality in the home is expressed in our love for the suffering and those who are in the vice of poverty, through no fault of their own, even when their loved one is dying. In a world where money is the bottom line, influencing so many of our choices, may we always strive to remember the person behind the pain and the words of Hippocrates, 300 years before Christ: 'It is more important to know the person who has the disease, than to know the disease that the person has.'

Spirituality

We have had mixed religions amongst staff and patients. And at Hospice Africa Uganda, we welcome all in need. While helping people in the transition towards death, it is always important to respect their God, realising that God is bountiful for 'in His house there are many mansions'. May you remember your spirituality, beyond that of religion or the Church. May the love and kindness you share for others go beyond the Church you attend and your Sunday rituals. May you also continue to grow deep in your spirituality as a clinician, for in this work, spiritual questions are important topics to patients and their families.

The Ugandan Team

I thank God every day for my Ugandan team. Our HAU team commenced with a few, and at one stage reached 130 between our three sites! But now, due to financial cuts have been reduced to 70+. I know our team members face their own hardships, but they continue to rise and persevere so they can be there for their patients. I believe in doing so, they follow Christ's example described by the apostles in the New Testament. I believe they have taken on a special calling to assist our brothers and sisters during their transition in death. I believe this crossing over is as special of a time as birth! in which we depart from this world and everyone we love and are familiar with.

A Message to My Team

May you remember Bishop Kevin Dowling from South Africa when he explained that our God is within us, and we are never alone when facing a critical decision or need for our patients. Because we can always call on Him and leave our patients in peace knowing the He has taken over.

And when I am no longer on this earth, I need you all who have learned this message to carry this ethos and the spirit of Hospice forward to patients and families, the team and each other.

My Ugandan Family: Where Am I Now?

I have a long-standing family here with me in Andrew Kaggwa House (AKH), which belongs to HAU on condition that I would live here as long as needed. So, I write this from AKH.

I love my family, and I am their JaaJaa (grandmother)! It began when 'Little Anne' joined me twenty-nine years ago to help with the house and its duties. Her daughter Mary, born and raised in this house, is now entering her fourth year in a Nursing degree! Little Anne also has a son, Solomon, who has a degree in Accounting and Business Studies, who is our Administrator with our new support organisation for child survivors of cancer who are now adults but are left with disabilities. This is to ensure that they receive sufficient training to support themselves, their carers and even to contribute to Uganda Society.

Margaret joined us in 2000 when Little Anne was pregnant with Mary. She has a son, Ryan who is at boarding school. This makes me very sad as we are limited as to when we can see him. He arrives home thin, and we fatten him up just in time to send him back to school!

Alice joined us when we had an influx of visitors. She has three children, all doing very well academically. Her eldest, Joseph, is now doing Civil Engineering at university. The next two are much younger, Vicky is ten and Frankie is seven and they are both as bright as buttons.

The 'little ones' are all Immaculate Conceptions. I have never seen the fathers of our children here in the house, and none of them seem to be contributing to their wives or children. (It is not uncommon for women to be treated badly by fathers and husbands, especially after a night out drinking local brew.) But am grateful I can support these women and their children, mainly through the money I earned teaching in the National University of Singapore. (They ensured you left with 50 per cent of your salary saved in their Central Provident Fund (CPF) for later withdrawals.) Many of the children's school fees are paid by other volunteers that have come throughout the years.

Surrounded by so many wonderful women and girls I cannot but help and reflect on the challenges facing our gender. Women must push forward to have equality with men in life's decisions. The Catholic Church and other Faiths, must not remain the last portal of Mans dominance over Women, demonstrated still in many countries and reflected as right, by the example of a male-dominated Church. Let them realise they are losing 50 per cent of God's wisdom which comes through the gentle wisdom endowed on women by God himself.

And so it is I will live out my last days in Uganda with my Ugandan family. I am so lucky they are happy to have me, even when I am crotchety! I love them all dearly and know the sacrifices they have made throughout the years to support my work and this mission. I feel blessed as I enter my final days, to be cared for so greatly by such wonderful women. May God watch over you when I am gone.

Final Thoughts

Mountains cannot be surmounted except by winding paths.
Johann Wolfgang Von Goethe

One day you will look back and see that all along, you were blooming.
Morgan Harper Nichols

W HEN I REFLECT on my journey. It amazes me that God managed to get me from point A to point Z. A wild, undisciplined schoolgirl drawn to the life of God and then against all odds given the chance to become a doctor. My wild heart led me to wild places and gave me the strength to face hard realities. My heart also led me back into the civilian life where I think God knew I'd do more outside the religious life than in it. But this was no easy road to journey. Sometimes, sun shone above but just as often the path lay covered in thick fog. I had no idea where it was leading. There was pain. Hard times. Heartbreak. Tears and loneliness. There still is! But that's how the light got in. And through my own cracks, I am better able to see the light of others. The cracks revealed the road of compassion and led me to the path I was meant to walk. Because of my imperfections, I was worthy to be a tool of a greater plan.

And so are you. Deeply worthy. Be without fear and feel God's love in all you do. May you look at your own cracks and those of others with grace. Find the peace and joy even when it rains. For 'Joy is like the rain!' And by staying connected to your heart, may you walk the path that is meant for you.

I thank God for my great life and my opportunities on this earth.

Thankyous

People that I have immense gratitude for that may have gone unnamed in this book are:

Rose Kiwanuka, my first PC Ugandan nurse in early 1994,

Martha Rabwoni, my second PC Ugandan nurse in late 1994.

Rachael Dipio, my third Uganda PC nurse in 1995.

Fazal Mbaraka, for her wonderful support and friendship over the years.

Eddie Mwebesa, palliative care physician who has been trained through HAU, who has remained dedicated to our vision and ethos, while taking on many responsibilities both clinical and in international programmes. He has served twenty years.

And all our clinical doctors and nurses since who carry out this hopitality to our patients in Uganda and demonstrate it to African countries on placements learning clinical palliative care. To our dedicated drivers, we could not do without them for their driving and their support with patients and families.

To our HA and HAU team members past and present, who have all contributed in their own ways to build, support and administrate our world.

The wonderful women who have looked after me over the years, and care for me during my ending days: Anne Bisasso, Margaret Kazibwe and Alice Kabeseke in Andrew Kaggwa House. They are major HAU team members. And their children, Joseph, Mary, Ryan, Victoria and Francesca, who are gradually taking on responsibilities, during their studies, for me and our home.

All of the wonderful volunteers who have joined us as community volunteers and support in so many ways including:

- daycare led by Catherine Wambuya and Sister Patricia, Sister of the Blue Nuns, now back in Melbourne; after volunteering with us for some time in the early years, Sr Patricia started Hospice Africa Australia, which has sadly folded for lack of support from Australians who understandably support SE Asia which is nearer and in need of financial support;
- Lucy Finch who then commenced Ndi Moyo[16] and community palliative care in Malawi;
- and many others who stayed short and longer times with us, entertaining and providing for our daycare patients.

To the Ugandan leadership for carrying on the palliative care flag and all their support in getting to where we have got to today.

To all our HA & HAU Board Members, past and present, who have dedicated hundreds and thousands of hours fundraising and raising awareness in the UK, Ireland, USA, France, Australia and Uganda.

To the international volunteers who have given so much of their time and expertise to this cause and HAU. Also to those working in HAU charity shops in Liverpool and France to raise funds for HAU.

To Abby Narvaez for photo credit for the cover photo and Photo 27.

---

[16] https://www.ndimoyo.org/

While working on this book, several people allowed us to stay in their homes. Special thanks to Aiden Eames, Ged Faulks, and Yvonne Molony-O'Caoimh and Aindrias O'Caoimh.

To all our patients who have given us their love once they realise we are their friends and extensions of their families with our care. They encourage us with their love.

But much gratitude to Autumn, for spending years spearheading the writing of this book. To Martin for encouraging us to not give up despite the years of broken deadlines! To both of you, *thank you so much for your patient and acceptance of my failures to meet the deadlines and keep up with you both!*

To Bishop Tutu and Nelson Mandela for their care for the maintenance of Ubuntu values; Hospitality to all, and 'if you want to go fast go alone: if you want to go far go together!'

Thanks for all who joined me on my entire journey of life!

To our God, who has led us all in the following of Christ, Mohammed and other founders of religious who were inspired by the need for compassion for the poor and suffering. We are following you.

Dr Anne Merriman

Anne loves her Ugandan family, including her growing number of Ugandan dogs and cats. She also loves her British and Irish families and her so many friends. She loves milk chocolate and a good pastry. She can be found watching her favourite movies and shows in between meetings and work. The ultimate world traveller, she has family all around the world and continues to host friends and volunteers from all around the world. She loves to dress in the latest fashion, with matching accessories and painted nails. Her stories have mesmerised hundreds over dinner tables and parties.

Awards and degrees

Nominated for Nobel Peace Prize, 2014, Founder and Director of Policy and Initiator (2000) and leader of International Programmes for 20 years, Hospice Africa Uganda; Honorary Teaching Fellow, International Observatory on End of Life Care in the Institute for Health Research, Lancaster University; Honorary Professor of Palliative Care at Makerere University in Kampala, Uganda; Founder Member and the Founding Vice Chair of the Board of the Palliative Care Association of Uganda (formed in 1999); Chair of Steering Committee of IHPCA and later Founder Member and the Founding Vice Chair of the Board of the African Palliative Care Association (formed in 2005); Board Member of Hospice Africa UK and Hospice Africa; Past Board Member of the International Association for Hospice and Palliative Care (IAHPC); Vice President for East Africa of the African Organisations for Research and Training in Cancer (AORTIC); MBE: Member of

British Empire, honorary for contribution to health in Uganda; Irish Presidential award recipient for bringing peace to suffering in Africa.

MBE: Member of British Empire
MB BCh: Basic medical degrees in UK and Ireland
DCH: Diploma in Child Health (Dublin: RCS 1965)
DTM&H: Diploma in Tropical Medicine and Hygiene. LSTM, 1972
MComm H: Master's in International Community Health (1982)
FRCM (Nig): Fellow of the College of Medicine in Nigeria
AM(Sing): Member of the Academy of Medicine in Singapore
FRCP (Edin) Fellow of the Royal College of Physicians in Edinburgh
FRCP(Ire): Fellow of the Royal College of Physicians in Ireland
FJMU: Fellow of John Moore's University, Liverpool – for her contribution to the relief of pain in the world
DSc(Hon): Honorary Doctor of Science at Edge Hill University, Liverpool – for her contribution to palliative care in Africa
Honorary fellowship from University of College Dublin for her accomplishments in palliative care
Medical Alumni of the year, UCD 2014

Autumn Fielding-Monson

Autumn received a MA in conflict resolution at the University of Bradford, UK (2009); she returned home to the Tri-Cities, WA, US, and worked for over five years as an analyst for a nonprofit mediation organization that resolved complex safety, health, environmental and related retaliatory issues at the Hanford nuclear site. In 2008 she volunteered with HAU and helped Anne write *Audacity to Love*, which provides an explanation and early history of palliative care in Africa. In 2014, she helped write Anne's Nobel Peace Price nomination. In 2017, she spent a year with Anne as an assistant/advisor and started working on this book. In 2018, she began a career in real estate. In 2022, she opened her own real estate company Pathway Realty in Washington State.

Autumn grew up in the Tri-Cities, WA, US and played basketball at Kennewick High school, University of Idaho and went on to finish her undergrad at Seattle Pacific University where they competed at Nationals every year and in the National Championship game. She loves animals, riding horses, triathlons, reading, travelling and spending time with her husband, family and friends.